THE POLITICS
OF POSTANARCHISM

To Zuzana

THE POLITICS OF POSTANARCHISM

Saul Newman

Edinburgh University Press

First published in 2010 by
Edinburgh University Press Ltd
22 George Square, Edinburgh
www.euppublishing.com

This paperback edition 2011

Typeset in 11/13pt Palatino by
Servis Filmsetting Ltd, Stockport, Cheshire, and
printed and bound in Great Britain by
CPI Group (UK) Ltd, Croydon CR0 4YY

A CIP record for this book is available from the British
Library

ISBN 978 0 7486 3496 5 (paperback)

CONTENTS

ACKNOWLEDGEMENTS

There are several people whom I would like to thank, and whose help in formulating ideas and commenting on drafts was invaluable. These include James Martin, Benjamin Noys, Todd May, Nicola Montagna, Stephanie Koerner, Carl Levy and Bernadette Buckley.

Disobedience in the eyes of anyone who has read history, is man's original virtue. It is through disobedience that progress has been made, through disobedience and rebellion.

Oscar Wilde, *The Soul of Man Under Socialism*

The seven degrees of human happiness. First, to die fighting for liberty; second, love and friendship; third, art and science; fourth, smoking; fifth, drinking; sixth, eating; seventh, sleeping.

Mikhail Bakunin

INTRODUCTION

Why be interested in anarchism today? Why be interested in this most heretical of political traditions, whose shadowy existence on the margins of revolutionary politics has lead many to dismiss it as a form of ideological mental illness? The central claim of anarchism – that life can be lived without a state, without centralised authority – has been an anathema not only to more mainstream understandings of politics, which bear the legacy of the sovereign tradition, but also to other radical and revolutionary forms of politics, which see the state as a useful tool for transforming society.

Furthermore, anarchism has often lacked the ideological and political coherence of other political traditions. While there is a certain body of thought that is unified around principles of anti-authoritarianism and egalitarianism, anarchism has always been heterodox and diffuse; while it has had its key exponents, anarchism is not constituted around a particular name, unlike Marxism. Indeed, despite the startling originality of some classical anarchist thinkers – and it is my intention in this book to bring this theoretical innovation to light – anarchists have usually been more concerned with revolutionary practice than with theory.[1] Moreover, while anarchism has historically had a certain influence on workers' movements, as well as on other radical struggles, it has not been as politically hegemonic as Marxism. Anarchism has flared up in brilliant flashes of insurrection – revolts and autonomous projects throughout the nineteenth and twentieth centuries – but these have just as quickly died down again, or have been savagely repressed.

Yet, despite these defeats, and despite anarchism's marginality, we can perhaps point to what might be called an 'anarchist invariant':[2] the recurring desire for life without government that haunts the political imagination. The rejection of political authority in the name of equality

1

and liberty will always be part of the vocabulary of emancipation. One can see an expression of this desire now in contemporary struggles against global capitalism, which are also struggles for autonomy. The vision of anarchy – of life without government – which for the sovereign tradition is the ultimate nightmare, is the eternal aspiration of the radical tradition. My central aim in this book, then, is to affirm anarchism's place *as* the very horizon of radical politics.

This is a bold claim. Anarchism would be considered utopian by many, indeed most, on the political left. Yet, there is an inevitable utopian dimension in radical politics; indeed, this is what makes it radical. I shall argue that utopianism – or a certain articulation of it – should therefore be asserted rather than disavowed. Moreover, we should recall that a society of free association without a state was also Marx's dream. Anarchism embodies the most radical expression of the principles of liberty and equality, proclaiming their inextricability, as well as showing that they cannot be adequately realised within a statist framework: both liberty and equality are constrained in different ways by the state. Nor, according to anarchism, can democracy be truly conceived within the state. Democracy – which is the motor for generating new and radical articulations of equality and liberty – always exceeds the limitations of the state and opposes the very principle of state sovereignty. However, for anarchists, democracy has to be more than just majority rule, because this can threaten individual liberty. Rather, it has to be imagined as a democracy of singularities.

For these reasons, anarchism is central to the politics of emancipation; indeed, it can be seen as the very compass of radical politics. It is also my contention that anarchism has important lessons to teach other forms of politics. Anarchists, for instance, highlight the ultimate inconsistency of liberalism: that individual liberty and rights cannot be properly expressed within a state order, despite the institutional checks and balances that are supposed to restrain state power. The politics of security and the prerogative, which have always been part of liberalism, going back to Locke, ultimately intensify the power of the state and thus pose a threat to individual freedom. Liberalism has always foundered on the impossible project of reconciling freedom and security. Furthermore, anarchists show that liberalism's attempts to justify state authority through notions of consent and the social contract are unconvincing sleights of hand and that, therefore, the state remains an illegitimate imposition of power. Yet, there is an anarchist dimension within liberalism: in the moment of rebellion in Locke's political philosophy, for instance, or in the radical libertarianism found in J. S. Mill's thought. Anarchism might be seen as the wild underside of liberalism, seeking to extend the realm of individual liberty, while showing that this can be realised only in the absence of the state and amid social and economic equality.

To socialists, anarchists teach the vital lesson that social equality cannot come at the expense of liberty; that not only does this trade-off violate individual freedom and autonomy, but it also violates in a different way, equality itself. This is because an equality that is imposed coercively on individuals entails some authoritarian mechanism of power, and this in itself is a form of inequality, a hierarchical relationship of command and obedience which makes a mockery of the very idea of equality. Equality is meaningless and self-contradictory unless people can determine it freely for themselves, without the intervention of a centralised state apparatus. The nineteenth-century Russian anarchist, Mikhail Bakunin, in his debates with Marx in the First International, warned that if the state itself was not destroyed in a socialist revolution, there would emerge a dictatorship of bureaucrats and scientists who would lord it over the peasants and workers, imposing a new tyranny – a prediction that was confirmed in the experience of the Bolshevik revolution and its aftermath.

We have seen in recent times the collapse of these two competing ideologies. Political liberalism – to the extent that it ever existed as anything other than a theory – has been eroded not only by market fundamentalism (neoliberalism), where the market subsumes the political space, but also by the politics of security, in which the totalitarian logic of emergency and control has displaced the language of rights, freedoms and the accountability of power. Liberalism has been devoured by its own offspring, security and the market. As for socialism, the revolutionary Marxist form has been largely discredited by the experience of the Soviet Union, and its parliamentary social democratic form, in imagining that it can temper the cold passions of the capitalist market, has ended up in an absolute capitulation to it.

However, in considering whether anarchism can offer any kind of alternative to these ideologies we must pose the question: what is anarchism as a form of politics? Is there an anarchist political theory as such? Is anarchism more than simply the rejection of political authority, the rebellious impulse or Bakunin's famous 'urge to destroy' – valuable

as they are? Does anarchism have something distinct to offer political thought? This question, however, brings to the surface a certain
paradox in anarchism, since anarchism has always considered itself
an *anti*-politics. Anarchism has consciously sought the abolition of
politics, and has imagined a sort of Manichean opposition between
the *social principle* – constituted by natural law, and moral and rational
conditions – and the *political principle* – which was the unnatural order
of power. Therefore, the abolition of the state was seen as the very
abolition of politics itself, the revolt of the social against the political.
If this is the case, can anarchism still be considered a politics? Yes –
because while calling for the abolition of politics, anarchists like Bakunin
and Kropotkin also discussed revolutionary strategy, the organisation
and mobilisation of the masses, political programmes, and the shape of
postrevolutionary societies, all of which are, of course, *political* questions. What this paradox gives rise to, then, is a different conception
of politics: a *politics that is conceived outside of, and in opposition to, the
state*. The tension, central to anarchism, between anti-politics and politics thus effects a dislodgement of politics from the state framework.
The central challenge of this book, then, is to think what politics means
outside the ontological order of state sovereignty.

A POLITICS OF ANTI-POLITICS?

We have, therefore, to recognise that anarchism is not simply an anti-
politics – it is also a politics. Let us formulate anarchism, then, as a
politics of anti-politics, or an *anti-political politics*. However, this formulation raises certain conceptual difficulties for classical anarchism. We
must investigate more closely the meaning of this aporia: what does
politics mean in the context of anti-politics, and what does anti-politics
mean in the context of politics? What kinds of constraints and limitations does one side of this formulation apply to the other; and what
kinds of possibilities does it open up *for* the other?

Postanarchism might be seen as an exploration of this aporetic
moment in anarchism. Postanarchism is not a specific form of politics;
it offers no actual programme or directives. It is not even a particular
theory of politics as such. Nor should it be seen as an abandonment
or movement beyond anarchism; it does not signify a 'being after'
anarchism. On the contrary, postanarchism is a project of radicalising
and renewing the politics of anarchism – of thinking anarchism *as* a

politics. Let us understand postanarchism as a kind of *deconstruction*. Deconstruction is, for Derrida, a 'methodology' aimed at interrogating and unmasking the conceptual hierarchies, binary oppositions and aporias in philosophy – its moments of inconsistency and self-contradiction. This is an operation which takes place on the horizon of the 'closure of metaphysics' (*la clôture de la metaphysique*), and its purpose is to reveal what Derrida terms the metaphysics of presence that continues to haunt philosophical discourse. In undermining this metaphysics of presence, a deconstructive reading shows that no concept is a self-contained or self-sufficient unity: its identity is always dependent on another term which is disavowed, and whose presence at the same time destabilises the dominant term.[3] Yet, as Derrida makes clear, deconstruction should not be thought of as a simple transgression of philosophy:

> There is not a transgression, if one understands by that a pure and simple landing into a beyond of metaphysics . . . Now, even in aggressions or transgressions, we are consorting with a code to which metaphysics is tied irreducibly, such that every transgressive gesture reencloses us – precisely by giving us a hold on the closure of metaphysics – within the closure. But, by means of the work done on one side and the other of the limit the field inside is modified, and a transgression is produced that consequently nowhere is present as a *fait accompli*.[4]

Similarly, postanarchism is not a transgression or a movement beyond the terms of anarchism; it does not leave anarchism behind but, instead, works within it as a constant engagement with its limits, invoking a moment of an outside in order to rethink and transform these limits. In doing so, it modifies the discursive field of anarchism without actually abandoning it.

Chiefly, postanarchism interrogates the metaphysics of presence that continues to haunt anarchism; it seeks to destabilise the foundationalism on which the discourse of classical anarchism rests. Its deconstructive tools are poststructuralist thought and elements of psychoanalytic theory; tools through which I develop a critique of essentialist identities and deep ontological foundations. As I will show, some of the central categories and claims of classical anarchist thought are based on presuppositions which can no longer be theoretically sustained. These include: an essentialist conception of the subject; the universality of morality and reason, and the idea of the progressive enlightenment of humankind; a conception of the social order as naturally constituted (by natural laws, for instance) and rationally determined; a dialectical view of history; and a certain positivism, whereby science could reveal the truth of social relations. These ideas derive from the discourse of Enlightenment humanism, which the anarchism of the eighteenth and nineteenth centuries was very much influenced by. My claim is that these ideas no longer have their full force; that they are part of a certain epistemological paradigm, a certain way of thinking and seeing the world which is increasingly problematic and difficult to sustain. This is not to say that the Enlightenment is out of date, but rather that its central tendencies must be reconsidered.

However, the postanarchist critique of foundationalism does not mean that we must abandon the politics of emancipation and the principles of liberty and equality which motivate anarchism. Quite the contrary. I simply contend that anarchism today does not need these deep foundations in human nature and moral and rational enlightenment to advance a radical politics and ethics of equal-liberty.

If we explore this aporetic tension between politics and anti-politics as it applies to anarchism, we see that the moment of politics generates a number of conditions for anarchism. Politics suggests, for instance, some sort of engagement with relations of power. Following Michel Foucault's insight that power relations are both pervasive and constitutive of social identities, practices and discourses, politics – even radical politics – is an activity conducted within a field structured by power. However, although we can never transcend power entirely – because there will always be power relations of some kind in any society – we can radically modify this field of power through ongoing practices of freedom. Furthermore, all forms of radical politics – especially anarchism, which claims that power and authority are unnatural and inhuman – must contend with the possibility of the subject's psychic attachment to power, a desire for authority and self-domination that was revealed by psychoanalysis from, Freud to Reich. Therefore, if the problem of voluntary servitude – so often neglected in radical political theory – is to be countered, the revolution against power and authority must involve a micro-political revolution which takes place at the level of the subject's desire. Also, emphasising the political moment in anarchism would affirm the idea of contingency and the event, rather than a revolutionary narrative determined by the rational unfolding of social relations or historical laws. Revolutions and insurrections – even those which seek the abolition of the state – are political events which must be made; spontaneity requires conscious organisation and political mobilisation.

Where the political pole imposes certain limits – the realities of power, the dangers of voluntary servitude, and so on – the anti-political pole, by contrast, invokes an outside, a movement beyond limits. It is the signification of the infinite, of the limitless horizon in which everything is possible. This is both the moment of utopia, and, in a different sense, also the moment of ethics. As I have suggested, anarchism has an important utopian dimension, even if the classical anarchists themselves claimed not to be utopians but materialists and rationalists. Indeed, some utopian element – whether acknowledged or not – is an essential part of any form of radical politics; to oppose the current order, one inevitably invokes an alternative, utopian imagination. However, I will try to formulate a different approach to utopianism in this book: the importance of imagining an alternative to the current order is not to lay down a precise programme for the future, but rather to provide a point of alterity or exteriority as a way of interrogating the limits of this order. Moreover, we should think about utopia in terms of action in the immediate sense, of creating alternatives within the present, at localised points, rather than waiting for the revolution. Utopia is something which emerges in political struggles themselves.

Ethics also implies an outside to the existing order, but in a different sense. Ethics, as I understand it here, involves the opening up of existing political identities, practices, institutions and discourses to an Other which is beyond their terms. Ethics is more than the application of moral and rational norms – it is rather the continual disturbance of the sovereignty of these norms, and the identities and institutions which draw their legitimacy from them, in the name of something that exceeds their grasp. Importantly, then, ethics is what disturbs politics from the outside. Here I shall develop an 'an-archic' understanding of ethics that I derive, in part, from Emmanuel Levinas.

The point is, however, that politics cannot do without anti-politics, and vice versa. The two must go together. There must always be an anti-political outside, a utopian moment of rupture and excess which disturbs the limits of politics. The ethical moment cannot be eclipsed by the political dimension, nor can it be separated from it as some like Carl Schmitt have maintained. If there is to be a concept of the political, it can be thought only through a certain constitutive tension with ethics. At the same time, anti-politics needs to be articulated politically; it needs to be put into action through actual struggles and engagements with different forms of domination. There must be some way of measuring politically the anti-political imaginary, through victories, defeats and strategic gains and reversals. So while anti-politics points to a transcendence of the current order, it cannot be an escape from it – it must involve an encounter with its limits, and this is where politics comes in. The transcendence of power involves an active engagement with power, not an avoidance of it; the realisation of freedom requires an ongoing elaboration of new practices of freedom within the context of power relations. So we can say that there is a certain paradoxical inextricability between the political and the anti-political moment in anarchism; a certain productive tension that postanarchism uses to formulate new approaches to radical politics.

THE AUTONOMY OF THE POLITICAL

Indeed, in working through the aporia between politics and anti-politics, postanarchism gestures towards a new understanding of 'the political'. Here Chantal Mouffe provides a useful definition of the political, distinguishing it from politics:

> By 'the political', I refer to the dimension of antagonism that is inherent in human relations, antagonism that can take many forms and emerge in different types of social relations. 'Politics', on the other side, indicates an ensemble of practices, discourses and institutions which seek to establish a certain order and organize human coexistence in conditions that are potentially conflictual because they are affected by the dimension of 'the political'.[5]

So, in this conception, the political might be seen as the repressed unconscious of politics – the dimension of antagonism and conflict at the heart of social relations – that threatens to destabilise the established political order, and which must, therefore, be domesticated.

Mouffe's conception of the political dimension as the realm of antagonism and conflict derives from Schmitt's formulation of the political relation in terms of the friend/enemy opposition.[6] The existential threat posed to a certain political identity by the figure of the enemy, a threat which presupposes the possibility of war, and which unites a collective association in opposition to this enemy, is what distinguishes, for Schmitt, the political relationship from other relationships, such as economics, religion, morality and ethics.

This understanding of the political is fundamentally opposed, in Schmitt's account, to liberalism, which is an attempt to evade or disavow the political dimension. According to Schmitt, liberalism is an anti-politics: in its distrust of the state it negates the political, displacing it with civil society, the sphere of individual private interests, law, economics, morality and rights:

> there exists a liberal policy in the form of a polemical antithesis against the state, church, or other institutions which restrict individual freedom. There exists a liberal policy of trade, church, education, but absolutely no liberal politics, only a liberal critique of politics.[7]

A similar critique is made by Schmitt of anarchism, which is also seen as an anti-politics that opposes the political state in the name of an intrinsically benign human nature: 'Indigenous anarchism reveals that the belief in the natural goodness of man is closely tied to the radical denial of the state.'[8]

How should a postanarchist approach respond to Schmitt's challenge? Does the opposition to the state, which is at the very core of anarchism, consign it to an apolitical liberalism, in which the sphere of individual interests eclipses the political dimension? My argument, to the contrary, is that postanarchism provides us with a new conception of the autonomy of the political, which transcends both the Schmittian and liberal paradigms.

The politics of postanarchism goes beyond the Schmittian conception in insisting that the appropriate domain of politics is not the state, but autonomous spaces that define themselves in opposition to it. For Schmitt, the nation-state is the primary locus of politics because it is the sovereign state which decides on the friend/enemy distinction. However, from a postanarchist perspective, the state is actually the order of depoliticisation: it is the structure of power that polices politics, regulating, controlling and repressing the insurgent dimension that is proper to the political; it is a forgetting of the conflict and antagonism at the base of its own foundations. This critique of the circumscription of the political within the state order applies also to Mouffe, who, although seeming to embrace the idea of antagonism and disruption, particularly with her idea of agonistic democracy,[9] confines this conflict implicitly to the national state framework. My contention would be that the democratic agonism, which Mouffe locates within the state as a conflict over the boundaries of inclusion and exclusion, actually realises itself only in opposition to the state. Thus, to speak of the autonomy of the political, as Schmitt and Mouffe do, necessarily invokes the idea of the *politics of autonomy*: the idea that politics seeks to define spaces of autonomy from the state, spaces in which people can determine their own lives, free from the looming shadow of Leviathan. Postanarchism points to a different conception of the autonomy of the political, one that turns on its head the neo-Hobbesian, as well as Jacobin, traditions of political thought, for whom the political is nothing but the affirmation of the state.

Furthermore, postanarchism resists the Schmittian hyperpoliticisation of politics, which seeks to evacuate ethics from the political domain. As I have said, politics has always to be thought of in relation to ethics, as that which disturbs the sovereignty of politics (as well as the politics of sovereignty). Indeed, the moment of ethics acts to restrain the imperium of politics, the filling out of the ontological space by politics – something which leads not only to nihilism, but also to a paradoxical depoliticisation, as if politics expands everywhere to the point where it loses any sort of meaning. There can be no pure or total politics; or if there can, it can only have disastrous consequences. The intensification of the political threatens to produce a closed, claustrophobic, even totalitarian space in which politics itself disappears. Paradoxically, then, the autonomy of the political depends not on its separation from the ethical domain but on its constant engagement with, and openness to, it. The postanarchist conception of the political emphasises the necessary and constitutive ontological gap between politics and ethics. Just as Schmitt believes that the political space of the nation-state acts as a *katechon* or restrainer to the global imperium of a new liberal regime of humanitarianism and international law,[10] I would argue that ethics – which embodies an anti-political (rather than apolitical) dimension – acts as a katechon to politics.

However, its anti-authoritarian impulse and its refusal of the purification of politics, does not make postanarchism liberalism. While postanarchism encompasses a certain moment of anti-politics, and while it shares with liberalism a suspicion of state authority and an insistence on individual freedom, it cannot be equated with liberalism. From a postanarchist point of view, liberalism does indeed subordinate the political to the orders of economics, morality and law – it leads to a certain depoliticisation, in which the political moment of action and contestation is swallowed up by the private interests and market pre-occupations of civil society. Indeed, the problem with liberalism is that it naturalises society as a domain of individual freedom and market exchanges, without recognising the constraints that the latter impose on the former. Liberalism also subordinates the political domain to notions of universal human rights and humanitarianism. Schmitt was entirely right to be suspicious of such notions, saying that they conceal a new form of imperialism.[11] At same time, one could say that liberalism is not anti-political enough in the sense that it is not sufficiently opposed to the state. Liberalism's paean to individual freedom is contradicted by its acceptance of the state as the guardian of this freedom. So liberalism, from a postanarchist perspective, is neither sufficiently political, nor sufficiently anti-political.

It is obvious here that I am using the terms *political* and *anti-political* in a radically different sense to Schmitt. As I have said, I disagree with Schmitt in seeing the state as the privileged site of the political: the political is the constitution of a space of autonomy which takes its distance from the state, and thus calls into question the very principle of state sovereignty. At the same time, the notion of the anti-political refers to the moment of both ethics and utopia, in which the boundaries of our political reality are challenged. And in this sense, the anti-political also implies a form of political engagement. One of the problems with the standard conceptions of the autonomy of the political – not only Schmitt's and Mouffe's, but also in a different sense, Hannah Arendt's[12] – is that they forget, or actively disavow, this anti-political dimension. Anti-politics should not be confused with an indifference to politics, with a quiet passivity or a turning away from political engagement. Rather, it should be seen as an active refusal of the limits of what is in the name of what could be – and this is, of course, a highly political gesture. I see anti-politics as the *unconscious* of politics, and, in this sense, any conception of the political must include the anti-political and must wrestle with the paradoxical relation between these terms. This is why anarchism – whose politics of anti-politics is rendered explicit by postanarchism – gives us new a formulation of the autonomy of the political.

THE STRUCTURE OF THE BOOK

In the chapters that follow, I shall elaborate a postanarchist approach
to the political through an exploration of anarchism and its place within
political theory.

In Chapter 1, I revisit the classical anarchism of thinkers like Godwin,
Bakunin, Proudhon and Kropokin, examining the key elements of their
political philosophy: the rejection of the state and centralised political
authority; the scepticism about democracy, the social contract and other
legitimating discourses of the state; and the critique of property and
inequality. I argue that anarchism's central political and ethical impulse
is the desire for equal-liberty, in which the two principles of equality
and liberty – which in liberal theory are often separated or seen to be
in tension with one another – are, for anarchists, inextricably bound
together, animating and giving meaning to one another. Furthermore, I
show that classical anarchism is based on a certain conception of society
and the social principle as inherently natural and rationally ordered,
in opposition to power and authority, which are seen as unnatural
and morally corrupting, and whose intervention disrupts the natural
functions of society.

Chapter 2 explores certain problems with this conceptualisation
of social relations. I engage in an interrogation of the Enlightenment
humanist paradigm in which classical anarchism is conceived, showing
that the deep ontological foundations which form the basis of its philosophy – foundations in human nature, scientific enquiry, and the
immanent rationality and morality of a free-formed social body – are
ultimately problematic and unstable. Here I develop a concept of
an-archy from Levinas, as well as the Heideggerian thinker, Reiner
Schürmann: an-archy points to the disturbance and ultimate impossibility of stable ontological foundations, including those of anarchism
itself. I suggest, however, that this an-archic moment – which is also
the moment of ethics – is not ultimately inconsistent with anarchism,
and that anarchism can be re-articulated through an-archy in order
to develop new, postanarchist understandings of political subjectivity,
power relations, ethics, insurrectionary politics and utopia.

In Chapter 3, I re-examine the debate between anarchism and
Marxism. I argue that anarchism provides an alternative theory of state
power, one that sees the state as a largely autonomous political dimension that is not reducible to a class analysis or to the dominant mode

of production. This alternative conceptualisation of the state – along with different approaches to questions of class, the vanguard party and technology – led, during the nineteenth century, to a major dispute between anarchists and Marxists over revolutionary strategy and political organisation, a controversy that has become more significant today with the exhaustion of the Marxist–Leninist project. Here I develop a (post)anarchist approach to the autonomy of the political, contrasting this with various post-Marxist and neo-Schmittian perspectives which, I argue, do not adequately address the problem of state sovereignty.

Chapter 4 takes up this notion of politics outside the state, showing the relevance of this idea to continental radical thought today. The purpose of this chapter is, therefore, to situate anarchism within debates among continental thinkers such as Alain Badiou, Jacques Rancière, Slavoj Žižek and Michael Hardt and Antonio Negri. I will show that many of the themes and preoccupations of these thinkers – with a politics beyond the state, political subjectivity beyond class and political organisation beyond the Party – reflect an unacknowledged anarchism. I show, furthermore, how anarchism can make important interventions around these questions. It is here that I argue that radical politics today should be conceived of in terms of rupture with the existing order, rather than emerging as an immanent dimension within it. However, the politics of the 'event', which this notion of rupture implies, should be conceived of in ways that avoid the violent, terroristic and potentially authoritarian revolutionary forms of the past.

In Chapter 5, I engage in a different set of theoretical debates – on this occasion with contemporary anarchist theorists, whose thought, I argue, displays a continuity with classical anarchism. Indeed, despite their substantial differences, Murray Bookchin and John Zerzan are united in their rejection of postmodernism/poststructuralism, and rely instead on an essentialist ontology. In pointing out the limitations of their approaches, I seek to develop further the idea of a politics of anarchism – or a postanarchism – that does not base itself on essentialist identities, processes of dialectical unfolding or on a certain organic conception of the social body; rather the possibilities of radical transformation should be seen as contingent moments of openness that break with the idea of a naturally determined order. I also engage here more fully with the question of ethics, responding to the charge that postanarchism, which draws a certain influence from the existentialist philosophy of Max Stirner, amounts to nihilism or relativism. I construct a different conception of ethical action and practices of freedom that are no longer reliant on fixed identities and universal moral categories. Here the question of utopia becomes important, but in a new sense: no longer as prescribing a programme of revolutionary political change, or as an idealisation of a future, post-revolutionary society, but as a moment of rupture and heterogeneity.

In the final chapter I explore these utopian moments of rupture and contestation as they emerge on the terrain of radical politics today, particularly in struggles against globalised capitalism. I argue that these diverse movements of resistance – indigenous groups, anti-capitalist networks, environmental activists, anti-war movements and so on – are ultimately struggles for autonomy; they open up new political spaces, characterised by 'anarchist' forms of organisation, which are outside the ontological order of state sovereignty, even if they impose demands upon the state. Furthermore, they can also be seen as symptomatic of the current regime of 'post-politics' and its democratic deficit; in developing new, decentralised and non-authoritarian political practices and decision-making structures, these movements and struggles invoke a new 'anarchic' understanding of democracy which is no longer tied to the sovereign state order. My argument here, and indeed, throughout the book, is that not only does anarchism form the horizon of radical politics today in its maximisation of the politics and ethics of equal-liberty, but that it also forms the ultimate horizon of democracy itself.

Notes

1 Indeed, anarchism has at times been characterised by a kind of radical anti-theory. Errico Malatesta, for instance, saw anarchism as the direct practice of insurrection, and was critical of attempts to turn it into a theoretical and scientific project. See his critique of Kropotkin in *Errico Malatesta: His Life & Ideas*, Vernon Richards (ed.) (London: Freedom Press, 1993), p. 41.
2 I owe this term to Benjamin Noys. See 'Anarchy-without-Anarchism' (October 2006), available at: http://leniency.blogspot.com/2009/06/anarchywithoutanarchism.html.
3 See Jacques Derrida, *Positions*, trans. Alan Bass (Chicago, IL: University of Chicago Press, 1971), p. 57.
4 Derrida, *Positions*, p. 12.
5 Chantal Mouffe, *The Democratic Paradox* (London: Verso, 2000), p. 101.
6 See Carl Schmitt, *The Concept of the Political*, trans. George Schwab (Chicago, IL: University of Chicago Press), 1996.

7 Schmitt, *The Concept of the Political*, p. 70.

8 Schmitt, *The Concept of the Political*, p. 60.

9 See Mouffe, *The Democratic Paradox.*

10 See Carl Schmitt, *The* Nomos *of the Earth in the International Law of the* Jus Publicum Europeaum, trans. G. L. Ulmen (New York: Telos Press, 2003).

11 Here Schmitt invokes Proudhon's aphorism, 'whoever invokes humanity wants to cheat' (*The Concept of the Political*, p. 54). Indeed, Schmitt is entirely right to point out the very illiberal forms of politics that liberals have historically supported (see p. 69).

12 See Hannah Arendt, *The Human Condition* (Chicago, IL: University of Chicago Press, 1958).

Chapter 1

THE EUTHANASIA OF GOVERNMENT[1]:
CLASSICAL ANARCHISM RECONSIDERED

In his seventeenth-century radical pamphlet, *The New Law of Righteousness*, Gerrard Winstanley declared war on the political and social arrangements of his time. In the name of an intransigent liberty and equality, he denounced the injustices of political authority, the iniquities of private property and their ideological support in the Church. Such pernicious institutions and mystifications must submit to a more fundamental and universal law – the law of equity – and would be swept away before a new communist vision of society:

> When this universal law of equity rises up in every man and woman, then none shall lay claim to any creature and say, This is mine, and that is yours. This is my work and that is yours. But everyone shall put their hands to till the earth and bring up cattle, and the blessing of the earth shall be common to all; . . . There shall be none lords over others, but everyone shall be a lord over himself, subject to the law of righteousness, reason and equity, which shall dwell and rule in him, which is the Lord.[2]

The law of righteousness was sanctioned by God, but would be implemented directly by the people. Real equality and liberty – each implicated in the other – would be realised in utopian experiments in common ownership and communal life and work, in which neither private property nor government authority would be recognised.[3] It was only in such an environment that liberty could be imagined, that each could be lord over him- or herself. It was only in a society of non-domination and equality that the wrongs of the world would be righted, and that the millennial dream of the true community would be realised.

This radical vision can be seen as part of what might be termed an 'anarchist invariant'. From the millenarian movements and heretical sects – the Anabaptists of Munster, the Taborites of Bohemia – in the Middle Ages, to the peasant rebellions across Europe in the fifteenth and sixteenth centuries, to the sailors of Kronstadt and the libertarian collectives of Spain, to the Zapatistas and the anti-capitalists of our time – we see imagined and enacted a heretical politics. This is a politics of insurrection in which is asserted a desire for total emancipation from political authority. While this revolt sometimes expressed itself in the language of religion, it was usually of the antinomian kind – in other words, it rejected the formal laws and established practices of religion, advocating instead individual freedom and self-expression.[4] It is anarchist because it expresses the aspiration for life which is not organised by central government, law, private property or formal religion, and in which social arrangements can be established voluntarily and without coercion. Because it rejects the principle of government and political authority, such a politics is precisely heretical – it goes against the entire tradition of politics and political thought that maintains that we cannot do without sovereignty.

This book is an exploration of anarchism as a political heresy, as a heterodox political philosophy and praxis animated by an insurrectionary desire, a utopian energy and a fundamental rejection of political authority. This anti-authoritarianism sets anarchism apart from most, if not all, other political philosophies. In this sense, it cannot be reduced to a combination of liberalism and socialism, even though it draws upon and radicalises elements of these doctrines. While anarchism would seem to share with liberalism an insistence on individual freedom and self-determination, it exposes in this the very inconsistency of liberalism itself: individual autonomy cannot be realised in conditions of inequality, nor under the dominion of private property. Nor can it be realised through the state and law. While liberalism has always claimed to be the standard bearer of individual liberty, it has also been an ideology of security: individual liberty must be guarded and protected, fenced off from the appetites and aggressive drives of others, and this security can be provided only by a sovereign state and through the application of law. While for liberals, liberty must come with security, for anarchists, security is always hostile to liberty: security is a mask for political domination; it takes on its own logic and develops its own prerogatives, regardless of liberal checks and balances. Indeed, individual liberty and state security are ultimately irreconcilable and antagonistic principles. It could be argued that this contradiction within liberal political rationality is being ruthlessly exposed today as the modern state securitizes itself in the name of the 'War on Terror'.

As for socialism, a tradition to which anarchism is in some respects closer, it has at times sacrificed liberty to the principle of equality. Anarchists share with socialists the desire for economic and social equality, but not at the expense of individual freedom and autonomy. There have always been authoritarian and centralist tendencies in socialism – from Marx's and Engels' willingness to use and intensify state power in the revolutionary period, to the 'democratic centralism' and vanguard politics of Lenin, to the statist and parliamentary fetish of reformist socialists and social democrats. As we shall see, the main objection that anarchists make to socialism – in both its revolutionary Marxist and democratic variants – is that it often neglects the dangers of political power and state authority. And what an ignominious end for socialism today! After the collapse of the state Communist project in the Soviet Union and elsewhere, and after the withering away of the welfare state model in the West, the so-called socialist parties of today have nothing better to do than reconcile themselves with the requirements of the global market. It might be noticed that in this they seem to take considerable relish.

So, while anarchism resonates with certain aspects of liberalism and socialism, it is also a distinct tradition of political thought – one that will be elaborated further in this chapter. At the same time, I want to suggest that anarchism can be seen as the ultimate horizon of *all* forms of radical politics. What I mean by this is that because anarchism combines liberty and equality to the greatest possible degree, it serves as an end point or limit condition for the politics of emancipation. All forms of radical politics – including most revolutionary forms of socialism and Marxism – aspire, consciously or unconsciously, whether realised or unrealised, to a kind of anarchism – even if understood only in the utopian sense. For instance, the postrevolutionary societies depicted by Marx and even Lenin – communist societies of abundance and freedom, liberated from forced work, property and centralised government, where 'the free development of each is the condition for the free development of all'[5] – are precisely anarchist societies, and are virtually indistinguishable from many of the aspirations of anarchist thinkers and revolutionaries. The celebration by Engels of the radical and decentralised democracy of the Paris Commune of 1871, is mirrored in the admiration for the same event expressed by anarchists like Bakunin and Kropotkin, even though the interpretations differed (for Engels it was the first example of the 'dictatorship of the proletariat';[6] whereas for Bakunin it signified something different, an anarchist social revolution). I will explore the relationship between anarchism and Marxism later on, as well as the question of radical democracy, to which anarchism has a necessarily ambiguous relationship. But we can say at this stage that the radical and decentralised democracy invoked at times by the Marxist tradition, points towards, and seems to aspire to, a form of anarchism. Marx claimed in his early writings that 'democracy is the solved *riddle* of all constitutions'; and that 'all forms of state have democracy for their truth and that they are untrue insofar as they are not democracy'.[7] Can we not say the same about anarchism? Perhaps, in other words, anarchism itself is like democracy in this sense – a sort of excess or limit condition which is, at the same time, the ultimate truth of all radical politics, the ground from which it springs and the final standard from which it is judged. Can we can say that just as democracy is the solved riddle of all constitutions, that anarchism is the solved riddle of radical politics? Can we say that just as all forms of state are untrue insofar as they are not democracy, that all forms of radical politics (and, indeed, all forms of democracy) are untrue insofar as they are not anarchy?

I will elaborate and justify these claims as the book progresses, but what I want to hint at here are two possible readings of anarchism – two interpretations that are intertwined and yet, as we shall see, are also to some extent in tension. Anarchism will be seen, first, as a certain political and theoretical tradition – not a doctrine or dogma, because it is too diverse and heterogeneous for that, but a body of thought and praxis which is united by certain principles, which has its key thinkers and activists, which has a unique history, which has its debates and controversies and which makes certain political, philosophical and ethical claims. Secondly, I will try to arrive at a broader and more transcendent reading of anarchism – an *anarchy-beyond-anarchism* if you like. This will be not so much an alternative theory of radical politics, but rather a kind of interrogation of anarchism itself, a deconstruction of its discursive limits and an investigation of its ontological foundations. This anarchy-beyond-anarchism (or postanarchism as it will come to be termed) will be a theoretical and critical work conducted at the limits of anarchism, one that will incorporate insights from different thinkers and perspectives not commonly associated with the anarchist tradition. However, I want to stress that this alternative critical reading does not have the intention of dismissing anarchism; on the contrary, it seeks to radicalise it, to broaden its scope and expand its possibilities, as well as to update it and make it more relevant to the radical political struggles of today. My contention, then, is that anarchism is more than a political and philosophical tradition – it also constitutes a universal horizon of emancipation which all forms of radical politics must necessarily speak to if they are to remain radical. Anarchism, in other words, contains a beyond, a moment of its own transcendence, when it exceeds the discursive limits and ontological foundations within which it was originally conceived and opens itself up to a multitude of different voices and possibilities. Once again, this is not to suggest that anarchism has been in the past a closed, dormant doctrine. On the contrary, it is because anarchism has been so heterodox and so resistant to doctrine – more so than most other political and theoretical traditions – that it remains contemporary and open to innovation.

DEFINING ANARCHISM: EQUAL-LIBERTY

There are numerous ways of defining anarchism – most see it as anti-statism or as a general scepticism towards political authority.[8] It is certainly true that for the anarchist a minimum basic requirement is that state authority justifies its own existence in more convincing terms than it currently does; it cannot be simply assumed, and cannot plausibly claim to be based on mystifications like the social contract. Nor can it be legitimised through democracy, as we shall see. However, what I think is more fundamental to anarchism is the idea of equal-liberty – a proposition through which all forms of domination and hierarchy come under interrogation. Equal-liberty is simply the idea that liberty and equality are inextricably linked, that one cannot be had without the other; that, in Bakunin's words:

> I am free only when all human beings surrounding me – men and women alike – are equally free. The freedom of others, far from limiting or negating my liberty, is on the contrary its necessary condition and confirmation. I become free in the true sense only by virtue of the liberty of others, so much so that the greater the number of free people surrounding me the deeper and greater

and more extensive their liberty, the deeper and larger becomes my liberty.[9]

This generous formulation of equal-liberty does not see another's liberty as potentially threatening but, rather, mutually enhancing. Nor does it see equality and liberty as two opposed or ultimately irreconcilable principles, or as imposing limits upon one another – as tends to be the case in the liberal understanding. On the contrary, the radical formulation of equal-liberty sees these two principles as part of the same category of emancipation: a person cannot be fully free unless others around him or her are equally free; moreover, one cannot be said to be emancipated unless this freedom is accompanied by equality, which, from this perspective, is not confined to formal or political equality, but includes all forms of social and economic equality. Equal-liberty, therefore, not only combines these two principles so that they mutually resonate; it also situates them in a social or collective context in which one is forced to consider the conditions of others around one.

It is in this sense that the radical reading of equal-liberty differs markedly from the liberal reading. The liberal understanding of equal-liberty generally derives from the nineteenth-century thinker Herbert Spencer's law of equal freedom, that states that 'Every man has the freedom to do all that he wills, provided he infringes not the equal freedom of any other man.'[10] The principle outlined here is that we all have an equal right to be free, and, therefore, that no free action should constrain or limit the freedom of another. This laissez-faire doctrine might in some ways be seen as a healthy corrective to over-bearing, over-legislating governments today that harass us with all sorts of petty, excessive and draconian laws and restrictions. Indeed, Spencer advocated in his early writings a form of libertarianism which says that all government institutions must be subordinated to the equal-liberty principle, and that therefore we have the right to simply ignore and disobey the state when its directives would lead to a violation of this principle.[11] Moreover, this doctrine of equal-liberty should obviously be supported as a bare minimum condition for politics. However, when it is examined more closely it reveals several shortcomings: mainly that equality is seen as being secondary to liberty. This is not only in the sense that in Spencer's formulation, equality is narrowly understood as formal equality (equality of rights, legal equality and the equal claim to non-interference), thus excluding broader claims for social and economic equality;[12] but also that there is seen to be an internal tension between liberty and the equality of liberty, a tension in which liberty itself must take priority. In other words, for Spencer, the threat that equality – even the very narrow equality of liberty – can pose to liberty is seen to be more serious than the threat that liberty can pose to equality, and therefore the principle of equality must be subordinate to that of liberty.[13]

This is not to suggest that liberalism always sacrifices equality to liberty; and, indeed, thinkers like Rawls[14] and Dworkin have obviously made important contributions to the theorisation of a liberalism that accommodates certain forms of social and economic equality. However, the general problem with liberal conceptions of equal liberty is that they usually presuppose and are imagined within a capitalist market – one whose inequalities can perhaps be ameliorated through social democratic measures, but never entirely overcome. Furthermore, liberalism always presupposes a state: whether it is the minimal and non-interventionist state of Spencer or Nozick, or the distributive state of Rawls, the state is always there to protect liberties or to provide social goods. Liberalism, from its inception, has always been a state project: from the protecting and securing Hobbesian state, to various conceptions of the 'night-watchman' state, to modern socially liberal states, to the contemporary neoliberal 'competition' state. This is because the liberal notion of equal-liberty is always premised on the individual, the individual whose liberties must be reconciled with, or protected against, those of other individuals; whose liberty must be traded off against equality; or whose disadvantaged status or bad luck in life must be compensated for through social welfare measures. This is problematic for two reasons. First, as Todd May points out, the subject in this paradigm is positioned as a passive recipient of either state protection or redistributive rights: there is no notion of the subject seizing, constructing and organising for him- or herself, in collaboration with others, egalitarian and libertarian social arrangements.[15] Secondly, what is largely absent in the liberal tradition is any real conception of collective liberty or autonomy, not necessarily in the sense of the right to self-determination for certain minority groups in society, but more broadly conceived as a collective realisation of liberty: one in which liberty can be shared without being diminished; in which the liberty of one is only imaginable in the context of the liberty of all; and in which liberty must come not only with formal equality (of liberty), but with social and economic equality. It is at this point that the difference between liberty and equality becomes indistinct, one term merging into the other. Because liberalism is based on the sovereign self-interested individual, it does not have the conceptual language to think in these terms – it sees only a competition of liberties that must be balanced with one another. Unlike anarchism, it cannot imagine liberty as a collective entity, as a social being.

We need, then, an alternative theorisation of equal-liberty, one that goes beyond the limits of the liberal formulation. A more radical understanding of equal-liberty would see it as a kind of open-ended horizon that allows for endless permutations and elaborations, so that, for instance, political equality is meaningful only with economic equality; civil liberty makes sense only if it also comes with political equality; economic equality is desirable only if it is accompanied by civil liberty and full political equality, and so on. Here Étienne Balibar provides a more productive formulation of equal-liberty, seeing it as central to the very autonomy of politics:

> The proposition of equal liberty as stated in revolutionary terms, has a remarkable logical form which has, since the Greeks, been termed as *elegkhos* or, in other words, a self-refutation of its negation. It states the fact that it is *impossible* to maintain to a logical conclusion, without absurdity, the idea of perfect civil liberty based on discrimination, privilege and inequalities of condition (and, *a fortiori*, to institute such liberty), just as it is impossible to conceive and institute equality between humans based on despotism (even 'enlightened' despotism) or on a monopoly of power. Equal liberty is therefore *unconditional*.[16]

We see here that the link between liberty and equality is not only established politically, but has a kind of logical coherence which is best understood negatively. In other words, on a more superficial reading, liberty and equality would seem to be mutually limiting concepts – so that the more liberty one has, the more one poses a potential threat to the liberty of others; and that equality (particularly social and economic) will usually come at the expense of, or at least endanger, individual liberty. Yet, on this more radical reading, the equation is turned around so that each principle becomes logically inconsistent *without* the other.

I would suggest that this radical understanding of equal-liberty is the one that is closer to the political ethics of anarchism.[17] Indeed, we might say that anarchism provides the fullest development and the most radical expression of equal-liberty, one that transcends both the socialist and liberal traditions: for anarchists, quite simply, equality and liberty cannot be fully implemented or even logically conceived within the framework of the state and political sovereignty. This is not only because the state violates and impinges upon individual liberty – through all sorts of laws and coercive and violent measures – but also because it violates equality, creating a concentrated monopoly on power, claiming sole legitimacy and authority, as well as supporting unequal class hierarchies, inequalities of wealth and economically exploitative practices. Political authority, therefore, denies both liberty and equality. This argument becomes evident in Bakunin's critique of the democratic state, which he sees as a contradiction in terms because it conceives of a democratic equality of rights within a sovereign state framework:

> [E]quality of *political rights*, or *a democratic State*, constitute in themselves the most glaring contradiction in terms. The State, or political right, denotes force, authority, predominance; it presupposes inequality in fact. Where all rule, there are no more ruled, and there is no State. Where all equally enjoy the same human rights, there all political right loses its reason for being. Political right connotes privilege, and where all are privileged, there privilege vanishes, and along with it goes political right. Therefore the terms *'democratic State'* and *'equality of political rights'* denote no less than the destruction of the State and the abolition of all political right.[18]

In other words, the equality of political rights entailed by democracy is fundamentally incompatible with *political right*: the principle of sovereignty which grants authority over these rights to the state. At its most basic level, political equality can exist only in tension with a right that stands above society and determines the conditions under which this political equality can be exercised. Political equality – and indeed democracy – if taken seriously and understood radically, can only mean the abolition of state sovereignty. That is why anarchists want to see not simply a society of egalitarian economic and social arrangements, but also to see these arrangements achieved by the people themselves, without coercion and without the need for centralised political authority.

CRITIQUE OF GOVERNMENT

Anarchism is, as I have said, a broad and diverse philosophical tradition with a long history – libertarian ideas stretch back as far as Taoism in third-century BC China.[19] However, in the context of this discussion, I am interested in a more recent collection of ideas, those which were part of eighteenth- and nineteenth-century radical thought; ideas which were influenced and conditioned by the Enlightenment, and inspired by the French Revolution. This is the body of thought commonly referred to as 'classical' anarchism, and is characterised by thinking which is more systematically and consciously anarchist. It should be noted, however, that classical anarchism is not defined by a particular historical period but, rather, as we shall see, by a certain rational-humanist paradigm of thought: a paradigm which frames not only the discourse of anarchism but also other radical political discourses and theories as well; a paradigm which is, moreover, to some extent still with us, although its cracks have been showing for some time now. Therefore, in the classical anarchist tradition I would include thinkers such as William Godwin, Pierre-Joseph Proudhon, Mikhail Bakunin and Peter Kropotkin.[20] What follows below will by no means be a comprehensive survey of all these thinkers, but rather an attempt to highlight certain key themes that are common to them, and to explore the ontological and epistemological foundations of their political philosophy.

One of the central themes of classical anarchism – and, indeed, of anarchism generally – is the rejection of the idea of government[21] and the contention that life can function perfectly well without it. This is the most radical claim that anarchists make, and it is what distinguishes anarchism from most other political philosophies, even radical ones. Indeed, one could say that the idea of government, the idea that we must have some institution like the state which is sovereign, is one of the most basic and fundamental assumptions of political thought. The central claim made by theorists of sovereignty, from Jean Bodin and Hobbes through to Carl Schmitt, is that politics as a collective activity cannot take place outside a state framework and is meaningless without sovereignty. Without government, we are told, society would fall apart.

The nightmare of the anarchic state of nature, whose insecurity is so intolerable that we rush headlong into the protective arms of the sovereign, is something that has haunted, and continues to haunt, political philosophy. The fear of anarchy and insecurity is a powerful political force and rhetorical device, something that legitimises state authority irrespective of its abuses. The fear of terrorism, the fear of crime or 'illegal' immigration, fear of 'financial anarchy' on Wall Street: for all these fears – fears which an anarchist analysis shows are actually fostered by government – the only remedy is seen to be government itself.

Anarchists have a very different view: government is seen not only to be unnecessary, but as actually having a pernicious, corrupting and destructive influence on social relations. In the words of the eighteenth-century thinker, William Godwin, governments 'lay their hand on the spring there is in society, and put a stop to its motion'.[22] In other words, governments interfere with society in destructive and artificial ways, disrupting its natural processes and arrangements. I will say more about this picture of social relations as self-regulating later, but the central idea here is that society has no need of government: government is an encumbrance upon society, regulating the lives of people excessively, exploiting and oppressing them, stealing their resources, limiting their freedom, and disrupting communal practices, arrangements and ways of life that they have fostered organically.

For anarchists, government and the state are an unbearable imposition on both the individual and society as a whole. For Godwin, government authority interferes with the individual's right of private judgement, which for him is the essential right, forming the basis for individual virtue. We cannot hope to arrive at a more virtuous existence unless we can make our own decisions freely on the basis of our own moral and rational judgement. This – and not any external compulsion – should be the only thing that determines our actions and that can legitimately impose obligations upon the individual. Any interference with this right is something that diminishes the sanctity of the human being. That is why this right of private judgement should translate into civil affairs as well as simply matters of individual conscience; indeed, the two domains are inseparable.[23] However, this right to freely form one's own opinions and to shape the conditions in which one lives, always runs up against the 'brute machine' of government: '"I have deeply reflected", suppose, "upon the nature of virtue, and am convinced that a certain proceeding is incumbent upon me. But the hangman, supported by an act of parliament, assures me I am mistaken"'.[24] Thus, the imposition of obligations that contravene private judgement is something that does a profound violence to the individual. Similarly, for Bakunin, that self-proclaimed fanatical lover of liberty, political authority and freedom are irreconcilable: political institutions are 'hostile and fatal to the liberty of the masses, for they impose upon them a system of external and therefore despotic laws'.[25] For anarchists, the very principle of political authority violates that of individual freedom and must, therefore, be abolished: liberty can be realised only when the individual is no longer governed by external political institutions.

How this idea jars with conventional politics today! For all the (neo) liberal rhetoric of individual responsibility and personal freedom, things seem to be going in precisely the opposite direction, with more and more government constraints being placed upon individuals, more regulations, more intrusive surveillance measures and the general intensification of state power. The spaces for individual autonomy – if things like personal privacy, self-determination, civil liberties and free political expression are any measure – seem to be shrinking rather than expanding. Whether such restrictions go under the name of security, or the 'prevention of harm', or discouraging 'anti-social' behaviour, there seems to be a passion for authority and an intense distrust of individual freedom and self-determination. The individual is seen as a potential source of harm or risk; a site of constant crisis which must be guided, protected, regulated, monitored, secured and secured against. Tocqueville's description of the despotism of nineteenth-century American democracy, in which an immense and protective power stands above people and keeps them in perpetual childhood and servitude[26] – seems to apply ever more so today.

Furthermore, government and the principle of political authority interfere with freely formed social relations. The individual liberty that anarchists celebrate does not exist in a vacuum, but emerges, as we have seen, in relations with others and presupposes the equal freedom of others. What anarchists object to is the way that governments act to repress any expression of collective liberty, and inhibit the emergence of autonomous social arrangements and communities. For instance, Kropotkin describes how in sixteenth-century Europe, independent entities such as guilds, free associations, village communities and medieval cities started to be taken over and displaced by an increasingly centralised and absolutist state apparatus – a process which was accomplished through violence rather than consent, and led to the annihilation of these autonomous social entities.[27] It was this process of state capture which, moreover, fostered more hierarchical and unequal forms of society, and led to a domination by political, religious and economic elites. The political domination of the state interferes with the principle of sociability and mutual assistance, which Kropotkin believed was immanent in social relations and implicit in nature – evidence of which he found in all sorts of cooperative and voluntary associations that existed in society.[28] So, for anarchists, not only do the state and centralised government suppress or prevent the emergence of autonomous self-organised communities – the state cannot tolerate even the slightest challenge to its sovereignty – but they also have a distorting effect on social relations, generating and actively sustaining hierarchical social structures. The unequal relationships entailed by capitalism and the reign of private property – the tyranny of the capitalist over the worker, the tyranny of the rich over the poor, the domination of the principle of capitalist accumulation and modern technology over the natural environment[29] – can survive only with the active support and intervention of the state. The 'free market' is not self-regulating, as the right-wing libertarians contend[30] – this is simply an illusion. Rather, the market is of necessity constantly propped up by the state – witness the recent massive government bail-outs of the banking sector – and protected and sustained through state coercion and violence. The process that Marx termed 'primitive accumulation', to refer to the violent integration of societies in different periods into capitalist relations, accomplished with the support of state power, is being repeated today in the process that we refer to as economic globalisation. Once again, state force – used against indigenous people, workers, environmental activists – is a crucial element. For anarchists, then, the state is destructive of organic social relations, suppressing its egalitarian and libertarian energies. To quote Bakunin: 'the State is like a vast slaughterhouse and an enormous cemetery, where under the shadow and the pretext of this abstraction (the common good) all the best aspirations, all the living forces of a country, are sanctimoniously immolated and interred'.[31]

LEGITIMISING POWER

This implacable critique of government and the state implies a fundamental scepticism about the ways in which political authority seeks to justify itself. Anarchists reject, for instance, notions of the social contract, which they regard as ideological mystifications. The social contract, for Bakunin, was an 'unworthy hoax' and an 'absurd fiction' – a cheap trick that has been foisted on people to make them believe the state to be legitimate and based on their consent. The contradiction in social contract theories detected by Bakunin, was that while they painted a picture of people in a state of either primitive savagery or egotistical competition, at the same time they claim that people suddenly have the foresight to come together to form a rational collective agreement.[32] The origins of our supposed consent to government are highly dubious and paradoxical, then, and Locke's notion of 'tacit consent'[33] is even more suspect. Rather than having given our consent to government and freely sacrificing our liberties, anarchists claim that government has been violently imposed upon us through conquest, or through various kinds of trickery, deceit and political fraud. The perfect liberty and equality that Hobbes found in the state of nature, and which he saw as so destructive of human coexistence, are precisely the conditions which anarchists see as the basis of ethical community – conditions which have been obscured beneath the looming shadow of Leviathan. Rather, the violent state of nature, based on egotistical competition, exists now, and has been fostered by the state and capitalism. For anarchists, then, consent or social contract explanations of the state and political obligation have no credibility, and are simply ideological masks which we must peer through to see the real workings of power and the true visage of the sovereign.

Indeed, one might say that these ideological masks are wearing a little thin these days. With the current era that is defined by the global 'War on Terror' – a war that continues in the post-Bush era – the trappings of consent, democratic accountability and liberal checks and balances seem to have fallen away, and what is revealed increasingly is naked power. Where was the 'consent of the governed' when millions marched against the impending war in Iraq in 2003, only to be met with the utter contempt of their political elites? Where was the liberal notion of limited government and the protection of rights when there has been an unprecedented expansion in the powers of the state over the citizen, when the most basic civil liberties have been eroded, when one can be arrested and imprisoned, in some cases for an indefinite period, without even knowing the reason why, when liberal democratic states practice torture, when governments openly lie to their people, when the old doctrine of divine right is invoked once again to justify war?[34] Liberal-democratic states founded, supposedly, on the consent of their people and on the requirement to protect their rights, seem to have turned upon their own people – perversely in the name of guaranteeing their security – and have become all but indistinguishable from authoritarian police states. Indeed, the claim that political elites make about the open, free and democratic nature of their societies, in contradistinction to those of Iran and elsewhere, becomes less and less convincing. So we see, then, the paradox of security that is central to justifications of state sovereignty: the logic of security – originally imagined to protect liberty – becomes so all-encompassing that it ultimately turns against liberty itself. From an anarchist perspective, the notion of the state of exception – characterised by Schmitt as an extraordinary situation in which constitutional rule is suspended[35] – is the very truth of the state, no matter what its constitutional arrangements are. Indeed, one might say that the state of exception, embodying the hyper-politicised 'total state' – so far from being opposed to liberalism as Schmitt believed – is actually the permanent underside of liberal societies, an underside which is now becoming increasingly explicit.

What is central to the anarchist critique of the state is that the state embodies a certain structure and logic of domination regardless of the form it takes; that, in other words, all states are in essence the same, whether they are monarchical states, authoritarian states, workers' states or even democratic states. The form a particular state takes is simply a kind of disguise which masks its drive to domination, or at best articulates it in a slightly different way. Therefore, for Kropotkin, 'there are those who, like us, see in the State, not only its actual form and in all forms of domination that it might assume, but in its very essence, an obstacle to the social revolution'.[36] Indeed, this was at the heart of the theoretical and political dispute between anarchists and Marxists during the nineteenth century: anarchists accused Marx of neglecting this central truth about political power, and claimed that the workers' state would simply perpetuate state domination. I will go into this in greater detail in a subsequent chapter; the point here is that, for anarchists, at the heart of all states, no matter how they are constituted, there is the same sovereign principle and, therefore, the same political inequality and the same project of infinite expansion.

DEMOCRACY AND THE STATE

Formal democracy does not change this. Formal democracy is simply another ideological trapping, another guise, another regime through which state power is expressed. Therefore, democracy in itself cannot serve as a legitimate justification for state authority. It is not that a democratic state would not be in itself preferable to, say, a monarchical state – although Bakunin believed that essentially there was no difference, and that democratic states may possibly be *more* pernicious because they more effectively disguise power[37] – but that mechanisms of universal suffrage and elected representation do not, in fact, guarantee equality and liberty and, indeed, often act to deny them. Notions of democratic accountability and the government representing the will and interests of the people, is simply an illusion which masks the absolute gulf between the people and power.[38] For example, our contemporary situation is characterised by a strange reversal in the status of democracy. In the eighteenth and nineteenth centuries, when campaigns for democratic suffrage where underway, the demand for democracy was perceived as a genuine threat by political elites, who were reluctant to grant even the most basic democratic rights. Today, however, the situation has been almost entirely reversed: political elites seek to outdo one another in their claim to be democratic and answerable to the people, trumpeting their democratic credentials. The people are encouraged, exhorted to involve themselves in democratic processes, to get out and vote; we are bombarded with what are seen as amazing democratic innovations, such as e-democracy and e-government, which are supposedly all about making government more accessible and accountable to its citizens. Democracy, moreover, is seen to be the only legitimate political system, to the point where wars are fought supposedly to spread democracy. Democracy, in other words, is virtually forced down our throats. At the same time, there has never been such resounding cynicism about democracy, such high levels of voter disinterest, such a sense of disillusionment about the efficacy and adequacy of democratic mechanisms and processes, such an alienation from formal politics.[39] What does this paradox tell us about the nature of democracy today? Democracy has gone from being something which challenged the power of political and economic elites, to something which now legitimises their rule. In other words, the power of elites is today expressed and justified through democracy, which is precisely why there is this insistence on democratic involvement and the virtues of the Western democratic model. Voting has become a symbolic act which legitimises political power, and a change of government, as the elite theorists have always told us, is a game of revolving oligarchies – something which is more evident now when there is no longer any real ideological difference between major political parties.[40] Indeed, one could suggest, without too much exaggeration, that Western, supposedly plural, democracies are effectively one-party states in which there are competing factions who vie for power, yet who all subscribe to the same economic and security agenda.

So, from the anarchist perspective, democracy is a system that both disguises and legitimises power, thus sustaining political and economic inequality. This is not to diminish the importance and achievements of democratic struggles during the nineteenth century, or even those of contemporary times (such as Burma, China and Iran, for instance); struggles which were and are essentially an expression of the popular demand for equal-liberty against power. It is, however, to suggest that there is a kind of underside to democracy: it is a mechanism through which collective movements and struggles are co-opted into the structures of the state through the category of citizenship.

Central to anarchists' scepticism about democracy, moreover, is the critique of representation: both in terms of the extremely limited and inadequate fashion in which current parliamentary arrangements represent the will of the people, and in the more general sense that the idea of representation itself inevitably distorts this will. This is why anarchists are opposed not only to representative democratic assemblies, but also to revolutionary vanguard parties which claim to speak for and represent the interests of the people. This was a major point of contention between anarchists and Marxists and Leninists. For anarchists, the emphasis is on the direct expression of the popular will, which is why anarchist revolutionary tactics tend to stress spontaneous revolt, self-organisation and direct action. To speak for people, to claim to represent their will and interests, establishes an unequal power relationship over the people. Moreover, representation always binds democracy to the state – it is a way of channelling the will of the people into state structures: this applies not only to mass political parties, but also to the revolutionary vanguard party which aims to take over state power, and that anarchists see as a mini state-in-waiting. That is why, for Proudhon, representative government is a 'perpetual abuse of power for the profit of the reigning cast and the interests of the representatives, against the interests of the represented'.[41]

This position on democracy becomes more ambiguous, however, when we consider the question of radical democracy. Even though this form of decision making is more direct and egalitarian, removing, or at least more tightly controlling, the relationship of representation, anarchists have remained sceptical of radical democracy, pointing out the dangers of majoritarianism and the tyranny of the majority. Anarchists are not Rousseauians and, indeed they point to the authoritarianism of the General Will to show that democracy – even if it is direct – is not guarantee of liberty, and often entails the unjust sacrifice of individual rights and dissenting minority voices to the will of the majority. It might be argued that anarchists do not seek a democracy but, rather, an *aristocracy of all*, where the liberty and autonomy of each is fully and equally respected. Indeed, Uri Gordon has argued that anarchism entails an entirely different form of politics that is based on consensus building rather than democratic decision making.[42]

At other times, however, anarchists have been more favourably disposed to democracy: Godwin considered it the best of existing systems, not only because it presupposed political equality, but also because – unlike more authoritarian systems – it granted to the individual a moral and rational autonomy, the ability to make decisions for him- or herself, that in turn fostered more open and cooperative relations between people.[43] Bakunin admired the radical democracy of the Paris Commune, and claimed, furthermore, that because democracy denotes government of, by and for the people, that we are all democrats.[44] Moreover, it is hard to imagine an anarchist society which would not involve some form of democratic decision making: here I think it is more accurate to see consensus-style decision making as an extension of democracy, rather than being qualitatively different from it. Democracy, as I see it, does not mean simple majoritarianism; what is much more fundamental to democracy is not majority rule, but rather the questioning of all forms of political power and social hierarchies and the assertion of collective autonomy or equal-liberty. So there is something in the democratic promise which always exceeds the limits of its current articulations, something which suggests an open horizon of political experimentation and endless articulations of equal-liberty – in which, for instance, individual liberty and the right to dissent are as much a part of the language of democracy as is political equality.

Furthermore, as I will try to show, democracy does not necessarily bind us to the state, but can be imagined outside it and as working against it. So the relationship between anarchism and democracy is one of fundamental and necessary ambivalence;[45] democracy, radically conceived, *is* anarchy. Anarchism seeks an ongoing democratisation of society, of power relations: it always seeks more democracy, and at the same time, democracy of a different kind. It points to a *beyond of democracy*, which in itself is part of the democratic promise. Bakunin perhaps puts it best when he says that although anarchists must support democracy, they must also find the term *insufficient*.[46]

PROPERTY AND EQUALITY

For anarchists, if democracy is to mean anything, then it must go beyond political equality and involve full social and economic equality; it must be the motor that generates different articulations of equal-liberty. There can be neither equality nor liberty under the current conditions of capitalism and the tyranny of private property – not only does the concentration of property in the hands of an elite in effect deny property to a majority of people, it also reproduces relations of social and political domination in which those without property are subordinated, and through which they are deprived of liberty. The subordination of the worker to the boss is as much a relationship of political domination as it is one of economic exploitation. Moreover, unequal relations of property always necessitate a strong and authoritarian state, a state which acts in the interests of the wealthy and economically powerful, and which perpetuates the conditions for their ongoing enrichment and accumulation of power; although, as we shall see later on, there is an important difference between the anarchist theory of the state and the Marxist class analysis of the state. Godwin had no doubt about the artificiality of property and inequality: in other words, the way that it was actually propped up and supported through the intervention of political institutions, without which it would collapse.[47] Furthermore, property and inequality – and particularly the desire for luxury and superfluity – had a corrupting influence on social relations as well as on individual subjectivity. It was the source of moral corruption, criminality and especially servility: 'Observe the pauper, fawning with abject vileness upon his rich benefactor, speechless with sensations of gratitude . . .'[48] Indeed, it is the 'spectacle of injustice'[49] and ostentation which fosters selfishness, jealousy, greed and idleness amid ignorance and poverty, thus sowing the seeds of social division. Moreover, for Godwin, accumulated wealth was always based on the most brutal exploitation of labour, something that was affirmed by Proudhon in his famous slogan, 'Property is Theft'.[50] Although Proudhon allowed for limited possession of property, seeing it as important to one's security and liberty, he remained opposed to large accumulations of wealth, claiming that these were precisely what endangered security, equality and liberty.

Anarchists, therefore, want to see the limitation of private property, and the transformation of property relations so that they are no longer exploitative. There have been numerous proposals and formulas for this: from the mutualism of Proudhon, in which workers would retain possession of the means to their labour and would organise economic exchanges based on voluntary contracts; to the collectivism of Bakunin, in which wages would reflect the amount of work done; to Kropotkin's communist formula for wealth distribution on the basis of human need.[51] Even Godwin, who was opposed to the idea of any sort of coercive socialisation of wealth, believed that society would eventually be rational and enlightened enough to agree to a voluntary transfer of wealth and a more equal distribution of property.[52] The relative equalisation and democratisation of wealth and property is thus seen as an important component in the liberation of society from both economic inequality and political domination.

THE REVOLT OF SOCIETY AGAINST THE STATE

Anarchists rejected other forms of domination apart from property and statism, including religion, patriarchal relations (Proudhon was the exception here), technology and scientific elitism. Indeed, it is perhaps more accurate to see classical anarchism as a critique of the relationship of domination generally, rather than just a critique of the state. However, for anarchists, the state is not simply a political institution or series of political institutions, nor is it simply the site where power relations are at their most concentrated and one-sided; it is also a series of arrangements and hierarchies which, to speak in Deleuzo–Guattarian terms, 'overcodes'[53] other social relations. In other words, the state is an abstract principle of authority and domination – a rationality of power – which sustains, even constitutes, other relationships of domination in society. It is almost as if the hierarchical and authoritarian

structures of the state provide a kind of model for other social, economic and personal relationships, allowing them to be articulated in
unequal ways. It is difficult, then, in the anarchist conceptual analysis
to see a particular relation of domination in isolation: it is something
that can be understood only in relation to the state which sustains it.
That is why the focus of the anarchist political critique tends to be on
the state, why anarchists seek the abolition of the state above all else
and why anarchists see as achievable a society without a state: a society
of decentralised, free communities. Central to anarchism, therefore, is a
revolt of society against the state, a revolt of the 'social principle' against
the political principle of power. Society and humanity cannot hope to
flourish unless they are liberated from the state. As Kropotkin says:

> Either the State will be destroyed and a new life will begin in thou-
> sands of centers . . . or else the State must crush the individual and
> local life, it must become master of all domains of human activity,
> must bring with it wars and internal struggles for the possession
> of power, surface revolutions which only change one tyrant for
> another, and inevitably, at the end of this evolution – death.[54]

What is presupposed here is a sort of moral and conceptual division
between society and the state, between humanity and political power,
a kind of Manicheanism: society, which is oppressed, distorted and corrupted by the operation of political power, will rise up against the state,
and, upon the state's destruction, free and egalitarian relations will be
allowed to flourish. This division between social life and the political
order is evident, for instance, in Bakunin's conception of the difference
between the natural laws of the material world – the laws which affirm
our place within the natural social order – and the artificial authority of
man-made laws and institutions that characterise political power, and
that act as a constraint upon our freedom.[55] In other words, there is a
division between a kind of organic natural order – which is fundamental
to society – and an artificial political order – the order of power, political
institutions, laws and so on – that is alien and hostile to society. This
natural order is rational and contains the foundations of morality; the
order of political power, on the other hand, is violent, irrational and
immoral. It is not simply that, as the old saying goes, power corrupts,
but that political power distorts and stultifies what would otherwise be
free human relations.

Classical anarchism can therefore be described as an *anti-politics*: anarchists call into question the principle of state sovereignty and refuse to see participation in formal structures political power as a means of achieving social change. It is in this sense that Bakunin distinguished between political revolution and social revolution: the latter sought not only to collectivise economic relations, but also to abolish political power, in contradistinction to bourgeois social democrats, Marxists and Leninists who wanted to engage with and use political power to further their ends. The anarchists were different because they sought the *total abolition of politics*.[56]

THE RATIONAL SOCIAL OBJECT

This idea of anarchism as an anti-politics is not as straightforward as it sounds, however, and, as I shall show in later chapters, it is open to a number of different interpretations. Even for Bakunin, anarchism was still a politics and, indeed, in the same passage in which he talks about the abolition of politics, he also talks about the 'politics of the Social Revolution' and discusses the politics of the International Workingmen's Association.[57] It is clear, then, that the anarchist desire to abolish politics simply suggests an alternative form of politics, one that is equal-libertarian and anti-authoritarian.

At the same time, anarchist anti-political politics is based on a certain conceptualisation of social relations. Central here is the idea, already introduced above, that society is constituted by self-regulating natural mechanisms, relations and processes that are rational and that, if left alone, allow a more harmonious social order to emerge. This idea, which is part of an Enlightenment-based rationalist and human-ist discourse that influenced other political philosophies as well, can be seen in a number of different aspects of classical anarchist thought. For instance, Bakunin, as we have seen already, posited the idea of 'immutable' natural laws and processes, whose truth would be revealed through science, and whose unfolding determined social progress and the intellectual, moral and material development of humanity. As part of a critique of religious idealism, he proposes a scientific-materialist account of man's development:

> Having shown how idealism, starting with the absurd ideas of God, immortality and the soul, the *original* freedom of individuals,

and their morality independent of society, inevitably arrives at the consecration of slavery, I now have to show how real science, materialism and socialism – the second term being but the true and complete development of the first, precisely because they take as their starting point the material nature and the natural and primitive slavery of men, and because they bind themselves to seek the emancipation of men not outside but within society, not against it but by means of it – are bound to end in the establishment of the greatest freedom of individuals and the highest form of human morality.[58]

Bakunin's political thought can be seen as a scientific-materialist philosophy combined with a dialectical view of historical development. A similar idea might be found in Godwin's rationalist anarchism, in which social improvements and the emergence of a more just and equal society is closely bound up with the progress of science, as well as with the inevitable development of people's moral and intellectual capacities.[59]

This positivist philosophy is further emphasised in Kropotkin's theory of social relations as being based on an innate tendency towards mutual aid and assistance, which we have inherited from the animal world and which is a major factor in evolutionary survival. In his critique of what he sees as a crude interpretation and application of Darwin to a 'survival of the fittest' model of social relations, Kropotkin argues that it was actually Darwin who first discovered an instinctive sociability in animals of the same species, a tendency towards cooperation rather than competition.[60] Moreover, this 'permanent instinct' towards mutual aid was also carried through into human society, and could be found in numerous cooperative organisations, voluntary associations and mutual assistance societies which operated without any involvement from the state – the Lifeboat Association, trades unions, social and sporting clubs and so on. Indeed, this social principle – the principle of cooperation, solidarity and mutuality – could be traced throughout human history, existing in a permanent tension with increasingly centralised political institutions. Kropotkin believed that this social principle would eventually prevail over the state, and form the social and ethical basis for a more cooperative society formed through voluntary arrangements. Indeed, the very foundations of anarchist ethics are to be found in this simple biological fact of mutual assistance: in struggling to survive, people must work and cooperate with one another out of necessity, and this forms the basis of our notions of morality, justice and altruism. Thus, as Kropotkin says:

> Nature has thus to be recognized as the *first ethical teacher of man*. The social instinct innate in men as well as in all the social animals – this is the origin of all ethical conceptions and all the subsequent development of morality.[61]

It is important to realise that in making arguments such as this, anarchists do not have a one-sided or naively benign concept of human nature.[62] However, even though there are also egotistical aspects of human nature which have the potential to work against the principles of sociability and cooperation, the point is that for anarchists, people are intrinsically and organically part of a social whole, and that their cooperative instincts tend come to the fore in this social context. There is a kind of social essentialism here, the idea that society embodies a rationality and a morality which is immanent, whose laws and processes are scientifically observable; a logic (of collectivity, sociability) that is unfolding and emerging in opposition to the logic of power. Thus, this rational social object forms a kind of moral pivot in the anarchist argument against political power: society contains, as we see, the seeds of its own emancipation, as well as the potential to organise itself without political power. It also provides the basis for the anarchist understanding of equal-liberty: freedom understood collectively and realised on the basis of an essential human commonality between people, forming the foundations for solidarity and community.

ANARCHISM AND UTOPIANISM

This particular conception of social relations provides the foundations for a future anarchist society. Anarchists were always wary about laying down precise blueprints for future social arrangements, emphasising instead revolutionary spontaneity and free acts of creation. At the same time, however, there is a definite utopian tendency in classical anarchism – a certain vision of a society without a state, a society based on free, voluntary arrangements and decentralised social structures. Bakunin, who followed Marx in criticising the utopian socialists, himself proposed a society of collectives based on work, from which class structures would be absent, in which scientific education would become available to all, and in which the care of children would become a communal responsibility. Proudhon believed that a federalist system in which relations were to be based on mutual contracts, would be the best way of preserving liberty and security; whereas Kropotkin went into considerable technical detail about how agriculture and industry would be organised, and how produce would be distributed.[63] Godwin, as we have seen, believed in the progressive perfection of human society through education and intellectual improvement.

Contrary to what many critics have argued, however, anarchism is not necessarily more utopian than other political philosophies – all political theories and projects have a utopian moment, based on certain pre-conceptions about either human nature or social relations.[64] To project any sort of ideal vision of what society could look like or what human relations could be, and to seek to implement either revolutionary or reformist programmes in the achievement of this end, is a utopianism – and could apply just as easily to liberalism, with its idealised free-market exchanges, utility-maximising models of rational behaviour or 'original positions', as it could to anarchism. Moreover, there is nothing wrong with utopianism as such – a utopian moment is central to all radical politics – although I will propose an alternative understanding of utopianism in later chapters. The utopia of classical anarchism, however, emerges as the result of this immanent social rationality that I have described. This is not to say that, for anarchists, a society without political authority would emerge inevitably; more so than most radical political philosophies, anarchism emphasised spontaneous human action and the urge to rebel. However, this revolutionary transformation to a libertarian-egalitarian society is seen as part of an immanent social process that is determined – or at least conditioned – by either natural laws, the dialectic, the progressive enlightenment of mankind, or the realisation of our innate sociability.

In this chapter I have argued that anarchism is an insurrectionary political philosophy driven by a desire for unconditional equal-liberty – a desire which calls into question all forms of political authority, social hierarchy and economic inequality. In this sense, anarchism is the ultimate horizon for radical politics. However, the politics and ethics of classical anarchism can be understood only within a certain Enlightenment rationalist–humanist paradigm, that which supposes there to be an objective truth to social relations that is suppressed by power and yet will be revealed; a rational and ethical potential within the human subject that is discovered in his or her relations with others. There is a certain narrative of liberation here, in which society rebels against power, in which humanity rebels against politics. In the next chapter I shall show that there are certain problems with this discourse, problems which make it necessary for us to rethink key aspects of classical anarchism.

Notes

1 A reference to William Godwin's philosophical critique of government in *Enquiry Concerning Political Justice*, where he talks about the triumph of rational human understanding over ignorance, weakness and blind confidence, the tendencies upon which government relies. Such a triumph would result in the 'the true euthanasia of government', something which Godwin assures us should not be contemplated with undue alarm. See pp. 247–8 (Harmondsworth: Penguin, 1985 [1793]).

2 'The New Law of Righteousness'. Cited from George Woodcock, *Anarchism: A History of Libertarian Ideas and Movements* (Harmondsworth: Penguin, 1986), p. 42.

3 The Diggers or The True Levellers, led by Winstanley, did attempt such experiments – most famously the colony on St George's Hill in Surrey in 1649. See Fenner Brockway, *Britain's First Socialists: the Levellers, Agitators and Diggers of the English Revolution* (London: Quartet Books, 1983).

4 Indeed, Engels believed that the sixteenth-century German revolutionary Thomas Müntzer's Christian theological discourse was a sort of cloak for a more radical pantheism and even atheism, as well as a communist militancy. His revolt against the Church, monarchy and feudal lords was an expression of class struggle – the struggle of the peasant-proletariat against their conditions of economic exploitation and political domination. See Friedrich Engels, *The German Revolutions: the Peasant War in Germany* (Chicago, IL: University of Chicago Press, 1967), p. 46.

5 Karl Marx and Friedrich Engels, *The Manifesto of the Communist Party*, in Robert Tucker (ed.) *The Marx–Engels Reader* (New York: Princeton University Press, 1978), pp. 473–500 at 490.

6 See Friedrich Engels, *The Civil War in France*, in *The Marx–Engels Reader*, pp. 618–19.

7 Karl Marx, 'Contribution to the Critique of Hegel's Philosophy of Law', Karl Marx and Friedrich Engels, *Collected Works*, Vol. 3 (London: Lawrence & Wishart, 1975), pp. 29, 31.

8 See Robert Paul Wolff, *In Defense of Anarchism* (Berkeley, CA: University

of California Press, 1998). Here he contributes towards a philosophical anarchism by suggesting that the moral autonomy of the individual is ultimately incompatible with state authority.

9   Mikhail Bakunin, *Political Philosophy of Mikhail Bakunin: Scientific Anarchism*, G. P. Maximoff (ed.) (London: Free Press of Glencoe, 1953), p. 267.

10 Herbert Spencer, *Social Statics* (London: Chapman, 1851), p. 103.

11 See Spencer, *Social Statics*, ch. XIX.

12 The main thrust of Spencer's critique of the state is against its attempts to regulate the market and address certain social inequalities. Such measures, he believed, encouraged laziness, violated individual freedom and would lead only to despotism. See Spencer, *The Man versus the State* (Harmondsworth: Penguin, 1969 [1884]).

13 See Tim Gray, 'Spencer, Steiner and Hart on the Equal Liberty Principle', *Journal of Applied Philosophy*, 10 (1), 1993, pp. 91–104.

14 Curiously enough, as Thomas Pogge shows, there are potential authoritarian implications in Rawls conception of the equality of liberty as constituted by the principle that liberty can be restricted only for the sake of liberty – implications which become evident, Pogge argues, in considering questions of crime, law enforcement and punishment. See 'Equal Liberty for All?', *Midwest Studies in Philosophy*, XXVIII, 2004, pp. 266–81.

15 See Todd May, *The Political Thought of Jacques Rancière, Creating Equality* (Edinburgh: Edinburgh University Press, 2008).

16 Étienne Balibar, *Politics and the Other Scene*, trans. Christine Jones, James Swenson and Chris Turner (London: Verso, 2002), p. 3.

17 Todd May arrives at a slightly different formulation of anarchist political ethics, in which equality is primary and foregrounds liberty. See *The Political Thought of Jacques Rancière*, p. 89.

18 Bakunin, *Political Philosophy*, pp. 222–3.

19 See Peter Marshall, *Demanding the Impossible: A History of Anarchism* (London: Harper Perennial, 2008).

20 This is by no means a complete list – one could also include Emma Goldman, Errico Malatesta, Élisée Reclus, and Max Stirner.

21 Here I am referring to government in the broad sense to include the idea of sovereign state authority, i.e., government in the sense of being governed.

22 William Godwin, *Anarchist Writings*, Peter Marshall (ed.) (London: Freedom Press, 1968), p. 92.

23 Godwin, *Enquiry Concerning Political Justice*, p. 204.

24 Godwin, *Enquiry Concerning Political Justice*, p. 205.

25 Bakunin, *Political Philosophy*, p. 240.

26 Alexis de Tocqueville, *Democracy in America*, trans. G. Lawrence, J. P Mayer (ed.) (London: Fontana Press, 1994), p. 692.

27 See Peter Kropotkin, *The State: Its Historic Role* (London: Freedom Press, 1943).

28 See Peter Kropokin, *Mutual Aid: A Factor of Evolution*, Paul Avrich (ed.) (New York: New York University Press, 1972).

29 Indeed, Murray Bookchin argues that the domination of nature is a direct outcome and a reflection of social and political hierarchies: 'The notion that man must dominate nature emerges directly from the domination of man by man.' See *Post-Scarcity Anarchism* (London: Wildwood House, 1974), p. 63.

30 At this point it is important to distinguish between anarchism and certain strands of right-wing libertarianism which at times go by the same name (for example, Murray Rothbard's anarcho-capitalism). There is a complex debate within this tradition between those like Robert Nozick, who advocate a 'minimal state', and those like Rothbard who want to do away with the state altogether and allow all transactions to be governed by the market alone (see Rothbard, 'Robert Nozick and the Immaculate Conception of the State', *Journal of Libertarian Studies*, 1 (1), 1977, pp. 45–57). From an anarchist perspective, however, both positions – the minimal state (minarchist) and the no-state ('anarchist') positions – neglect the problem of economic domination; in other words, they neglect the hierarchies, oppressions and forms of exploitation that would inevitably arise in a laissez-faire 'free' market. Economic inequality, therefore, would not only produce violence and instability, but would also lead to concentrations in power and influence: economic inequality thus becomes political inequality, economic domination thus translates into political domination. Furthermore, the problem with the minimal state such as that advocated by Nozick, is that it is never minimal in practice: on the contrary, a state which preoccupies itself with security functions – military and police force – is in fact highly interventionist, intrusive and authoritarian. The state apparatus under Bush – while not exactly a minimal state in Nozick's terms – may be seen as an example of this tendency: while the Bush Administration ideologically signed up to the fundamentals of economic libertarianism – tax cuts and privatisation, for instance – it also presided over a massive expansion in the state's security, surveillance and war-making operations, running up the biggest government deficit in US history. The libertarian minimal state always ends up as a Leviathan state. Anarchism, therefore, has no truck with this sort of right-wing libertarianism, not only because it neglects economic inequality and domination, but also because in practice (and indeed in theory) it is highly inconsistent and contradictory. The individual freedom invoked by right-wing libertarians is only a narrow economic freedom within the constraints of a capitalist market, which, as anarchists show, is no freedom at all.

31 Bakunin, *Political Philosophy*, p. 207.
32 Bakunin, *Political Philosophy*, p. 165.
33 See John Locke, *The Second Treatise of Government*, J. W Gough (ed.) (Oxford: Basil Blackwell, 1956), pp. 61–2 [119–20]
34 Tony Blair, in a TV interview in 2006, said that God would judge him on his decision to go to war in Iraq. George W. Bush made similar anti-democratic statements.
35 See Carl Schmitt, *Political Theology: Four Chapters on the Concept of Sovereignty*, trans. G. Schwab (Chicago, IL: University of Chicago Press, 2005).
36 Kropotkin, *The State*, p. 9.
37 This would be in contrast to someone like Norberto Bobbio, who argues that what is central to democracy is the visibility of power. See *Democracy and Dictatorship: the Nature and Limits of State Power*, trans. P. Kennealy (Cambridge: Polity Press, 1989).
38 See Bakunin, *Political Philosophy*, pp. 217–18.
39 Notwithstanding the enthusiasm surrounding the 2008 election of Obama in the United States, the general diagnosis for democracy is not good. Indeed, many now speak of 'post-democracy'. See Colin Crouch, *Post-Democracy* (Cambridge: Polity Press, 2004).
40 The current scandal in the UK over MPs' expenses – in which the most petty and grasping avariciousness has been displayed by political representatives – symbolises the nihilism at the heart of contemporary democracy.
41 Cited in Marshall, *Demanding the Impossible*, p. 246.
42 See Uri Gordon, *Anarchy Alive!: Anti-authoritarian Politics from Practice to Theory* (London: Pluto Press, 2008).
43 See Godwin, *Enquiry Concerning Political Justice*, p. 490.
44 See Bakunin, *Political Philosophy*, p. 223.
45 See Amedeo Bertolo, 'Democracy and Beyond', *Democracy & Nature*, 5 (2), 1999, pp. 311–23.
46 Bakunin, *Political Philosophy*, p. 223.
47 Godwin, *Enquiry Concerning Political Justice*, p. 720.
48 Godwin, *Enquiry Concerning Political Justice*, p. 725.
49 Godwin, *Enquiry Concerning Political Justice*, pp. 727–9.
50 Indeed, Proudhon claims that not only is the property of one based on the theft of the property of the other, but that it is, in fact, a contradiction in terms in the sense that the idea of free and equal exchange on which property is in theory based, depends in fact on external force and fraud: 'Finally, property does not exist by itself. In order to produce and to act it requires extraneous cause, which is force or fraud. In other words, property is not equal to property: it is a negation, a delusion, NOTHING' (emphasis is Proudhon's). See *What is Property?*, Donald R. Kelley and Bonnie G. Smith (eds) (Cambridge: Cambridge University Press, 1994), p. 169.

51 See Peter Kropotkin, *The Conquest of Bread, and Other Writings*, Marshall S. Shatz (ed.) (Cambridge: Cambridge University Press, 1995).

52 Godwin, *Enquiry Concerning Political Justice*, p. 736.

53 See Gilles Deleuze, 'Many Politics,' in Gilles Deleuze and Claire Parnet (eds), trans. Hugh Tomlinson, *Dialogues* (New York: Columbia University Press, 1987), pp. 124–53.

54 Kropotkin, *The State*, p. 44.

55 Bakunin, *Political Philosophy*, pp. 239–40.

56 Bakunin, *Political Philosophy*, p. 314.

57 Bakunin, *Political Philosophy*, p. 314.

58 Bakunin, *Political Philosophy*, p. 146.

59 See Godwin, *Enquiry Concerning Political Justice*, p. 740.

60 See Kropotkin, *Mutual Aid*.

61 Peter Kropotkin, *Ethics: Origin and Development*, trans. L. S. Friedland (New York: Tudor Publishing, 1947), p. 45.

62 As David Morland points out, classical anarchist thinkers recognised troubling egotistical and destructive tendencies in human nature, which created problems for their own utopian conceptions of future anarchist societies. See *Demanding the Impossible? Human Nature and Politics in Nineteenth-Century Social Anarchism* (London: Cassell, 1997).

63 See Peter Kropotkin, *Fields, Factories and Workshops Tomorrow*, Colin Ward (ed.) (London: Freedom Press, 1998).

64 For a discussion and defence of anarchist utopianism see Samuel Clark, *Living without Domination: the Possibility of an Anarchist Utopia* (Farnham: Ashgate, 2007).

Chapter 2

CROWNED ANARCHY[1]: TOWARDS A POSTANARCHIST ONTOLOGY[2]

In the previous chapter, anarchism was described as a revolutionary anti-politics that rejects political, social and economic domination and hierarchy in the name of an unconditional principle of equal-liberty. However, this position presupposed a certain organic vision of social relations and a notion of rational enlightenment, which served as the moral pivot against the distortions, obfuscations and injustices of political power. Anarchism, therefore, bases its critique of political authority on moral and rational foundations that derive from a social essence or being which is objectively understood. Whether this is understood in terms of the individual's progressive enlightenment, or the determination of material forces by historical laws and dialectical processes, or the discovery of man's innate sociality through the principle of mutual aid – there is the idea of a moral and rational basis to social relations, a natural foundation that is obscured by the workings of power and religion, yet which can be revealed through scientific enquiry.

Classical anarchism is, therefore, a political philosophy that is framed within an Enlightenment rationalist-humanist discourse. Central to anarchism is the idea of rational progress, the unfolding of an immanent social logic, and the emancipation of the subject from external constraints and oppressions – motifs which are incorporated also into liberalism and Marxism, albeit in different ways and with different emphases. While anarchism, as I have suggested, is the most radical of these political philosophies – and in its treatment of political power certainly the most sophisticated – it nevertheless shares with them an indebtedness to Enlightenment thought.

The problem is, however, that aspects of the Enlightenment paradigm have broken down and are no longer sustainable; that there is, as Jean-François Lyotard put it, an 'incredulity towards metanarratives'.[2]

46

It is not so much that ideas of emancipation and rational enlightenment have been relinquished, but there is a certain scepticism regarding their universality, that is, the sense in which they are understood by everyone in the same way. Yet it is not my intention here to call for an abandonment of the Enlightenment, or to pronounce its death sentence. On the contrary, a certain fidelity to key elements of the Enlightenment is more important now than ever. Rather, the Enlightenment paradigm must be reconsidered; its discursive limits must be interrogated. That is precisely what poststructuralist thinkers like Derrida, Lacan, Lyotard and Foucault have tried to do. It is entirely incorrect to say that poststructuralist thought is anti-Enlightenment. Rather, it sees the attempt to transcend the limitations of Enlightenment thought as being part of the very project of the Enlightenment. Central to the Enlightenment, in other words, is a critical reflection on its own limits. The Enlightenment, as Foucault showed with respect to Kant, embodies a critical ethos and the free and autonomous use of reason – something that can work against other rigidifying tendencies within Enlightenment thought. It is this ethos which allows us, as Foucault says, to refuse the 'blackmail of the Enlightenment':

> Yet that does not mean that one has to be 'for' or 'against' the Enlightenment. It even means precisely that one must refuse everything that might present itself in the form of a simplistic and authoritarian alternative: you either accept the Enlightenment and remain within the tradition of its rationalism . . . or else you criticize the Enlightenment and then try to escape from its principles of rationality . . .[3]

Instead, we must conduct, through precise historical inquiries, an exploration of the limits of our present, the conditions in which we live, conditions which are still determined by the Enlightenment. We must be aware, as Foucault says, of the historicity of the Enlightenment, and the sense in which the Enlightenment is an event and a complex and heterogeneous set of processes, transformations, discourses, institutions and practices which constitute us as subjects, as well as providing conditions and possibilities for our escape from subjectification. For this reason, we must also interrogate the historical link between the Enlightenment and humanism. Humanism is the discourse which has imposed certain identities and constraints upon us in the name of Man.

The Enlightenment – in the radical sense that Foucault conceives of it – is what allows us to explore the limits of this figure of Man and to gain greater autonomy from it.

It is exactly in this spirit of critical interrogation – this double move *within and against* the limits of the Enlightenment – that I would like to approach the question of the ontological foundations of classical anarchism. To unpack the Enlightenment, to explore its limits, is to not to jettison it but to *radicalise* it. In the same way, to interrogate the Enlightenment foundations of anarchist thought, to explore the limits of its humanism and rationalism, is not to abandon anarchism or even to transcend it – it is rather to move within it, being faithful to it, but to expand its terms and radicalise its possibilities. In this chapter, I would like to explore the possibilities of an anarchism that takes a certain distance from the rationalist-humanist foundations according to which it was classically theorised. This would mean a move beyond the ontological terrain of classical anarchism, particularly its organicist vision of social life and its essentialist conception of the human subject. To accomplish this move, I will be drawing upon a series of thinkers and approaches not commonly associated with anarchism, although I shall try to point out their ultimate continuity with it.

POSTMODERNITY AND THE CRITIQUE OF FOUNDATIONALISM

The general interrogation of ontological foundations – the questioning of their coherence, unity, stability, universality and so on – is part of what is often referred to as postmodernism or the postmodern condition. I will not spend much time defining postmodernism – inasmuch as a general definition of postmodernism *can* be offered – or in describing the different ways in which it is understood in art, architecture, literary criticism, cultural studies, social theory and so on. Nor do I see postmodernism as providing, in itself, a sufficient way of thinking about politics. Rather, I am interested in understanding the implications that postmodernism – as a certain cultural and philosophical condition – has for anarchism: to what extent does postmodernism allow us to rethink and, indeed *force* us to rethink, certain elements of anarchism?

It is important to stress at the outset that postmodernism is not an historical period as such. It does not mean that we have somehow left modernity behind and entered a new historical era. It is more accurately seen as a kind of critical reflection upon the limits of modernity, and a moment of transcendence which is, at the same time, *within* modernity. Moreover, as Gianni Vattimo argues, the reason why thinkers like Nietzsche and Heidegger do not propose a way of 'overcoming' modernity is precisely because to do so would be to affirm the very logic of development that is central to modernity.[4] In other words, the most effective way of transcending modernity is not to propose a moment beyond it, because this simply invents a new set of foundations, and conforms to ideas of progress, telos and origins that are central to the modern experience. Rather, it is to engage in a critical deconstruction of the very idea of foundations, without proposing a new set of foundations in their place.

Let us take as an example the status of knowledge: rather than the progressive development and expansion of systems of knowledge based on scientific observation, a postmodern approach would unveil instead a clash of interpretations, a series of struggles over meaning and knowledge. The hegemonic claims of knowledge, the claims to universal truth made by scientific discourses in particular, are thus undermined. Knowledge cannot be disassociated from power and power struggles, and therefore its proclaimed neutrality and universality is a fiction. Postmodernity can be seen in terms of a certain approach to knowledge: it takes its distance from grand narratives, from the notion of a scientifically verifiable objective truth and from the idea that the world is becoming more intelligible through advances in science.

This theme is taken up by Paul Feyerabend, who proposes an 'anarchist' approach to scientific knowledge. His argument is that the methodological rules imposed by science are ultimately arbitrary and historically contingent, that they are not based on any firm claim to truth. Indeed, many of the most important scientific discoveries – the Copernican Revolution for instance – were only possible through a breaking, whether intentional or accidental, of existing methodological rules.[5] This tells us that the authority of scientific knowledge, based on rigid rules of enquiry – which determines what knowledge is included or excluded – is on much shakier ground than it would like to admit. It is much more productive, according to Feyerabend and, indeed, much closer to the truth of scientific enquiry, to take an *anarchist* view of science: to question the authority and legitimacy of scientific knowledge, and to break its methodological rules. Indeed, he finds it extraordinary that anarchist political thinkers – and here he cites Kropotkin – while questioning all forms of political authority, uphold unquestioningly the epistemological authority of science and, indeed, base their whole philosophy on its rather uncertain claims.[6] Why should the same freedom of thought, speech and action, and the same scepticism about authority that anarchists demand in the field of politics, not also translate into the field of scientific inquiry?

Similar attempts to unseat the authority of existing systems of knowledge can be found in a number of fields: for instance, in mathematics, with Gödel's 'incompleteness theorem', which points to the inadequacy and incompleteness of the axioms making up any given branch of mathematics; and in structuralist and particularly poststructuralist theories of language, from Jakobson to Barthes, Derrida, Lacan and Kristeva, where there is no necessary correspondence between linguistic signs and external 'reality', and where the structural relationship between signifiers is itself unstable and incomplete. It is this project of questioning the consistency, stability and totality of foundations – foundations of knowledge, science, experience, identity – that is central to the postmodern condition. And it is this theoretical move – or series of moves – that allows for a critical engagement with some of the central categories of classical anarchist thought: in particular, its positivistic faith in scientific enquiry to reveal the workings of the social world, and its incorporation of humanist ideas about the discovery of a human essence and the progressive enlightenment of the subject. As we shall see, these are the foundational categories that are increasingly problematic and difficult to sustain in the wake of postmodernism. Postmodernism, therefore, throws down a challenge to anarchism: *if you are anarchists, then you must at least question your own foundations; you must question the authority not only of the state and capitalism, but also of the systems of knowledge and thought and the stable identities upon which your anti-authoritarian political project is based.* In other words, for anarchism to be consistent, it must also engage in – or at least consider the implications of – an *epistemic and ontological anarchism.* I do not want to suggest, however, that such a project is alien or hostile to anarchism, that it involves the imposition of an unbearable demand from outside its own terms. Rather, I would argue that the anti-authoritarian ethos of anarchism – that of a permanent suspicion towards authority – contains already the possibility of this sort of deconstructive move.

AN-ARCHY: ANARCHISM WITHOUT FOUNDATIONS

What does it mean to think anarchism without firm foundations? We know that classical anarchists based their critique of power on certain ontological foundations – such as human essence, a certain view of historical development (whether dialectical, materialist or evolutionary) and a rationalist vision of social relations – which were seen to be part of a natural order outside the world of power. In other words, even though political power distorted and repressed the free development of social forces, even though it thwarted the full expression of man's moral and rational capacities, these forces and capacities were part of an ontological order that was exterior to power; an order determined by natural laws or biological and evolutionary tendencies, that unfolded in a rational way and provided the point of departure for a critique of power. Querying such foundationalism might involve showing that social relations are opaque, unstable and even antagonistic, rather than transparent and immanently harmonious; or unmasking the much more ambiguous relationship between power and the human subject. These are points which will be explored later. Crucially, though, the critique of foundations opens politics to the moment of contingency, to the uncertainty of – not complete groundlessness – but ever-shifting grounds.[7] What this theoretical move allows us to do is to think anarchism in a different way. It allows us – indeed *compels* us – to cast doubt on the stability, totality and coherence of its ontological foundations. This is not to suggest that the anarchist project can no longer be motivated by principles and ethics, or by the critique of power and the idea of the emancipation of the subject and communities. This would be to make anarchism nihilism, a move that I would oppose. Rather, what I am suggesting is that the deconstructive strategy outlined above would mean that the rational and moral foundations of anarchism are never completely naturalised or essentialised, that they are never graspable by us in their totality.

It is here that I would like to develop the idea of *an-archy*, which I understand as a kind of ontological anarchism.[8] In other words, an-anarchy implies the notion of a critique or questioning of the authority of ontological foundations, *including those of anarchism itself*. What I want to suggest here is the idea of a transcendental moment within anarchism itself: that there is, within the potentiality of anarchism, an an-archy that exceeds and transcends it. If *arché* can be seen as an overall rule or guiding principle (something like the first truth, or rational principium), then an-archy can be defined as the absence of this rule. According to Reiner Schürmann, the 'withering away' of *arché* is related to Heidegger's idea of the closure of metaphysics, the dissolution of the epochal rules that guide actions in different historical periods. It is this weakening of determining rational principles for action that Schürmann terms the 'anarchy principle'. Unlike in metaphysical thinking, where action has always to be derived from and determined by a first principle, '"anarchy" on the other hand always designates the withering away of such a rule, the relaxing of its hold'.[9] Importantly, Schürmann explicitly distinguishes his notion of 'anarchy' from anarchism:

> Needless to say, here it will not be a question of anarchy in the sense of Proudhon, Bakunin and their disciples. What these masters sought was to *displace* the origin, to substitute the 'rational power', *principium*, for the power of authority, *princeps* – as metaphysical an operation as there has been. They sought to replace one focal point with another.[10]

In other words, the classical anarchists sought to do away with political power; but as we have seen, their critique of power was based on certain rational and natural principles, a certain conception of human nature and natural social relations, which power violated, disrupted and imposed itself upon. Furthermore, the system of state power and authority would be overcome and in its place would emerge a much more rational form of social organisation. Thus, unnatural political authority was counterposed to the legitimate authority of natural laws; irrational political authority would be replaced by rational social authority. From the perspective of the 'an-archy principle', this is to simply replace one mode of authority with another (the political authority of the state with the scientific authority of reason) and, therefore, one foundation with another. By contrast, for Schürmann,

> The anarchy that will be at issue here is the name of a history affecting the ground or foundation of action, a history where the bedrock yields and where it becomes obvious that the principle of cohesion, be it authoritarian or 'rational', is no longer anything more than a blank space deprived of legislative, normative, power.[11]

We can see here the anti-authoritarian potential of this an-archic deconstruction of anarchism: it implies a questioning of the authority of any guiding principles or foundations, even if they are employed in an anarchist critique of political authority. Such principles or foundations are thus deprived of normative power, and they can no longer easily serve as a natural basis for the establishment of a new system of rules and institutions, even if they are those of an anarchist society. Yet far from being hostile or inimical to anarchism, I interpret the an-anarchy principle as being thoroughly compatible with the anarchist ethos of permanent suspicion towards authority. Indeed, it may be seen as an extension of it – it poses an ethical challenge to anarchism to examine the potential authoritarianism of its own philosophical foundations as well that which may be inherent in the vision of the anarchist society that will replace the state.

So, even though an-archy is not a political principle in itself – rather it is an ontological principle – it nevertheless has important political implications, particularly for an anarchist politics. Indeed, according to Schürmann, 'anarchy' is what makes it impossible to sustain the idea of domination: anarchy is precisely what destabilises any idea of a natural inequality between people that forms the justification for political or economic oppression. Such domination is based on the 'original hubris' of the attempt to subordinate being to principles.[12]

Moreover, for Schürmann, anarchy gives us a new understanding of freedom, which he describes in terms of an action without *arché* or rational principle, 'acting "without a why"': 'a life "without why" certainly means a life without a goal, without *telos* . . .'[13] I am slightly less convinced by this idea, however. It is not that I believe that we need *telos* or ultimate goals in order to act, but that this conception seems to leave out the question of ethics. Surely action, and particularly anti-authoritarian action, must at least engage with ethics; surely, it must be informed by some sort of ethical position. I am not suggesting that Schürmann's formulation of anarchy amounts to a nihilism, but rather that it is insufficient in itself as a way of thinking about political and ethical action. Indeed, I would prefer to see anti-authoritarian action as acting *with* a why. But what is this 'why' and how does it emerge? We have already established through the an-anarchy principle that action can no longer be seen as being guided by deep foundations or an overall rational *principium* – and this is what Schürmann is getting at with his notion of acting 'without why'. However, there are other ways of conceiving of ethics, other ways of thinking about the reasons why we should act in a certain way.

ETHICAL ANARCHY

This is where the thinking of Emmanuel Levinas becomes important. For Levinas, the ethical terrain emerges through an encounter – or what he calls an assignation – with the other. This encounter is with the other in his or her sheer exteriority. It is, moreover, something which is deeply unsettling to the ego because the other cannot be reduced to our rational idealisations or assimilated into our structures of consciousness, so conditioned are they by logos and rational thought. Thus, the encounter with this outside produces something akin to an obsession, a disequilibrium or delirium. Indeed, for Levinas, the encounter is an-archical in the sense that it unsettles the 'sovereignty' of the self-transparent, self-coinciding ego. This anarchy, for Levinas, though, is not the same as disorder or chaos; rather it leads to a kind of 'persecution' or radical self-questioning, an interrogation of one's own self-contained sovereignty:

> But anarchy is not disorder as opposed to order, as the eclipse of themes is not, as is said, a return to a diffuse 'field of consciousness' prior to attention. Disorder is but another order . . . Anarchy troubles being over and beyond these alternatives.[14]

Levinas' idea of anarchy thus goes beyond the binary of order/disorder, which has so often served as a justification for unlimited state sovereignty. Indeed, Levinas suggests to us that the disorder of the 'state of nature' is always a certain construction of the political order itself – another order which functions as the ontological supplement to the order of the state. For Levinas, then, anarchy means something different: it refers to the sense in which we are disturbed by the encounter with the other. Moreover, this is an ethical moment because it imposes upon us a radical responsibility for the other.

The anarchy of the encounter is not a moment of freedom conceived in the strictly individualist sense: for Levinas, this is no freedom at all because it often leads to a kind of imperialist subjectivity, and thus to the domination of the other.[15] Indeed, in this encounter, there is a 'substitution' in which one now exists through and for the other, and here the limits of one's own identity are broken up. However, while this destabilisation of one's identity through a sense of radical responsibility to the other might sound like the very antithesis of freedom, Levinas contends that it allows a freedom of a different kind: 'Substitution frees the subject from ennui, that is, from the enchainment to itself, where the ego suffocates in itself due to the tautological way of identity . . .'[16] The freeing of the self from the self is really a getting away from essence; essence is not the basis for freedom – as it is claimed in the humanist tradition – but a limitation on it. For Levinas, then,

> Essence, in its seriousness as *persistence in essence*, fills every inter-val of nothingness that would interrupt it. It is a strict book-keeping where nothing is lost nor created. Freedom is compromised in this balance of accounts in an order where responsibilities correspond exactly to liberties taken . . . Freedom in a genuine sense can only be a contestation of this book-keeping by a gratuity.[17]

So, what is being proposed here in this liberation from essence, is a form of freedom which goes beyond the usual liberal formulation in which the individual's freedom is selfishly and jealously guarded, where it is balanced against responsibilities, where it is measured against the freedom of the other, as if in a zero-sum game – where the liberty gained by one is the liberty lost by the other. In the liberal paradigm, as we have seen in Chapter 1, freedom is often conceived in terms of a contestation between individual wills, so that not only is the liberty of one a potential threat to the other, but that the equality of the other is also a potential threat to liberty. This encourages a kind of book-keeping mentality, a constant and obsessive cost–benefit accounting of the freedom one has, or thinks one has, in a perpetual state of fear and competition with the other. By contrast, the more 'genuine' freedom that Levinas proposes through his idea of anarchy is one that is closer to the equal-libertarian ethos of anarchism. Here, an individual's freedom is thinkable only through the freedom of others; freedom is relational and communal – it is not something jealously guarded by the individual against other individuals, but shared freely and revelled in (a 'gratuity' as Levinas puts it). It implies a spendthrift's approach to freedom. It is a kind of generous excess that spills over the edges of individual self-interest. That is why this liberation does not emerge from one's own 'essence' or from an ontology.[18] It is, rather, a distancing from oneself through the encounter with what is outside his or her usual everyday experience.

The anarchical encounter is not a relationship between self-contained selves, but between singularities which are open to one another.

So, far from being a purely individual experience, the sort of anarchical ethics being proposed here is one that is relational and, therefore, political – albeit not in an obvious sense. It is political because it makes one consider oneself in relation to others, and it promotes a form of freedom which, as I have suggested, can be experienced *only* in relation to others, not in the sense of contestation or competition with others, but rather in the sense of community and solidarity with others. For Levinas, 'The unconditionality of being hostage is not the limit case of solidarity, but the condition for all solidarity.'[19]

The Levinasian conception of anarchy provides us with a new way of thinking about ethics and politics; or, to be more precise, a new way of thinking about the relationship between ethics and politics. As Miguel Abensour shows, ethics, understood in the Levinasian sense, is what cannot be reduced to politics. Indeed, it points to a kind of 'metapolitics' which is a departure from politics and a move towards the Other: 'It is as if the effect of metapolitics is to call to our attention an underneath (*en-deça*) that permits a leave of politics and that opens a passageway *beyond* politics.'[20] Anarchy, then, points to a kind of gap between ethics and politics. Here we see, once again, that anarchy is what goes beyond classical anarchism. Indeed, for Levinas, classical anarchism establishes a new *arché* in place of the old; it established the principle of rationality – the rational organisation of the social order – in the place of the irrational political authority of the state. Levinas' understanding of anarchy is *prior* to this anarchism, and points once again to the idea of the disturbance of ontological foundations:

> The notion of anarchy as we are introducing it here has a meaning prior to the political (or anti-political) meaning currently attributed to it. It would be self-contradictory to set it up as a principle (in the sense that anarchists understand it). Anarchy cannot be sovereign like an *arché*. It can only disturb the State – but in a radical way, making possible moments of negation *without* any affirmation. The State then cannot set itself up as a Whole. But, on the other hand, anarchy can be stated.[21]

So anarchy is not in itself a politics; it does not propose a particular form of social organisation, nor even any specific political strategy. Rather, it is only what disturbs the state from the outside. Indeed, anarchy is that which disturbs *any* political order. However, this does not mean, as Abensour shows, that anarchy is apolitical or has no relevance to politics:

> an-archy disturbs politics to the point where we can speak of the disturbance of politics . . . To separate an-archy from sovereignty, to separate it from a principle does not mean that an-archy doesn't affect politics or leaves it unchanged by abandoning it to its own determinations.[22]

So, an-archy is not a politics on its own, and certainly cannot serve as a sovereign principle of social organisation. But this does *not* mean that it has no political effects. It is a kind of ethical distance from politics which nevertheless disturbs the political order, opens it up to the Other that exceeds it, and this, from my point of view, is the political gesture *par excellence*.

This understanding of an-archy – as the distance or oscillation between ethics and politics – is particularly useful for rethinking anarchism. I am certainly not saying that an-archy should replace anarchism, or that anarchism should give up its political aspirations. Rather, that an-anarchy keeps alive the very necessary tension or moment of suspension between ethics and politics, preventing one from being eclipsed by the other. In this sense, it is the very condition for doing politics in an ethical way. An-archy, as I see it here, is what opens political practices and discourses to an ethical questioning as to their own limits, exclusions and authoritarian potentiality. So, rather than saying that ethics should replace politics, I see one as being the supplement of the other. In the same way, I would suggest that an-archy, in the different senses described above – not only in the Levinasian sense, but also in the very different Heideggerian sense (as elaborated by Schürmann) – should be seen as the supplement of anarchism. It refers to the moment within anarchism that *at the same time transcends and exceeds it*, allowing for a radicalisation of its terms and possibilities.

RETHINKING ANARCHISM

In the section above, I have explored two different figures of an-anarchy, both of which engage in a questioning of ontological foundations and universal guiding principles, and which provide us with alternative – and I think more radical – conceptions of freedom and ethics. Both give us a new way of approaching anarchism, allowing us to reflect more carefully on its limitations. They move us to re-situate anarchism – and indeed radical politics generally – no longer on the basis of founding principles or human essence, but rather through a kind of ontological gap or disjuncture: the withdrawal of *arché* or ultimate grounds, in Schürmann's case; and, for Levinas, the radically asymmetrical and destabilising encounter between the Self and the Other, as well as between politics and ethics. Both moves, as we have seen, are anti-sovereign: they destabilise the foundations and consistency of sovereign identities and the power relations based on them. However, neither version of an-archy provides in itself a sufficient way of thinking about politics. Rather, as I have argued, they should be seen as ways of supplementing anarchism as a political philosophy and practice.

It is here that I shall put forward a few tentative proposals that would contribute to a reworking of anarchist politics along the lines of the post-foundational an-archy 'principle' outlined above:

(1) *Is there an anarchist subject?*   The classical anarchists had a mostly essentialist view of the human subject: the subject had certain rational and moral tendencies – an innate sociability, for instance – which, while constrained by power, would flourish with his or her emancipation from power. Thus, the revolution of humanity against power, and the possibility of voluntary social cooperation and harmonious coexistence after the revolution, were based on these essential characteristics. As I pointed out in Chapter 1, this is not to suggest that anarchists were naive about human nature, acknowledging as they did the egotism and desire for power that at times corrupted and distorted our more cooperative and rational instincts. But the point is that in the context of relations with others, and given the right social conditions, the instincts for moral action and rational cooperation would take precedence. However, if we are to question this moral and rational foundation for human existence, then can we still speak of an anarchist subject in this way? To raise this question is not, of course, to deny the possibilities of moral or rational action – there would be no hope of a radical politics of emancipation if we were to do so. The point is, rather, that we cannot necessarily assume that rational and ethical action comes from positive properties which are essential to the subject or are inherent in social

relations. Rather, a post-foundational approach would offer a more contingent and situated view of political and ethical agency.

As part of this, the very idea of human essence must be re-examined. Here the thought of Max Stirner becomes crucial. As I have argued elsewhere, Stirner occupies a pivotal place within the anarchist tradition: he engages in an epistemological and ontological anarchism which breaks in a radical way with the conceptual categories and foundations of classical anarchism, particularly its reliance on humanist notions of essence.[23] Central here is his project of overturning Feuerbachian humanism: as Stirner alleged, the figure of Man, which Feuerbach put in the place of God, was simply a reinvention of God and a reaffirmation of the religious illusion in the new disguise of secular, rational humanism. Stirner showed that Feuerbach had merely endowed Man with a God-like divinity and thus invented a humanist religion in place of Christianity: 'The human *religion* is only the last metamorphosis of the Christian religion.'[24] The new human religion is alienating because it creates an abstract notion of human essence to which we as individuals must conform. Essence is an ideological illusion, an abstract spectre to which individuals are subordinated. Human essence, along with other abstractions like rationality and morality, become part of a spirit world of ideological 'spooks' or what Stirner calls 'fixed ideas': that is, impossible ideals that are alien to us, yet which we are expected to live up to because they are now believed to be an intrinsic part of us.[25] These 'fixed ideas' govern our thoughts and desires, imposing on us impossible demands, enclosing the uniqueness of the individual within a rigid generality. So, for Stirner, there is no essential truth to the human subject or to social relations more broadly.

If we take Stirner's critique on board, we must accept that essence cannot serve as an effective basis or stable ontological ground for political action, as it did for the classical anarchists. And yet this does not mean we cannot act politically. Indeed, for Stirner, it is precisely the removal of this apparition of human essence that allows the individual to act freely and, indeed, to recreate himself as he or she chooses:

> I on my part start from a presupposition in presupposing myself; but my presupposition does not struggle for its perfection like 'Man struggling for his perfection', but only serves me to enjoy it and consume it . . . I do not presuppose myself, because I am every moment just positing or creating myself.[26]

Stirner's radical egoism does not entail, as many have suggested, a liberal individualism defined by self-interest, but rather a form of existentialism where the ego is a kernel of nothingness out of which different articulations of freedom and even ethical action can emerge, and through which all stable identities are disrupted.

(2) *The desire for authority.* The crucial question raised by Deleuze and Guattari – 'how can desire desire its own repression . . .?'[27] – confronts all radical politics with a central ambiguity. The classical anarchists were not unaware of this problem; indeed, Kropotkin attributes the rise of the modern state in part to people becoming 'enamoured of authority' and to their self-enslavement to increasingly centralised systems law and punishment.[28] However, this problem, while acknowledged, was not sufficiently addressed or theorised in anarchism. Yet, it creates certain obvious difficulties for anti-authoritarian politics, unsettling the notion of the moral and rational agent who revolts against an immoral and irrational power. Indeed, it would seem that in our contemporary societies, rather than there being a general desire for insurrection and freedom from power, there is rather a desire for more control, more surveillance, more police powers – a passion for authority, and a resentful intolerance of the freedom of others, which leads to a dependence on and, indeed, a demand for all kinds of state intervention. Living in a state-dominated society certainly fosters an abrogation of individual responsibility and a disdain for freedom, but perhaps there is a deeper psychological attachment to power that must be more closely investigated.

It is here that psychoanalytic theory can provide some clues. Freud believed, for instance, that a desire for authority could be found in the psychodynamics of groups, which formed themselves around the figure of the Leader – the substitute father with whom the members of the group identified as an 'ideal type', and through whom the libidinous ties which hold the group together are formed.[29] This sort of psychological dependency on power – something that was also explored by Freudo-Marxists like Wilhelm Reich[30] – meant that the possibilities of emancipatory politics are at times compromised by hidden authoritarian desires; that there was always a risk of authoritarian and hierarchical practices and institutions emerging in post-revolutionary societies. The central place of the subject – in politics, philosophy – is not abandoned here, but complicated. Radical political projects, for instance, have to contend with the ambiguities of human desire, with irrational social behaviour, with violent and aggressive drives, and even with unconscious desires for authority and domination. This is not to suggest that psychoanalysis is necessarily politically or socially conservative. On the contrary, I would maintain that central to psychoanalysis is a libertarian ethos, by which the subject seeks to gain a greater autonomy (from authoritarian leaders and the groups constituted around them), and where the subject is encouraged, through the rules of 'free association', to speak the truth of the unconscious.[31] To insist on the 'dark side' of the human psyche – its dependence on power, its identification with authoritarian figures, even its sadistic and aggressive impulses – can serve as a warning to any revolutionary project which seeks to demolish political authority: *how can we be sure that the revolt against power will not simply reproduce it in another form; can a revolutionary politics at the same time work against our hidden desires for domination?*[32] Psychoanalysis by no means discounts the possibility of human emancipation, sociability and voluntary cooperation; indeed, it points to conflicting tendencies in the subject and in social interactions between the desire for harmonious coexistence and aggressive desires for power and domination. It nevertheless serves as a warning to radical politics about the difficulties associated with dislodging these more aggressive and authoritarian drives simply through a transformation in social and political conditions. In other words, the revolution must go 'all the way down' to the psyche. Indeed, as Judith Butler contends, the psyche – as a dimension of the subject that is not reducible to discourse and power and which exceeds it – is something that can explain not only our passionate attachment to power and to the modes of subjectification and regulatory behaviours that power imposes on us, but also our resistance to them:

> Thus the psyche, which includes the unconscious, is very different from the subject: the psyche is precisely what exceeds the imprisoning effects of the discursive demand to inhabit a coherent identity, to become a coherent subject. The psyche is what resists the regularization that Foucault ascribes to normalizing discourses.[33]

(3) *What is power? How does it operate?*   The point made by Butler, nevertheless points to a certain complicity or participation of the subject in power. If anarchism is a politics against power, an anti-politics, then the complexity of power relations in contemporary societies, and the

way that power is reproduced by the subject 'unconsciously' in every-day practices, is something which must be properly considered. When the classical anarchists in the nineteenth century called for the over-throw of the state, they had in mind a relatively crude apparatus; that is, the Prussian or Tsarist authoritarian state: 'pneumatic machines' as Bakunin described them, with their bureaucrats, policemen, sol-diers, gaolers, executioners and priests. We must admit that this state still largely exists today – perhaps without the priests, and with more sophisticated technologies of control – yet with the same centralising and expansionist tendencies, the same bureaucratic elitism and heavy-handedness, the same coercive and intimidating presence and the same contempt for ordinary people.

Yet as Foucault points out, if it is power that we are concerned with then its presence and operation are far more ubiquitous and pervasive. Power becomes coextensive with all social relationships and is not reducible to the state, even though the state is the site where power is at its most concentrated, excessive and brutal. In other words, we can no longer imagine a clear conceptual distinction between society and the state, between humanity and power, as power is reproduced through everyday relationships and practices – such as educating, healing, gov-erning – and through a variety of social institutions (power for Foucault was to be seen as a 'mode of action' upon the actions of others rather than as a property of centralised political institutions[34]). If power is seen in this way, it is more problematic to think in terms of a revolt of society against the state. It is, however, incorrect to say that Foucault rejects the notion of the state, even though he has at times questioned its unity and coherence as a political institution.[35] Indeed, many of his analyses – of state racism, biopolitics, liberalism/neoliberalism, security and dif-ferent rationalities of government – took the problem of the state and sovereignty as central. However, the key point that can be taken from Foucault's general approach to power is that there is a much closer and more paradoxical interaction between the state and society than clas-sical anarchists imagined; that the problem of power goes 'all the way down' into civil society, and any sort of emancipatory transformation of social relations must start with a transformation of power relations at an everyday micro-level.

Yet I contend that this emphasis on the micro-level at which power operates does not, as many critics have alleged, undermine the pos-sibilities of radical politics. On the contrary, emphasising the multiple, local and everyday acts of resistance allows us to think radical politics in a much more tangible way, rather than waiting for the great revolutionary event. It is simply that, for Foucault, power is never something that can be entirely transcended: there will always be power relations in society; power is implicit in all kinds of social practices and interactions. The intractability of power does not mean, however, that we cannot strive for and establish a series of power relationships that are less dominating than those that we currently have, and that allow for a much greater degree of equality, autonomy and reciprocity. This is why we should pay close attention to Foucault's distinction between power and domination:

> one sometimes encounters what may be called situations or states of domination in which power relations, instead of being mobile, allowing various participants to adopt strategies modifying them, remain blocked, frozen . . . In such a state, practices of freedom do not exist or exist only unilaterally or are extremely constrained and limited.[36]

In whatever social relationships we develop – even anarchist ones – there will always be power at some level; yet here power relations would (presumably) be more fluid, reciprocal and egalitarian. What we must watch out for is the risk of domination emerging, something that is always possible due to the instability and uncertainty of power relations.

It is for this reason that I argue that Foucault is a kind of anarchist – even though he would almost certainly have refused this label – and that the central ethos of his thinking is an anti-authoritarian one, one that incites us to be perpetually on our guard against the ever present possibility of domination. As Foucault says: 'My point is not that everything is bad, but that everything is dangerous . . . If everything is dangerous, then we always have something to do. So my position leads not to apathy but to a hyper- and pessimistic activism.'[37] Rather than providing concrete alternatives, however, Foucault's thinking can be described in terms of a continual problematisation of existing practices and institutions. His project is one of exposing the contingency and arbitrariness of our current social arrangements, the ways they are established through multiple dominations and exclusions. At the heart of power relations and institutions is a struggle that has become sedimented. In unmasking the conflict and war at the base of sovereign social and political institutions – the 'blood that has dried on the codes of law' – Foucault unsettles the very principle of sovereign authority. Indeed, Foucault may be seen, like the anarchists, as an anti-Hobbesian: the state is established not through a rational agreement, but through war and violence.[38]

At the same time, Foucault's anti-authoritarianism poses certain problems for classical anarchism. When, for instance, Foucault's critique of institutions is applied also to the discourses and modes of rationality – pointing to the way they operate to legitimise these institutions – certain blindspots are revealed in the positivist and rationalist approaches of classical anarchists like Kropotkin and Godwin. Hegemonic discourses of rational truth, science and even morality have to be seen, in themselves, as political institutions with potentially dominating effects. Moreover, their hegemony is often challenged by what Foucault refers to as an 'insurrection of subjugated knowledges' – the stubborn refusal of scientifically disqualified discourses (those of the psychiatric patient, for example) to be silenced.[39] From this perspective, it is rather more complicated to assert scientific and rational knowledge against the distortions and mystifications of political authority. While it is always necessary to speak truth to power, we must at the same time be aware of the potential power-effects of this truth, and the exclusions which made it possible.

(4) *What is revolution? What form should resistance take?* However, this scepticism about the project of liberation does not mean that insurrections and forms of resistance against power are impossible. It is rather that the idea of a revolution, as a totalising, all-encompassing phenomenon which reverses power everywhere, all at once, must be questioned; we cannot simply assume that the subject always refuses power, or refuses it in a uniform, total sense. As Foucault says, 'there is no single locus of great Refusal, no soul of revolt, source of all rebellions, or pure law of the revolutionary'.[40] Yet resistance occurs: people resist power all the time, in various ways and, moreover, the operation of power always produces its own localised forms of resistance.[41] General insurrections against structures of power can certainly occur, but they are not immanent within social relations, as the anarchists believed. An insurrection is something that must be constructed out of the multiple, localised resistances that take place on an everyday basis in society.

It is here that we can assert with the Situationists the 'revolution of everyday life'. For Guy Debord, although classical anarchism made a valuable contribution to revolutionary thought and practice by insisting on the revolutionary destruction of state power – in contrast to the Marxists – it also fell into the trap of seeing the Revolution as a kind of totalising end point, a grand overturning of existing society that must be achieved all at once; in this sense it disregarded important questions of method and organisation. This led to a kind of simplification and absolutism in its revolutionary politics: 'the doctrine requires no more than the reiteration, and the reintroduction into each particular struggle, of the same simple and all-encompassing idea – the same end point that anarchism has identified from the first as the movement's sole and entire goal'.[42] Instead, we must recognise that insurrections against power are more fragmented and uncertain, emerging from different points, and often subject to strategic reversals.

For Raoul Vaneigem, the revolution was multiple and everyday – it was something that occurred at the level of individual subjectivity and was based on lived experiences. It was a release of the excess energy invested in everyday actions, driven by the creative and poetic power of our imaginations. While the theme of revolutionary spontaneity is shared here with the anarchists, Vaneigem argues that the revolution cannot be founded on a unified communitarian project that is immanent in society – rather it is individual and often fragmented. Nor can it be founded on the idea of a natural order.[43] Rather, what is acknowledged here is the idea that the natural order is never outside power, and is always mediated socially and *through* power. In the same way, the individual is implicated at an infinitesimal level in the reproduction of power and social hierarchies through everyday interactions, through participation in the society of the spectacle, through work, consumption, and, importantly, through conforming to the identities and roles which power has conferred upon us. We thus willingly participate in our own domination and alienation in return for partial compensations – our very own place in the hierarchy of power: 'This is why some agree so readily to be governed. Wherever it is exercised, on every rung of the ladder, power is partial, not absolute. It is thus ubiquitous, but ever open to challenge.'[44] For this reason, the revolution against power must also be a revolution against identity and roles: a process of radical subjectivisation by which we work ourselves out of the bind of power.

Insurrectionary politics must, therefore, take place also at the molecular level of the subject: questioning the subject's involvement and complicity with the power that dominates him or her through fixed identities and places, and which is sustained by everyday practices. In other words, the aim of insurrections must be not only to transform one's immediate surroundings and social relations more broadly, but to work at the level of the individual psyche; indeed, the two projects are inseparable. Foucault, for instance, explored ethical strategies and 'practices of freedom' which were aimed at increasing one's autonomy from power.[45] It is with its focus on the transformation of the individual – the revolt of the self against fixed identities – that Stirner saw in the insurrection something vitally different from the traditional politics of revolution:

> Revolution and insurrection must not be looked upon as synonymous. The former consists in an overturning of conditions, of the established condition or *status,* the state or society, and is accordingly a *political* or *social* act; the latter has indeed for its unavoidable consequence a transformation of circumstances, yet does not start from it but from men's discontent with themselves, is not an armed rising but a rising of individuals, a getting up without regard to the *arrangements* that spring from it. The Revolution aimed at new arrangements; insurrection leads us no longer to *let* ourselves be arranged, but to arrange ourselves, and sets no glittering hopes on 'institutions'. It is not a fight against the established, since, if it prospers, the established collapses of itself; it is only a working forth of me out of the established.[46]

Radical political action must not be aimed *only* at overturning established institutions like the state, but also at attacking the much more problematic relation through which the subject is enthralled to and dependent upon power. The insurrection is, therefore, not only against external oppression, but, more fundamentally, against the self's internalised domination.

THE QUESTION OF UTOPIA

The points raised above are not ultimately inconsistent with anarchism, although they do necessitate a rethinking of some of the conceptual categories of classical anarchism. Nor should they be interpreted as a condemnation of classical anarchism as utopian, or as a rejection of anarchism's utopianism in the name of some 'reality' principle. On the contrary, I see the utopian moment of anarchism as a vital dimension of any politics that takes emancipation and radical transformation as central: this is not only to say that all forms of radical politics have a utopian aspect, but also that the vision of a society without government has to be taken as the ultimate ethical and political horizon of any radical politics worthy of its name. While classical anarchists professed to be anti-utopians, there is nevertheless a strong utopian current in their thought, and they proposed a number of visions of what a future anarchist society might look like: societies based on decentralised structures and free and voluntary social arrangements. Indeed, Kropotkin believed that 'No destruction of the existing order is possible, if at the time of the overthrow, or of the struggle leading to the overthrow, the idea of what is to take the place of what is destroyed is not always present in the mind.'[47] While I have argued above that power relations will never be entirely eliminated, and that anarchists must always be aware of the potential for new forms of domination that can emerge in any form of social arrangement – even in libertarian ones – I would also suggest that Kropotkin is correct in stressing the need for some sort of alternative vision of a social order in motivating political action against the current order.

However, it may be more productive to think about utopia in a slightly different way. Rather than utopia being seen as a blueprint for a future post-revolutionary society, as a set of processes and organisational measures to be implemented as part of a revolutionary programme, utopia might be seen as a (non)place of alterity – in other words, as a moment of exteriority which, like the Other in Levinasian ethics, punctures and displaces the existing sovereign order. The place of utopia – which is also a non-place, a future that is yet to be created, and no doubt never will be created in exactly the way it is envisaged – is something that allows us to distance ourselves from the existing order, to see its limits; to understand that it can be transcended, that there are alternative and vastly better ways of living one's life. As Abensour argues, utopia should be seen as a way of inciting desire – the desire for something else, for something other than what we currently have: 'Is it not proper to utopia to propose a new way of proceeding to a *displacement of what is* and what seems to go without saying in the crushing name of "reality"?'[48] We are crushed under the weight of the current order, which tells us that *this* is our reality, that what we have now is all there is and all there ever will be. Utopia provides an escape from this stifling reality by imagining an alternative to it; it opens up different possibilities, new 'lines of flight'. In this way, reality is shaken up and destabilised. Therefore, the potency of utopia lies not in providing a way of ordering society after the revolution, but in disordering society as it exists today, in providing a point of rupture in existing social relations, introducing into them an element of radical heterogeneity. The point about utopia, then, is not that it is a specific place that we get to, but rather a *non-place that unsettles the consistency of all places.* This idea of dreaming what is different should not be dismissed as an apolitical fantasy; on the contrary, the desire for a different reality, for different and unrealised ways of life, is something that draws attention to the limits and inadequacies of current institutions, and thus provides a point of radical critical reflection on them. As Abensour shows, the utopian drive – what he calls 'persistent utopia' – intersects with the desire to think democracy differently, to realise democracy beyond the state, which is precisely the project of anarchism:

> The two in fact have proximate emancipatory projects: on the side of democracy, the establishment of a collective power, a political community whose nature is permanent struggle against the domination of the powerful; on the side of utopia, the choice of association against hierarchically structured societies based on domination.[49]

Central to utopia, then, is a critique of domination: a politics of non-domination; not in the sense of providing a precise recipe for building a society in which domination is absent, but in the sense of allowing us to think outside domination, to think the outside *of* domination.

POSTANARCHISM: THE POLITICS OF ANTI-POLITICS

This new understanding of utopia gives us also a new way of thinking about anarchism itself. What I have been hinting at throughout this chapter is the idea of an anarchic moment of transcendence that goes beyond the limits of anarchism, and at the same time emerges from within it and is compatible with its anti-authoritarian ethos. The anarchy principle that I have explored implies a critical engagement with the ontological foundations of classical anarchism. Here, an-archy can be seen as a politico-ethical (or 'metapolitical') supplement to anarchism, something that works persistently at its limits, maintaining a kind of critical distance from it, while at the same time being motivated by the same anti-authoritarian ethos of anarchism.

What this an-archic anarchism points to is a politics of *postanarchism*, which implies, as I have said, a moment beyond anarchism that is at the same time part of anarchism. To formulate postanarchism more precisely, one could say that it refers to the *threshold between politics and anti-politics*. Postanarchism is both an anti-politics *and* a politics. As I suggested in Chapter 1, classical anarchism, in its rejection of the state and political representation, saw itself as a movement against politics – an anti-politics. However, in its desire to do away with politics, classical anarchism was also constructing a politics – it involved movements, organisations, strategies, programmes, ways of mobilising people against the state, ideas about the structure of future societies and so on. All of this implies a politics, even if it is aimed at the abolition of politics. Postanarchism plays upon this paradoxical position in which classical anarchism found itself, highlighting its moment of *aporia*. Postanarchism affirms the *anti-political* moment of anarchism – it affirms its rejection of the state and its suspicion of political representation, and it endorses its fundamental ethical critique of political power in the name of an unconditional equal-liberty. At the same time, postanarchism also affirms the *political* moment within anarchism: that is, the sense in which it must nevertheless engage with the realities of power; the extent to which revolutionary projects are complicated by the way that the subject who is to be liberated is at the same time caught up in diffuse networks of power; and the extent to which we can no longer rely on a series of ontological foundations (such as human essence, social objectivity, and rational and scientific discourses) to provide us with a pure point of departure from which to critique the workings of power.

This is where the question of utopia becomes important: postanarchism shares with anarchism its anti-authoritarian goal of a society without power. Indeed, it *intensifies* this dream, seeing as its fundamental aspiration, even ethical injunction, the transcendence of power. It always wants more freedom, more equality, more democracy. It reignites the hope for the eternal community. It dreams the same millenarian dreams as those heretical movements of the Middle Ages, the libertarian workers' dreams of the Communards, the libertarian-communist dreams of Marx himself – the dreams that, in fact, we all have of a society in harmony with itself, without violence and compulsion, where full autonomy resonates with full equality, where no one rules over another, where there is no more power or domination or exploitation, where the lion lies down with the lamb, like a garden of earthly delights before the intervention of an alienating and ferocious God. Such an impossible yet insistent desire has to be seen as the driving principle and eternal horizon of radical politics, especially anarchism. Postanarchism is in this sense an active anti-politics of utopian desire. On the other hand, postanarchism implies an awareness of the intractability of power, the need to engage with specific and local sites of power without a pure place of critique, the uncertainty and contingency of any political enterprise, the difficulties involved in mobilising people and building political movements, and the sense in which political projects and utopian aspirations are subject to dramatic reversals, setbacks and may even contain the seeds of a new kind of authoritarianism. This is not to say that the latter, political aspect of postanarchism is more 'realistic' than the former anti-political aspect: I have already pointed to the way in which the constraints of 'reality' must be questioned in the name of other possibilities, and that this questioning is entirely realistic. What is central to the political side of postanarchism is more an emphasis on limits and boundaries. So, we can say that postanarchism embodies, in this way, both the moment of a limitless horizon (the dimension of anti-political utopian desire) *and* the constitutive limit (the dimension of politics). It is thus an anti-political politics, and enshrines a necessary and constitutive tension, or aporetic moment, between these two poles.

This chapter has attempted to reformulate anarchism along postfoundational lines, and has, through a series of theoretical moves and philosophical strategies, arrived at postanarchism as a politics of antipolitics. Following chapters will seek to elaborate a politics of postanarchism which can intervene in both contemporary political situations as well as contemporary debates in political theory. Chapter 3, however, will be devoted to further exploring the implications of a politics of antipolitics through an engagement with Marxism.

Notes

1 This expression is a reference to Gilles Deleuze's monist idea that there is a univocal being in the sense that all beings are located on a single plane

of immanence, without any difference being privileged over any other: 'Univocity of being thus also signifies equality of being. Univocal being is at one and the same time nomadic distribution and crowned anarchy.' *Difference and Repetition*, trans. Paul Patton (London: Continuum, 2001), p. 37.

2 Jean-François Lyotard, *The Postmodern Condition: a Report on Knowledge*, trans. Geoffrey Bennington and Brian Massumi (Manchester: Manchester University Press, 1991), p. xxiv.

3 Michel Foucault, 'What is Enlightenment?', in *The Essential Works of Foucault 1954–1984: Ethics, Subjectivity and Truth, Vol. 1*, Paul Rabinow (ed.), trans. Robert Hurley (London: Penguin, 1994), p. 313.

4 Gianni Vattimo, *The End of Modernity: Nihilism and the Hermeneutics in Post-Modern Culture*, trans. Jon R. Snyder (Cambridge: Polity Press, 1988), p. 2.

5 See Paul Feyerabend, *Against Method* (London: Verso, 1993), p. 14.

6 Feyerabend, *Against Method*, pp. 12–13.

7 The distinction between the complete rejection of foundations (anti-foundationalism) and questioning of the coherence, stability and universality of foundations, is usefully supplied by Oliver Marchart, who draws upon Heidegger's idea of the way that the abyss forms the ground itself: '"Der Ab-*grund* is *Ab*-grund" is a chiasm which is supposed to mean: the ground is a-byss, and the a-byss is ground.' In other words, what Heidegger proposes is not the complete absence of ground or foundation, but rather a withdrawal of ground which at the same time operates as a kind of grounding. This is a post-foundationalism rather than a simple, relativist anti-foundationalism. See *Post-Foundational Political Thought: Political Difference in Nancy, Lefort, Badiou and Laclau* (Edinburgh: Edinburgh University Press, 2007), p. 20.

8 I borrow this term from Hakim Bey, who proposes a project based on *nothingness*, on a rejection of rational certainty, natural law or social law. See *Immediatism* (San Francisco, CA: AK Press, 1994), p. 1.

9 Reiner Schürmann, *Heidegger on Being and Acting: From Principles to Anarchy*, trans. Christine-Marie Gros (Bloomington, IN: Indiana University Press, 1987), p. 6.

10 Schürmann, *Heidegger on Being and Acting*, p. 6.

11 Schürmann, *Heidegger on Being and Acting*, p. 6.

12 See Schürmann, *Heidegger on Being and Acting*, p. 291.

13 Schürmann, *Heidegger on Being and Acting*, p. 10.

14 Emmanuel Levinas, 'Substitution', *The Levinas Reader*, Sean Hand (ed.) (Oxford: Blackwell, 1989), pp. 88–125 at 91.

15 Levinas, 'Substitution', p. 102.

16 Levinas, 'Substitution', p. 114.

17 Levinas, 'Substitution', p. 115.
18 Levinas, 'Substitution', p. 114.
19 Levinas, 'Substitution', p. 114.
20 Miguel Abensour, 'An-archy between Metapolitics and Politics', *Parallax*, 8(3), 2002, pp. 5–18 at 6.
21 Levinas, 'Substitution', p. 119 (see note 3)
22 Abensour, 'An-archy between Metapolitics and Politics', pp. 15–16.
23 See Saul Newman, *From Bakunin to Lacan: Anti-Authoritarianism and the Dislocation of Power* (Lanham, MD: Lexington Books, 2001).
24 Max Stirner, *The Ego and Its Own*, David Leopold (ed.) (Cambridge: Cambridge University Press, 1995), p. 158.
25 Stirner, *The Ego and Its Own*, p. 43.
26 Stirner, *The Ego and Its Own*, p. 150.
27 See Gilles Deleuze and Felix Guattari, *A Thousand Plateaus: Capitalism and Schizophrenia*, trans. Brian Massumi (London: Continuum, 2004), pp. 236–7.
28 Kropotkin, *The State*, p. 28.
29 See Sigmund Freud, 'Group Psychology and the Analysis of the Ego', *The Standard Edition of the Complete Psychological Works of Sigmund Freud*, vol. 18. trans. and ed. James Strachey (London: Hogarth, [1920–2] 1955).
30 See Wilhelm Reich, *The Mass Psychology of Fascism* (New York: Farrar, Straus & Giroux, 1980).
31 According to Mikkel Borch-Jacobsen, Freud's psychoanalytic theory of groups implies 'something like a revolt or an uprising against the hypnotist's unjustifiable power'. See *The Freudian Subject*, trans. Catherine Porter (Stanford, CA: Stanford University Press, 1988), p. 148.
32 This is really the same question that was posed by Jacques Lacan in response to the radicalism of May 1968: 'the revolutionary aspiration has only a single possible outcome – of ending up as the master's discourse. This is what experience has proved. What you aspire as revolutionaries to is a master. You will get one . . .' What Lacan is hinting at with this rather ominous statement – one that could be superficially, although, in my view, incorrectly, interpreted as politically conservative – is the hidden link, even dependency, between the revolutionary and authority; and the way that movements of resistance and even revolution may actually sustain the symbolic efficiency of the state, reaffirming of reinventing the position of authority. See Jacques Lacan, 'Analyticon', *The Seminar of Jacques Lacan, Book XVII: The Other Side of Psychoanalysis*, Jacques-Alain Miller (ed.), trans. Russell Grigg (New York: W. W. Norton, 2007), p. 207.
33 Judith Butler, *The Psychic Life of Power: Theories in Subjection* (Stanford, CA: Stanford University Press, 1997), p. 86.
34 See Michel Foucault, 'The Subject and Power', *The Essential Works of*

Foucault 1954–1984: Power Vol. 3, James Faubion (ed.), trans. Robert Hurley (London: Penguin, 2003, 326–48) at 340.

35 See Michel Foucault, 'Governmentality', *The Foucault Effect: Studies in Governmentality*, Colin Gordon (ed.) (Chicago, IL: University of Chicago Press, 1991), pp. 87–104 at 103.

36 Michel Foucault, 'The Ethics of the Concern of the Self as a Practice of Freedom', *Essential Works, Vol. 1. Ethics*, pp. 281–302 at 283.

37 Michel Foucault, 'On the Genealogy of Ethics: An Overview of Work in Progress', *Essential Works, Vol. 1: Ethics* pp. 253–80 at 256.

38 See Michel Foucault, *Society Must Be Defended: Lectures at the Collège De France 1975–76*, trans. David Macey (London: Allen Lane, 2003).

39 See Foucault, *Society Must Be Defended*, p. 7.

40 Michel Foucault, *The History of Sexuality Vol. 1: Introduction*, trans. R. Hunter (New York: Vintage Books, 1978), pp. 95–6.

41 Indeed, for Foucault, power and resistance were mutually implicated in a relationship of continual incitement and provocation, a field within which the 'game of freedom' was played out. See 'The Subject and Power'.

42 Guy Debord, *The Society of the Spectacle*, trans. Donald Nicholson-Smith (New York: Zone Books, 1995), p. 63.

43 Raoul Vaneigem, *The Revolution of Everyday Life*, trans. Donald Nicholson-Smith (London: Rebel Press, 2006), p. 86.

44 Vaneigem, *The Revolution of Everyday Life*, p. 132.

45 See Foucault, 'The Ethics of the Concern of the Self as a Practice of Freedom'.

46 Stirner, *The Ego and Its Own*, p. 279–80

47 Peter Kropotkin, *Revolutionary Pamphlets*, Roger N. Baldwin (ed.) (New York: Benjamin Blom, 1968), pp. 156–7.

48 Miguel Abensour, 'Persistent Utopia', *Constellations*, 15(3), 2008, 406–21 at 418.

49 Abensour, 'Persistent Utopia', p. 417.

Chapter 3

AN INFANTILE DISORDER[1]: ANARCHISM AND MARXISM

The Russian anarchist, whose pseudonym was Voline, recounts a meeting with Trotsky in New York in April 1917. Both men were discussing revolutionary conditions in Russia at the time. After listening to Voline's warning about how the Bolsheviks would, once in power, start persecuting the anarchists, Trotsky replied in reassuring tones of comradely conviviality: '"Can you really, for a single instant, entertain such nonsense: left-wing socialists in power turning their guns on the anarchists! Come, come, what do you take us for? Anyway, we are socialists, comrade Voline. So we are not your enemies . . .".' Two years after this encounter, in 1919, Voline finds himself arrested by the Bolshevik military authorities, who notified Trotsky by telegram, asking what should be done with him. Trotsky replied in his telegram: 'Shoot out of hand. – Trotsky.'[2] Fortunately, for Voline, he was not shot, due to intervening circumstances that he does not elaborate on. But this anecdote illustrates, in darkly comic tones, the fraught relationship between the authoritarian and libertarian strands of revolutionary politics – a conflict which goes back to the old debates between Marx and Bakunin, the conflict which split the First International in 1872 and whose impact on radical politics has never ceased to reverberate.

In Chapter 2, I developed a concept of postanarchism as an articulation of a post-foundational approach to anarchist theory. I suggested that postanarchism occupied a certain terrain at the threshold of politics and anti-politics, combining both the utopian desire to do away with all political structures based on power, with the awareness at the same time of the realities of power and the constitutive limits of political action. In this sense, postanarchism allows us to investigate the nature of the political in a new and unique way. In this chapter I will explore postanarchism's contribution to our understanding of the political by re-examining the relationship between Marxists and anarchists, uncovering the genealogy of their dispute over problems of power and state authority. As we shall see, this dispute is central to contemporary considerations of the political, largely because what is commonly invoked in the notion of 'the political' is the question of power and place of state sovereignty. Moreover, not only does the anarchist critique of Marxism contribute to debates around the 'relative autonomy of the state', but it also allows us to reflect more precisely on the mystery of state power today: what is this creature, the state; what role does it play in society; and what is its relationship to the economy? Indeed, one could say that in the light of both the so-called War on Terror and the current 'crisis of capitalism', it is the state itself that is emerging as the central problem for radical politics today.

MARX AND THE ANARCHISTS

In 1872, after the rift in the International Workingmen's Association between the followers of Marx and the followers of Bakunin, the latter wrote a letter to the newspaper *La Liberté* in which he expounded the matter which so 'profoundly separates' the libertarian socialists from the marxians:

> Our reckoning is that the, necessarily revolutionary, politics of the proletariat should have as its sole and immediate object the destruction of States . . . Nor can we comprehend talk of freedom of the proletariat or true deliverance of the masses within the State and by the State. State signifies domination, and all domination implies subjection of the masses, and as a result, their exploitation to the advantage of some governing minority . . . The marxians describe to quite contrary ideas. As befits good Germans, they worship the power of the State, and of necessity also the prophets of political and social discipline . . . The marxians acknowledge no other emancipation than the one they expect from their so-called people's State (*Volksstaat*).[3]

For Bakunin, then, the main difference between his position and that of Marx, Engels and Lassalle and other 'authoritarian socialists', is over the question of how a socialist revolution should approach the problem of state power: for anarchists, the masses cannot be liberated through the state because the state *always* entails domination, and, therefore, the state should be destroyed as the first act of revolution. For Marx, on the other hand, the state must be taken over and used as a tool of revolution – a position that, according to Bakunin, would lead only to a perpetuation of state power. This radical divergence in revolutionary theory would have major implications for radical politics. To fully understand its consequences, however, we must investigate more carefully the parameters of the disagreement.

CLASS INTEREST OR RELATIVE AUTONOMY?

The central question that is at the root of this controversy is the extent to which the state can be explained as a mechanism of class interest and domination. There is no doubt a real ambiguity here in Marx's thought, and I believe that Nicos Poulantzas is correct in his assessment that Marx neglected the problem of state power in its specificity because his main theoretical preoccupation was with the capitalist mode of production. Thus, the political dimension of state power is often reduced in Marxist theory, and in much of Marx's own analysis, to an effect of the capitalist economy.[4]

However, the precise way in which the capitalist mode of production determines the state is far less clear in Marx, and he tended to waver between two positions. The first was that the state was simply an instrument of the bourgeoisie as the economically dominant class, and directly reflected their interests. This position is expressed in its clearest and most succinct, if unsophisticated, form in *The Communist Manifesto*: 'the executive of the modern state is but a committee for managing the common affairs of the bourgeoisie'.[5] The other dominant position in Marx's thought is one that seems to allow the state a much greater degree of autonomy from class interests. This alternative position can be found in Marx's work, *The Eighteenth Brumaire of Louis Bonaparte*, where he describes a coup d'état in France in 1851 in which state forces led by Louis Bonaparte seized absolute power, achieving not only a considerable degree of independence from the bourgeoisie, but often acting directly against its immediate class interests. Nevertheless, the Bonapartist state served the long-term interests of the capitalist system, even if it often acted against the immediate interests and will of the bourgeoisie.[6]

Poulantzas argues that Bonapartism was, for Marx, more that simply a concrete instance of the capitalist state, but was actually the *constitutive theoretical characteristic* of it.[7] That is to say, the conception of the state as relatively autonomous from bourgeois class interests was the very truth of the state under capitalism, and, in opposition to Ralph Miliband who insisted on the direct influence of the bourgeoisie on the capitalist state – pointing to the class background of those who made up the personnel of the state – Poulantzas argues that it is precisely the *distance* of capitalist state from direct bourgeois interference that enables it to more effectively serve its long-term economic interests. For Poulantzas, then, the state has to be thought of as an autonomous series of relations and institutions, one that has its own internal unity and logic, and yet which acts to sustain the capitalist system by maintaining an equilibrium between different forces and providing a central organising structure for social relations.[8]

THE ANARCHIST THEORY OF THE STATE

Anarchists also argue that Marx, and indeed the majority of the Marxist tradition as a whole, neglects the autonomy of political power and particularly the power of the state. Bakunin claimed, for instance, that Marxists pay too much attention to the *forms* of state power while not taking enough account of the way in which state power actually operates, and its structural predominance in society: 'They (Marxists) do not know that despotism resides not so much in the form of the State but in the very principle of the State and political power.'[9] In other words, by focusing on the class character of political power – that is, the way that the state is either the political instrument of the bourgeoisie or simply serves bourgeois interests – Marx ignores the way that the state itself, as a structure of domination and sovereignty, has its own specific logic of self-perpetuation and expansion which is above and beyond class interests. That was why, for Kropotkin, we must look beyond the bourgeois form that the state currently takes under capitalism, and recognise that it is an autonomous structure of power and domination which will always act as an obstacle to revolution.[10] The state, in other words, constitutes its own locus of power: it is not merely an instrument or expression of class power; nor is it simply the political expression of the capitalist mode of production. Rather, state power has its own organising principles and prerogatives, its own tendency towards the domination of social forces. The key difference, then, between the anarchist and

Marxist approach to the state is that the latter tends to regard the class nature of the state as the source of its domination, whereas the former sees the state as dominating no matter which class is in control of it.

Let us examine more closely the state's relationship to capitalism and class in the anarchist analysis. While there are certain parallels between the Marxist and anarchist approaches to the state under capitalism, there are also important differences. As in the Marxist analysis, anarchists argue that the state operates to sustain the capitalist mode of production – it provides an environment, both coercive and regulatory, in which the bourgeois can continue to exploit the worker, thus perpetuating capitalist accumulation. However, this does not mean that the state is simply an epiphenomenon of capitalism, and certainly not an instrument of bourgeois class interests: behind the bourgeois accumulation of capital is the statist project of the infinite accumulation of power. In other words, rather than seeing the state simply as an instrument of capitalist accumulation, it may be the other way round – capitalism is a way for the state to accumulate power; relations of state power intersect with, intensify, and in turn are intensified by, relations of capitalism. So, rather than economic forces determining political forces, as in the Marxist analysis, the relationship between the political and the economic is more complex, and may indeed work the other way round. Alan Carter puts the question:

> But what is to stop us entertaining an alternative account: namely, the superstructure selects specific relations of production because they are functional for that superstructure? An authoritarian post-capitalist state might, for example, choose managerial relations rather than support factory committees, because the former enable a surplus to be extracted, which the state requires to enforce its rule (as opposed to allowing the proletariat to consume its own produce . . .).[11]

So the problem, according to Carter, is that Marxists, because of their economic reductionism, are unable to realise that the state always acts to protect its own interests, and that this imperative will be no less the case in a post-capitalist society. As a structure of power, the state has its own interests beyond those of the capitalist class, and it supports the set of economic relations that best enables it to expand its power through the generation of a surplus: this set of economic relations might be capitalism, but, under a different set of circumstances, it might even be socialism.

If we look at the so-called neoliberal 'rollback' of the state in many societies from the early 1980s up until just recently – something that might superficially suggest that the state is entirely beholden to bourgeois economic interests, up to its own 'withering away' under capitalism – what we find is just the opposite. So far from there being a minimisation of state power, there was an infinite expansion of it, particularly in its security, surveillance and war-making functions (while its welfare functions shrank). The quasi-libertarian rhetoric of 'getting government off our backs' hid precisely the opposite phenomenon: a state that was not only more violent and coercive, but also more intrusive and interventionist, regulating social interactions and individual behaviours through a form of state-market disciplining. The 'nanny state' that the conservative tabloids in the United Kingdom like to condemn – not without justification – is only the other side of the neoliberal state: it is a way of trying to iron over the social dislocations and antagonisms wrought by the neoliberal market through a fetishisation of some vague ideology of 'community', one that is under threat from all sorts of 'anti-social' behaviours and 'unhealthy' lifestyles – a discourse that legitimises more disciplinary, coercive and surveillance power for the state. So, far from being a withdrawal of the state, neoliberalism implies a much more complex interaction between the state and society, a more intensive state regulation of social interactions and moral behaviours that takes place at a molecular level. Neoliberalism has nothing to do with classical notions of laissez-faire, but is a political rationality that seeks to construct social relations and individual behaviours according to a market logic; a project which implies not the reduction or minimisation of state power but precisely the opposite. Foucault's extensive analyses of neoliberalism as a rationality of government show precisely that the 'withdrawal of the state' from society is at the same time a project of the state itself, a new way of articulating its power. As Thomas Lemke says in his synopsis of Foucault's lectures on neoliberal governmentality:

As regards the shift in delimitation between the state and society, the studies reveal that the neo-liberal forms of government do not simply lead to a shift in the capacity to act away from the state and onto the level of society, to a reduction in state or its limitation to some basic functions. The neo-liberal forms of government feature not only direct intervention by means of empowered and specialized state apparatuses, but also characteristically develop indirect techniques for leading and controlling individuals without at the same time being responsible for them.[12]

Moreover, we can see that with the current crisis of neoliberalism, the state is simply re-articulating itself in slightly different way, no doubt in some sort of quasi-Keynesian form, with bank bail-outs, cash injections, big spending packages and so on. It is not the case, however, that the state has now made a comeback. The state never went away. It simply interacted with society in different guises. For anarchists, then, whether the state takes a neoliberal form, or a neo-Keynesian form, or some other form altogether, it is always the same structure of domination and control, and it will always entail violence, oppression and inequality. Indeed, state power has intensified and expanded in recent times rather than contracted, to the point where the distinction between the state and civil society – the conceptual distinction that was central to liberalism and, in a different way, to Marxism – has all but collapsed. The phenomenon of so-called public–private partnerships that social democratic governments are so keen on, the ubiquitous surveillance of public spaces and the expansion of biopolitical systems of control – biometric scanning, DNA databases, finger-printing at airports etc. – where not even our bodily interior is any longer a private domain, point to the way that the state has in a sense been mapped on to civil society, to the extent that the two entities become coextensive. Michael Hardt puts this best when he refers to a post-civil condition in which 'Not the State but civil society has withered away!'[13] The fundamental insight that we can draw from the anarchist analysis is that the modern state project is a totalitarian one. The 'actually existing' totalitarian regimes of the early to mid twentieth century were but crude and ultimately unsuccessful attempts to institute what is currently being implemented in much more subtle and pervasive ways in contemporary societies. Our post-liberal and biopolitical security states are totalitarian precisely in the sense that we do not (yet) perceive them as such, exercising power through a technologically-assisted and –technologically-driven web of control and surveillance that permeates society at all levels. The mania that our governments today display for more control, more security, more surveillance, more information gathering and so on, points to the inexorable nature of this state project.

THE TRANSITIONAL STATE

I have outlined the central difference between the Marxist and anarchist approach to the state. Generally speaking, for Marxists, what really counts is the capitalist mode of production and class interests, and the state is largely a secondary epiphenomenon of this. For anarchists, by contrast, the state itself is the major source of domination in society, or at least one that is just as important as capitalism. This distance of the state from capitalism is even reflected in an alternative historical analysis of the state. Anarchists see the state as emerging from different, non-economic factors and developments: for Bakunin, the state emerges partly out of religious authority; Kropotkin points to factors such as the historical dominance of Roman law, the rise of feudal law and the growing authoritarianism of the Church.[14]

These differences in perspective were brought to a head in the major debate between Marx and the anarchists over the role of the state in the 'transitional' period after the revolution. The controversy over whether the state should be abolished as the first act of the revolution, as the anarchists urged, or whether it should be used as an instrument of revolution in order to build socialism under the conditions of the 'dictatorship of the proletariat', as Marx and Engels believed, is really the crux of the matter. For Marx, because state oppression lies in the way that it serves bourgeois class interests, if the proletariat – which was the 'universal class' – were to take control of the state, it could be used as a neutral tool to revolutionise society. That is why, in the transitional period after the revolution, Marx calls for a 'decisive centralisation of power in the hands of State authority'.[15] Moreover, Marx and Engels believed that 'when, in the course of development, class distinctions have disappeared, and all production has been concentrated in the hands of a vast association of the whole nation, public power will lose its political character'.[16] The state would, after the abolition of class distinctions, simply become a neutral administrative apparatus in the service of society, and would eventually, to use Engels' expression, wither away.

We must remember that Marx shared with the anarchists the same aspiration of a society of free association without a state. However, the problem lay precisely in his idea that the state under socialism would lose its political character and would no longer be repressive because class distinctions had been overcome. For anarchists like Bakunin, this position was naive because it neglected the way that the state has its own specific logic of domination which is beyond the immediate control of the bourgeoisie. Indeed, the state enacts its power through ruling classes, which are the state's material representatives; in other words, a ruling class was actually essential to the state. That was why the state would not lose its political character simply because existing class distinctions had disappeared, but would, on the contrary, actually lead to the creation of new ruling class – no longer the bourgeoisie but a class of bureaucrats who would come to dominate and exploit the rest of society. Rather than the state withering away under communism, its power is intensified and it comes with a new set of class divisions. Bakunin's prediction of the state in the transitional period is, thus, rather different from Marx's:

> and finally, when all other classes have exhausted themselves, the class of bureaucracy enters upon the stage and the State falls, or rises, if you please, to a position of a machine. But for the salvation of the State it is absolutely necessary that there be some privileged class interested in maintaining its existence.[17]

So Marx's vision of the state under communism as a neutral apparatus, free from class power and at the service of society, would translate, in Bakunin's eyes, to a totalitarian machine controlled by a new technocratic class that would exercise possibly an even greater domination over society than under the bourgeoisie. It is perhaps facile to say that Bakunin was proved right by the history of the Soviet Union – even he could not have predicted the monstrous nature of Stalinism and its total distortion of Marxist politics. And yet Bakunin does highlight accurately the blindspot in Marx's thought over the question of state power, the sense in which it can never be trusted as a neutral tool of revolutionary politics, and that it will always seek a perpetuation of its power no matter what the economic and class conditions are. The problem lies in the way that state power corrupts the subjectivity of revolutionaries – the way that involvement in the state creates a desire for power and a psychological bond with the structure that one becomes a part of: 'We of course are all sincere socialists and revolutionists and still, were we to be endowed with power . . . we would not be where we are now.'[18] It is, therefore, the height of naivety to imagine that one can revolutionise society from a position of power, that one can be involved in state power, either in the parliamentary sense – and this was one of the key strategies of the Marxist tradition – or in the revolutionary sense, without being corrupted by it. Indeed, the recent ignominious history of social democratic parties in Europe serves as just as vital a warning about the perils of state power as the history of the Bolshevik revolution. For anarchists, then, a revolution has to be libertarian in means as well as ends; it must not work through state power but outside and against it. Marx's accusation against the anarchists, that in their refusal of the state they had neglected the reality of political power,[19] should thus be turned around: it is precisely the Marxist tradition which, in its economic and class reductionism, neglected the reality of political power by imagining the state to be, in essence, neutral when it was anything but.

The controversy over the state in revolutionary politics is perhaps best exemplified in Lenin. His work, *State and Revolution*, is characterised by a strange ambivalence on the question of the state, a tension between the libertarian desire for the revolutionary destruction of state authority, and more authoritarian tendencies reflected in the notion of the dictatorship of the proletariat and the revolutionary vanguard. At times, Lenin seems to come close to an anarchist position. In opposition to what he sees as a social-democratic distortion of Marx's thought, he urges the violent overthrowing of state power, without which the liberation of the masses is impossible.[20] The state is a parasitic institution of domination which is synonymous with class antagonism and exploitation, and which cloaks bourgeois exploitation in ideas of universal suffrage. Indeed, he upbraids the more reformist-minded socialists for misinterpreting Engels' notion of the withering away of state power to mean a slow, gradual and piecemeal withering away of the *bourgeois* state – whereas it is precisely the *structure* of the state itself that would be transcended under communism. Moreover, he cites with approval the radical democracy of the Paris Commune of 1871 as precisely an instance of the overcoming of state power[21] – an example also celebrated for the same reasons by Bakunin and Kropotkin. However, after indicating a commonality with the anarchist position, Lenin also distances himself from their desire to abolish the state immediately:

> The proletariat needs the state only for a while. We do not at all disagree with the Anarchists on the question of the abolition of the state as an *aim*. We maintain that, to achieve this aim, temporary

use must be made of the instruments, means, and methods of state power against the exploiters, just as the dictatorship of the oppressed class is temporarily necessary for the annihilation of classes.[22]

While Lenin's position might sound reasonable – *let's not rush to abolish state power, let's use it for a while to revolutionise society and then we can do away with it* – the anarchist lesson is clear: this is the trap of political power, the temptation of every revolution. The revolutionary – despite his or her best intentions – will get caught up in the cult of power and authority, and will come to depend on the state's mechanisms more and more; and we will soon find that the temporary state is now a permanent and increasingly oppressive presence in post-revolutionary society. The problem with Lenin is that in his polemic against the anarchists, he uses the argument about the withering away of the state as a way of justifying the concentration and perpetuation of state power under the dictatorship of the proletariat. To avoid the trap of power, anarchists believed – naively perhaps – that the abolition of the state should really mean the abolition of the state, not its permanent 'temporariness'. So, from the anarchist perspective, the Marxist and Leninist revolutionary strategy of seizing and utilising state power in the transitional period was just as flawed as the strategy of seeking power through parliamentary and electoral means, which Lenin saw as the polar opposite of his own position. Indeed, both strategies are two sides of the same statist coin: both strategies, despite their differences, work within the paradigm of the state in the sense that they both have as their aim the control of state power. Anarchism seeks to carve out for radical politics an alternative position: a politics that works outside the state and seeks to transcend it.

PARTY AND CLASS

This distinction between the libertarian, and more statist and authoritarian, positions becomes clearer if one looks at the role of the revolutionary vanguard in Marxist and particularly Leninist politics. For Marx, the Communist Party would play a leadership role in the revolution because it had a certain epistemological authority over the masses – it alone understood the laws of history and matters of revolutionary tactics: 'they (Communists) have over the great mass of the proletariat the advantage of clearly understanding the line of march'.[23] Bakunin believed that this claim to epistemological authority was dangerous, that is, it would lead to an elitism of knowledge, a new dictatorship of scientists and savants.[24] Moreover, the military metaphor that Marx used to describe the role of the revolutionary party – 'line of march' – is continued in Lenin, who makes references to 'our troops' and 'military operations', and, moreover, argues that the revolutionary party should, due to Tsarist repression, operate in secret, something that would preclude it from being fully democratic and transparent.[25] Moreover, Lenin placed a strong emphasis on party discipline and unity. Certainly, some degree of democratic debate and decision making was allowed within the revolutionary party, under the principle of 'democratic centralism'. However, from an anarchist perspective, the very notion of a revolutionary vanguard is authoritarian: it embodies notions of leadership, control of the masses and the discouraging of revolutionary spontaneity; of speaking for the masses and interpreting their revolutionary desire in particular ways. Rather than this, anarchists focus on the spontaneous self-organisation of the masses, without the need for political parties of any kind. Furthermore, the revolutionary party – with its emphasis on discipline and unity, its leadership structures and hierarchical decision-making procedures and its permanent executives and bureaucracies – already mirrors the state apparatus that it is proposing to take over. This is a point made by Murray Bookchin:

> The party is structured along hierarchical lines that *reflect the very society it professes to oppose.* Despite its theoretical pretensions, it is a bourgeois organism, a miniature state, with an apparatus and a cadre whose function it is to *seize* power, not *dissolve* power.[26]

We find a similar critique also levelled against the Marxist idea of class. For anarchists, Marx's idea that the industrial proletariat – because of its specific place in the capitalist mode of production – was the universal and only truly revolutionary class, was actually exclusivist and hierarchical. It denied a radical political potential to other, even more subordinate classes in society, such as the peasantry and the lumpen-proletariat – classes which Marx regarded as essentially reactionary. By contrast, classical anarchists saw a real revolutionary potential in these other classes precisely because they had no connection to the factory system. Not only was the industrial proletariat actually numerically small compared with other groups and classes in society, but it was also thoroughly imbued with bourgeois ethics. Bakunin believed that the small elite of 'class-conscious' proletarians constituting the upper echelons of the working class, lived in a relatively comfortable and semi-bourgeois fashion, and had been, in fact, co-opted into the bourgeoisie. A similar point is made by Bookchin, who argues that the working class in modern societies has largely bought into conservative bourgeois values of factory discipline, hierarchy and respect for author- ity, values and everyday practices through which the capitalist system is reproduced.[27] We must acknowledge, of course, that for Marx the pro- letariat is as much of a political subjectivity as an actual socio-economic category, but it is precisely because its economic role in capitalism is the basis for its universal political role – it was thus the class that suppos- edly embodied the dissolution of all classes – that one should question this. There is no necessary or essential link between one's place in the productive process and one's political outlook or level of revolutionary 'consciousness', and this has been borne out by the industrial working class historically in many cases taking up politically and socially con- servative attitudes. For anarchists, then, it was much more productive to broaden the category of the revolutionary class to include other sub- ordinated groups in society. Bakunin speaks of 'that great rabble which being very nearly unpolluted by all bourgeois civilization carries in its heart, in its aspirations, in all necessities and the misery of its collective position, all the germs of the Socialism of the future . . .'[28] Here we have a notion of a rabble or mass rather than a class, an identity which is more heterogeneous as well as more spontaneously revolutionary.

THE LIBERTARIAN LEFT

As we have seen, the anarchist critique of the Marxist tradition is basi- cally on the grounds of its authoritarianism: something that is implicit – and often explicit[29] – not only in its neglect of the dangers of state power, but also in its ideas about revolutionary leadership and class identity. Anarchists were also sceptical of other authoritarian elements in Marxist thinking, such as the uncritical embrace of industrial tech- nology – which Marx regarded as a sign of progress – as well as systems of factory discipline like Taylorism, which Lenin particularly admired for its efficient organisation of labour. Of course, Marx believed that these technologies could be harnessed and utilised for socialist rather than capitalist ends; but anarchists were for the most part more sensitive to the destructive effect that these technologies had on traditional communal ways of life, as well as the threat they posed to freedom and autonomy. Anarchism, therefore, offers an alternative conception of radical politics, one that is revolutionary but non-statist, non-centralist and libertarian. Indeed, the anarchist critique of Marxism opened the way for a more heterodox tradition of radical left thinking and politics: one that which finds certain resonances today, for instance, with libertarian Marxists and Autonomists. The key themes to emerge out of the Autonomist Marxist tradition – the spontaneous self-organisation of the workers without, for the most part, the involvement of the party, and hence the critique of political representation; the uncompromising critique of the sovereign state as that which negates the creativity of social forces – show clear parallels with classical anarchism.[30] While there are important differences between anarchism and Autonomia, there is, nevertheless, a certain missing link between them that has yet to be properly explored or even acknowledged, as there is a missing link between anarchism and a number of other contemporary continental approaches to radical politics – a connection that will be discussed more fully in the following chapter.

Where one finds a clear compatibility between aspects of Autonomist/ libertarian Marxist thought and anarchism is around the notion of autonomy itself. There is a desire in both traditions for a form of revolutionary politics that is autonomous from the state – that does not try to take over state power, either through the revolutionary seizure of power or through involvement in party politics. In other words, there is a refusal of representation – a rejection of the idea that the masses can be represented through the state form and through political parties which seek to attach the masses to the state. This drive towards an autonomous politics is present in the thought of Antonio Negri who, working within a Spinozist ontology, explores the central tension between what he calls *constituent* power – that is, the radically democratic power of revolutionary desire – and *constituted* power – which is the uncertain crystallisation of this revolutionary desire into fixed constitutions and political systems, an arrangement in which constituent power is repressed and captured. There is, in other words, a paradoxical relationship between democratic innovation – embodied within the revolutionary force of the multitude – and the sovereign and constitutional regimes which draw on this constituent power and at the same time act to contain it:

But isn't closing constituent power within representation – where
the latter is merely a cog in the social machinery of the division
of labour – nothing but the negation of the reality of constituent
power, its congealment into a static system, the restoration of traditional sovereignty against the democratic innovation?[31]

That is why there is always a crisis of the juridical order – because it is
constituted and draws its force from something that at the same time
threatens to disrupt it, a revolutionary and radically democratic excess
which it tries to fix and represent, but which always threatens to spill
out over its edges. For instance, a revolution is always more than the
revolutionary regime that is newly established; the democratic imagination that made the revolution and the constituted new revolutionary
order can never be completely represented by it, and always exceeds it.
That is why revolutionary governments invariably end up turning on
the very revolutionary forces which made the revolution: we saw this in
the increasingly authoritarian and repressive character of the Bolshevik
regime in its consolidation of the Russian Revolution, repressing
the constituent power of the independent workers' councils (soviets),
whose democratic will was converted into a state apparatus under the
category of the 'dictatorship of the proletariat'. All regimes and juridical orders are thus based on a kind of repression or forgetting of their
own revolutionary origins. Thus, the mystery of the foundations of
sovereignty is precisely that which it cannot bear to acknowledge, the
constituent power of the people, something it tries to hide in mystifications like the social contract or abstract juridical notions.[32]
    This idea would seem to reflect the classical anarchist position on
the state – the way that the state, and indeed the mechanisms of political representation, including and especially the vanguard party – are
antithetical and hostile to revolutionary forces. This was particularly
evident in the Russian Revolution which, as Voline recounts in *The
Unknown Revolution*, was a libertarian social revolution that was eventually consolidated in a Bolshevik coup d'état. It was riven by conflicting ideas – the Bolshevik idea of using the state and establishing a
dictatorship of the proletariat, and the anarchist idea which was 'to
carry out the Revolution and resolve its difficulties, not by political and
state means, but by means of natural, unforced economic and social
activity of the workers' very own associations . . .'[33] Moreover, the
idea of a radically democratic power which cannot be represented and

which works outside or against the state, is also central to anarchists' revolutionary thought. Indeed, they saw the radical democracy of the Paris Commune as precisely an example of what Negri would consider constituent power. As we have seen, then, anarchism maintains that democracy is ultimately irreconcilable with state sovereignty and always exceeds it, something that is echoed in Negri: 'Everything, in sum, sets constituent power and sovereignty in opposition, even the absolute character that both categories lay claim to: the absoluteness of sovereignty is a totalitarian concept, whereas that of constituent power is the absoluteness of democratic government.'[34]

POST-MARXISM

The discussion of anarchism so far has pointed in a number of ways to what might be termed the *autonomy of the political*. As I have argued, anarchism highlights the importance and autonomy of the political power of the state much more effectively than does Marxism. In other words, in perceiving the state itself as a problem which is essentially irreducible to the economic domain, anarchism points to the autonomy of the political domain. Indeed, it was the danger presented specifically by the political power of the state which meant that it must be confronted head on in a revolution. Even though this revolution against the state was understood as a revolution of the social against the political, it still presents the political domain as a specific question to be addressed – even if only as something to be abolished. Furthermore, the notion of the autonomy of the political was explored in another sense, through anarchist (as well as libertarian-Marxist) ideas of autonomous self-organisation, the rejection of representation and vanguard politics, and the movement of radical democracy against the sovereign state. Once again, while these themes might – indeed *do* – suggest an anti-politics, they can be seen also as a different way of understanding the autonomy of the political: the *political disturbance of state sovereignty*.

The notion of the autonomy of the political is central to post-Marxism, a theoretical perspective – best typified by thinkers like Ernesto Laclau and Chantal Mouffe – that seeks to deconstruct a number of key conceptual and political categories within Marxism. Laclau and Mouffe address what they see as the crisis of Marxism – evident not only in the failure of Marxist-Leninist projects, but also in concrete social conditions of the shrinking working class in post-industrial societies, the fragmentation of the political domain and the rise of the 'new social movements' which bear little resemblance to the class struggle of the proletariat, at least as it was conceived by Marx. Added to these factors, they argue, is the cultural and epistemological condition of postmodernity, which entails a certain scepticism about the universal essentialist identities and positivistic categories on which Marxism was based. Their main contention is that the failure of Marxism as a political project was due to its general neglect of politics – to its insistence that the political domain was reducible to the economy.

The idea elaborated by Laclau and Mouffe about the autonomy of the political from strict economic and class determination has important connections with anarchism. Like the classical anarchists, Laclau and Mouffe see the political dimension – the dimension of power, struggle, antagonism – as not being fully explainable by, or reducible to, the economic mode of production. Also, they question the relevance, unity and coherence of the central Marxist category of class, arguing that, particularly in the later parts of the twentieth century, radical political identities are much more heterogeneous; that there is a multitude of struggles and social movements today – ethnic minorities, students, environmentalists, indigenous peoples, gays, feminists – that can no longer be expressed adequately by the concept of class, and whose interests and demands are no longer strictly economic. Indeed, as Laclau and Mouffe say, 'The common denominator of all of them would be their differentiation from workers' struggles, considered as "class" struggles.'[35] There is no longer a privileged revolutionary subject but rather a plurality of movements, identities and demands. Do we not see reflected here, for instance, Bakunin's criticism of the notion of class and his preference for the idea of a more heterogeneous and less exclusivist 'mass'? Moreover, Laclau and Mouffe show the way that even in Marx's time, the various struggles of workers and artisans tended to be against relations of subordination generally, and against the destruction of their organic, communal way of life through the introduction of the factory system and new forms of industrial technology, and thus did not conform to Marx's notion of the disciplined proletarian struggle.[36] The same point was made by the anarchists who, as we have seen, were critical of Marx's contempt for the peasantry and his enthusiastic embrace of modern industry and technology; they emphasised instead the libertarian and spontaneous character of popular rebellions against the factory system. Furthermore, many of the struggles during the second half of the twentieth century are explained by Laclau and Mouffe as struggles against domination, rather than as simply against economic exploitation. Indeed, they were often struggles generated around different forms of state intervention, and the way this has resulted in an increased bureaucratisation of life: 'In all the domains in which the state has intervened, a politicisation of social relations is at the base of numerous new antagonisms.'[37] This is not to say that such struggles do not contest capitalist exploitation, but rather that economic exploitation would be seen here as an aspect of broader relations of domination. This ties in with the multitude of struggles that we see today: struggles and movements which – while they are constructed in opposition to global capitalism – are no longer proletarian struggles in the traditional Marxist sense. Instead, they are anti-institutional and incorporate a diverse range of issues: the environment, cultural autonomy, indigenous rights, anti-war and anti-imperialism and so on. This is why, for Laclau and Mouffe, contemporary political, social and economic struggles are more accurately seen as radically democratic rather than Marxist; indeed, their proliferation during the twentieth century should be seen as part of an ongoing articulation of the democratic revolution and its horizon of equality and liberty.

We can detect, then, a strong resemblance between Laclau and Mouffe's post-Marxism and aspects of anarchism; a resemblance which is never acknowledged in their work. Anarchism, as we have seen, provides many resources for a critical move beyond Marxism, particularly in terms of its theorisation of the autonomy of the political. Moreover, many of the theoretical moves employed by Laclau and Mouffe in their deconstruction of Marxism – their incorporation, for instance, of elements of post-structuralism and psychoanalysis – are also deployed in my elaboration of postanarchism, particularly in its critique of essentialist foundations and identities, and its contention that political solidarities must be actively constructed rather than simply relied upon to emerge organically from social and economic processes. However, there are a number of important differences between post-Marxism and postanarchism. Indeed, it is my contention that an anarchist-based approach can serve as a more convincing basis for understanding contemporary radical political struggles than a Marxist-based approach – even one as far removed from a classical Marxist position as Laclau and Mouffe's post-Marxism.

The main difference between the two approaches is over the

question of the state. While in Laclau and Mouffe there is a close analysis of the political effects of the different articulations of the state – from the Keynesian welfare state to the neoliberal state – there is still the assumption that all politics takes place on a state-based terrain. This is not to say that, in their analysis, radical political struggles do not oppose particular state policies or even certain articulations of the state. But they still move on a territory which is conditioned by the problematic of state sovereignty: political and social movements make certain demands upon the state, seeking either to influence state policy or take over state power.[38]

This view of politics derives in large part from the Gramscian theory of hegemony, which was an attempt to explain the way that the bourgeoisie in capitalist societies maintained its dominant position not so much through a coercive state apparatus, but through a diffuse series of relationships, institutions, ideas and values that were coextensive with civil society. Not only the state, in other words, but also the Church, schools, universities, private associations, scientific discourses and cultural and moral values could all be seen as constructing a bourgeois hegemony – a general ideological domination that permeated society, and relied not on the direct use of force (although this was always available in the last instance) but on the everyday interactions, as well as the participation and consent of people in civil society. Indeed, from Gramsci's perspective, it no longer made any sense to separate civil society from the state – both were interlinked in a complex series of power relations that formed an 'integral State'. According to Gramsci, then, the Leninist strategy of seizing control of a centralised state apparatus was conceivable in societies such as Russia; while in the West, a different strategy had to be devised – no longer the 'war of maneuver' but the 'war of position'.[39] In other words, the working class and other subaltern groups in society had to develop, through the intellectual and moral leadership of the Communist Party, a counterhegemony which would rival that of the bourgeoisie: they had to develop their own institutions, culture, modes of identification, shared ideas and values – their own 'collective will'. The party, for Gramsci, is the Machiavellian prince, whose role was as political leader was to 'conquer a State, or to found a new type of State . . .'[40]

Now it is precisely this notion of party and class leadership from which Laclau and Mouffe distance themselves, seeing this as a part of the Marxist and Leninist legacy to which Gramsci remained attached.

Yet, what Laclau and Mouffe retain from Gramsci is the idea of the state as that which encompasses political and civil society, and thus the idea that hegemonic struggles take place within a state framework – they take place over and around the question of state power.[41] What is never really considered in their analysis is the question of the legitimacy of the principle of state sovereignty itself, and the idea that politics can be imagined outside the state. The idea of anarchism as a politics of anti-politics would be in a sense foreclosed from their theory, or would at least be at the very outer limits of it.

THE POLITICS OF SOVEREIGNTY

So, for Laclau and Mouffe, while they provide an innovative way of understanding how radical political identities are constituted, one that is an important advancement on Marxism, politics still largely takes place on the stage set by the state and sovereignty. This does not mean that political struggles do not challenge state power in radical ways, but they nevertheless presuppose the state, and particularly the nation-state, as the basic framework for politics.

This is particularly evident in Mouffe's scepticism towards the idea of transnational activism and cosmopolitan politics. While Mouffe is, of course, perfectly correct in her criticism of a certain neoliberal vision of cosmopolitan globalisation based on the unaccountable and undemocratic power of global financial institutions, and while she also makes certain valid points of criticism against the democratic cosmopolitan vision based on human rights norms and the rule of international law, her approach seems to reify the concept of state sovereignty and sees the nation-state as the only legitimate site of democratic politics. This position becomes more apparent in her condemnation of Hardt's and Negri's politics of the multitude, which invokes the idea of a form of global democracy beyond the nation-state.[42] While I, too, have certain reservations about Hardt's and Negri's understanding of the global order and their vision of politics – which I shall discuss in Chapter 4 – they at least try to think politics beyond state sovereignty. Mouffe's alternative to the cosmopolitan vision of politics is the idea of a 'pluriverse', which derives from Carl Schmitt:[43] a multi-polar world where competing regional blocs maintain a balance of power. Now I fully agree with Mouffe about the need to oppose US empire – an imperialism which clothes itself in the language of human rights, although perhaps not to the extent that Mouffe imagines: should one not, instead, place the emphasis on the inconsistency of this human rights ideology, on the numerous ways in which the United States, along with other Western powers, *violate* their own human rights commitments when it suits their national interest? A cosmopolitan order based on universal human rights is, of course, not sufficient, and Mouffe is perfectly correct to show that this will often conceal a particular position of imperial power. However, I am not sure that the alternative she proposes – competing regional power blocs like ASEAN and the EU maintaining a balance of power – is necessarily any more desirable than the cosmopolitan vision. It seems to me that regional groupings of nation-states, competing for power and resources, is a rather limited aspiration for radical politics. Mouffe says:

> Once it is acknowledged that there is no 'beyond hegemony', the only conceivable strategy for overcoming world dependence on a single power is to find ways to 'pluralize' hegemony. And this can be done only through the recognition of a multiplicity of regional powers. It is only in this context that no agent in the international order will be able, because of its power, to regard itself above the law and to arrogate to itself the role of the sovereign.[44]

So, to avoid the single imperial sovereign, Mouffe's alternative is to have multiple sovereigns. Yet, I fail to see why this is necessarily a better scenario: rather than having one single site of oppression and domination, we have several. Should one, for instance, welcome the rise of China as a rival superpower – as Mouffe seems to – with its authoritarian neocapitalist state and its terrible repression of its own people; should one celebrate the EU, with its expanding networks of surveillance and its ever more intensively controlled borders? If, indeed, this is the alternative that is being proposed, then some sort of human rights cosmopolitanism – as flawed as it would inevitably be – seems to me a more attractive proposition. Surely radical politics must not be condemned to a vision such as this. Anarchists want to see not a proliferation of sovereigns, but rather a transcendence of (state or regional) sovereignty altogether – a much deeper pluralisation and democratisation, at the level of communities rather than nation-states and regional groupings. Mouffe would see this idea as simply entailing another form of sovereignty, another set of exclusions. I am not so convinced of this, and, indeed, it is one of the challenges of this book to think politics beyond the problematic of sovereignty.

What is problematic about the 'pluriverse' position – in which any attempt to transcend the sovereign state in the name of something more universal is condemned as utopian, unrealistic and caught within the interminable logic of sovereignty – is that it invokes 'realpolitik', a cynical realism which is to my mind ultimately conservative. One finds this particularly in William Rasch, in whose neoSchmittian imaginary there is a fetishisation of borders, limits, exclusions, conflict. This is a kind of *ultra politics* in which the only guarantee of pluralism and democracy – indeed, of politics itself – is the sovereign state; where all notions of revolutionary politics, universal peace and democracy beyond the state are rejected as utopian, moralistic, quasi-religious and ultimately disingenuous, and where the idea of politics occurring at the level of civil society and autonomous associations rather than sovereign institutions, is dismissed as anti-political liberal pluralism. We can see this clearly in Rasch's critique of Giorgio Agamben (and Walter Benjamin): unlike Schmitt who 'locates himself firmly within the political as defined by the sovereign state of exception, both Benjamin and Agamben imagine the possibility of a politics that exceeds the political'.[45] For Rasch, who takes Schmitt's side, it is unthinkable to have a politics which exceeds the political, which exceeds, in other words, sovereignty; it is unthinkable to call into question the structure of sovereignty. A critique along similar lines is launched against Hardt's and Negri's notion of the anti-sovereign multitude, which, according to Rasch, neglects the ineluctable presence of sovereignty in any form of politics. The central argument here is, therefore, that sovereignty is the ineradicable dimension of politics, and that any attempt to think of politics in terms of a post-sovereign form of a community of non-violence disguises the inevitable question of 'who decides?': who or what, in other words, determines the limits or parameters of this community?; how will it be 'imposed' on those who might disagree with it? The answer, for Rasch, is the sovereign.[46] So, a politics of anti-politics – a politics aimed at the abolition of politics – is, for Rasch, a logical contradiction. However, as I have argued, anarchism is precisely such a politics, and its aspiration of overcoming state sovereignty is not in any sort of contradiction with the idea of politics – unless one locates politics always within the structure of state sovereignty, which Rasch clearly does. Rasch is correct to raise the question of how post-sovereign communities will be constituted, what their limits will be, who will decide on their parameters, etc.; these are questions which anarchists must themselves address. But I would argue that this does not mean that we are always caught within the paradigm of sovereignty – that there are other mechanisms for deciding political matters than the sovereign state; the various decentralised and autonomous forms of direct democracy that anarchists have suggested and, in different contexts experimented with, suggest that alternatives to state sovereignty are possible.

As I argued in Chapter 2, the question of limits and the difficulty of dislodging power relations must be acknowledged and addressed more seriously by classical anarchism in particular. However, this was understood as a kind of ethical injunction to continue to interrogate existing political structures in the name of an open horizon of equality and liberty. What concerns me about an approach like Rasch's is the way that it fetishises limits, exclusions and power, rather than attempting to transcend them – it glories in the conservative cynicism that says: *give up your utopian dreams of the eternal community without a sovereign; you will always have sovereignty, this is all we can hope for.* And worse, that this reification of the sovereign state is contorted into an argument for a progressive left politics. This is a kind of 'dirty hands' realism that I see as being entirely at odds with the idea of emancipation. The limiting of politics to the paradigm of sovereignty, and the warding off of any attempt to go beyond it, imposes an unnecessary and deeply conservative constraint upon radical politics. The challenge of emancipatory politics must be to transcend the sovereign state, to think beyond it.

I believe that, for instance, a certain re-articulation of democracy beyond the bind of sovereignty can suggest some answers here, a project that Derrida was engaged in with his notion of the 'democracy to come', something that I shall explore in the final chapter. Indeed, as I suggested in Chapter 1, I see this working against state sovereignty as being at the heart of democracy. In this sense, it is somewhat different from Mouffe's notion of agonistic plural democracy in which – in contrast to both liberal consensus and deliberative models of democracy – the mechanism of exclusion through which the democratic 'we' is constituted is made fully visible rather than being hidden, and which is based on a certain antagonistic Schmittian relationship between friend and enemy – albeit one where the figure of the enemy is transformed or sublimated into a worthy adversary.[47]

This approach does more than simply acknowledge the existence of borders, exclusions and antagonism in the construction of a democratic identity; it reifies them into the defining and ineluctable feature of politics. However, why is making borders visible and central necessarily emancipatory? Of course, it is better than leaving them hidden – if they are visible they can at least be contested and re-negotiated. But the point is that the 'we/they' distinction on which this model of democracy is based raises deeper questions about who exactly is being excluded, who is the enemy/adversary of the democratic we; and how do these discursive exclusions map on to the very real exclusions which constitute the identity of nation-states – the real borders that are often viciously enforced against those figures of the Other, such as the refugee or illegal immigrant? So what is being implied here, once again, is the idea that democratic and pluralist politics – indeed, politics itself – takes place primarily within the nation-state, and revolves continually around the problematic of state sovereignty and its borders. Perhaps this is also why in Mouffe's theory of democracy there is a strong defence of parliamentary institutions because of the way that they stage this antagonistic relationship, transforming it into a more 'safe' agonism.[48] This endorsement of parliamentary democracy seems to me like a somewhat limited model for a radically democratic politics to follow. Indeed, I prefer Abensour's notion of an-archic insurgent democracy, which he clearly distinguishes from 'conflictual democracy':

> Insurgent democracy is not a variant of conflictual democracy, but its exact opposite. Whereas conflictual democracy practices conflict within the State, a democratic State which in its very name presents itself as an avoidance of the original conflict, inclining as a result conflictuality towards permanent compromise, insurgent democracy situates conflict in another space, outside the State, against it, and far from practicing the avoidance of the major conflict – democracy against the State – it does not shrink from rupture, if need be.[49]

So, although Mouffe's model of democracy enshrines the idea of agonistic contestation, because it is ultimately conceived within the state it avoids the much more fundamental antagonism (or potential antagonism) between the state and democracy itself.

THE AUTONOMY OF THE POLITICAL OR THE POLITICS OF AUTONOMY?

These differing ideas of democracy revolve around two alternative approaches to the autonomy of the political. The understanding of the autonomy or 'primacy' of the political that is invoked in various ways in Mouffe and Rasch, derives from Schmitt. For Schmitt, what is specific to the political dimension – what makes it distinct from the economic, legal, religious and ethical domains – is a sort of existential antagonism between friend and enemy. The friend/enemy relation is at the heart of all distinctly political relationships and actions: 'The political is the most intense and extreme antagonism, and every concrete antagonism becomes that much more political the closer it approaches the most extreme point, that of the friend–enemy grouping.' Furthermore, 'In its entirety the state as an organized political entity that decides for itself the friend–enemy distinction.'[50] So, for Schmitt, this distinctly political relationship is primarily conceived within the state – indeed, the state defines itself in its sovereign decision on the friend–enemy antagonism: the state decides, in other words, who its enemies are, and this decision is what marks the borders of its identity. That is why, for Schmitt, war is the ultimate and most extreme articulation of the friend–enemy antago-nism.[51] One can see Schmitt's friend–enemy metaphor reflected in the motifs of agonism, conflict and pluralism that figure so prominently in both Rasch's and Mouffe's political thinking (although not entirely uncritically in Mouffe's case). Yet, as I have indicated, to think the politi-cal in this way is to chain it to the mast of state sovereignty. I would argue, then, that Schmitt's conceptualisation of politics is basically a reaction-ary one that has little to offer radical left thought. By contrast, I find Abensour's notion of the autonomy of the political much more fruitful:

> Instead of conceiving of emancipation as the victory of the social (a civil society reconciled) over the political, leading at the same time to the disappearance of the political, this form of democracy gives rise, works steadily towards giving rise to, a political community against the State. To the opposition of the social and the political, it substitutes that of the political and the State.[52]

So far, then, from movements of opposition to state sovereignty result-ing in the eclipse of politics and the subordination of the political to the social, as someone like Rasch would claim, what is being proposed here is a different notion of democratic politics – one whose opposition and exteriority to state sovereignty *is* the political relation *par excellence*. In other words, politics does not always have to be imagined within the limits of the state for it to be politics.

Furthermore, what is suggested here is an understanding of politics which is anarchist but which, at the same time, goes beyond the classical anarchist idea of the subordination of the political principle to the social principle. Earlier I suggested that for anarchists, the autonomy of the political signifies precisely the triumph of the organic and rational social principle over the artificiality of the political principle of state power. But perhaps there is a different way of thinking about the political principle – one that is detached from state sovereignty and works against it in the name of an entirely different kind of political community. This is where the autonomy of the political translates into the politics of autonomy – a politics and an understanding of the political community which is outside of, and autonomous from, the state. In this formulation, the autonomy of the political is retained – it is not subordinated to an organic social principle – but it is disconnected from the principle of state sovereignty which has for so long served as the prison house of politics. Is this new formulation of the autonomy of the political not much more appropriate for a radical politics of emancipation than the one conceived by Schmitt, where politics becomes a violent intensification of state power? All we get with Schmittian 'pure politics' is an empty, Hobbesian landscape from which all hope of emancipation has vanished, and where all we can do is wait for the looming shadow of the sovereign.

In this chapter I have tried to develop an alternative understanding of the autonomy of the political based on the anarchist critique of state sovereignty. In an examination of the debate between anarchists and Marxists over the question of state power, I showed that anarchism was much more sensitive to the dangers of political power and authority and therefore to the challenges of politics, than Marxism. I also suggested that, although there were certain important – yet unacknowledged – parallels between anarchism and post-Marxism, that anarchism is distinct in that it imagines forms of politics and democracy that are no longer positioned on the terrain of state sovereignty. It is here, then, that we arrive at an understanding of radical politics which is completely different from the neo-Schmittians; and yet which, rather than supplanting the political with the social dimension – as in the discourse of classical anarchism – still insists on the autonomy and primacy of politics. It is here that the anti-politics of anarchism meets the politics of postanarchism.

The following chapter will pursue this project of thinking about politics outside the state. It will do this through an exploration of debates over radical politics in contemporary continental theory, showing how postanarchism can intervene in them in important ways.

Notes

1 A reference to Lenin's famous critique of left-wing Communism and anarchism. See V. I. Lenin, *Left-wing Communism, an Infantile Disorder, Collected Works, 1870–1924*, vol. 31 (London: Lawrence & Wishart, 1966).

2 Voline, *The Unknown Revolution*. Cited in Daniel Guérin, *No Gods, No Masters: an Anthology of Anarchism* (Oakland, CA: AK Press, 2005), p. 477.

3 Mikhail Bakunin, 'The Excommunication of the Hague', *La Liberté*, 5 October 1872. Cited in Guérin, *No Gods, No Masters*, p. 191.

4 See Nicos Poulantzas, 'The Problem of the Capitalist State', *New Left Review*, 58, 1969, pp. 67–8.

5 Karl Marx and Friedrich Engels, 'Manifesto of the Communist Party', *The Marx–Engels Reader*, 2nd edn., Robert Tucker (ed.), pp. 473–500 at 475.

6 See Karl Marx, 'The Eighteenth Brumaire of Louis Bonaparte', in Karl Marx and Friedrich Engels, *Collected Works*, vol. 11 (London: Lawrence & Wishart, 1979).

7 See Nicos Poulantzas, *Political Power & Social Classes*, trans. Timothy O'Hagan (London: NLB and Sheed & Ward, 1973), p. 258.

8 See Poulantzas, *Political Power and Social Classes*, pp. 44–5.

9 Bakunin, *Political Philosophy*, p. 221.

10 See Kropotkin, *The State*, p. 9.

11 Alan Carter, 'Outline of an Anarchist Theory of History', in David Goodway (ed.) *For Anarchism: History, Theory and Practice*, (London: Routledge, 1989), pp. 176–97 at 180–1.

12 See Thomas Lemke, '"The birth of bio-politics": Michel Foucault's lecture at the Collège de France on neo-liberal governmentality', *Economy and Society*, 30(2), May 2001, pp. 190–207 at 201.

13 See Michael Hardt, 'The Withering of Civil Society', in E. Kaufman and K. J. Heller (eds), *Deleuze and Guattari: New Mappings in Politics, Philosophy and Culture* (Minneapolis, MN: University of Minnesota Press, 1998), pp. 23–39.

14 Kropotkin, *The State*, p. 28.

15 Karl Marx and Friedrich Engels, 'Address of the Central Council to the Communist League', in Tucker, *The Marx-Engels Reader*, pp. 501–11 at 509.

16 Marx and Engels, *Communist Manifesto*, p. 490

17 Bakunin, *Political Philosophy*, p. 208.

18 Bakunin, *Political Philosophy*, p. 249.

19 See Karl Marx, 'After the Revolution: Marx debates Bakunin', in Tucker, *The Marx–Engels Reader*, pp. 542–8.

20 See V. I Lenin, *State and Revolution* (New York: International Publishers, 1990 [1943]), p. 9.

21 Indeed, for Marx himself, the Paris Commune was a form of working-class government – of the people by the people – which 'breaks the modern State power'. See *The Paris Commune 1871*, Christopher Hitchens (ed.) (London: Sidgwick & Jackson, 1971), p. 95.

22 Lenin, *State and Revolution*, p. 52.

23 Marx and Engels, *Communist Manifesto*, p. 484.

24 See Bakunin, *Political Philosophy*, p. 300.

25 See V. I. Lenin, 'What is to be Done?', *Collected Works, Vol. 5, May 1901–February 1902* (London: Lawrence & Wishart, 1961), pp. 347–529 at 477.

26 Bookchin, *Post-scarcity Anarchism*, p. 196.

27 See Bookchin, *Post-scarcity Anarchism*, pp. 183–4.

28 Mikhail Bakunin, *Marxism, Freedom and the State*, trans. K. J. Kenafick (London: Freedom Press, 1984), p. 48.

29 See Engels' disparaging of those in the socialist movement who were critical of the principle of authoritarianism: 'Have these gentlemen ever seen a revolution? A revolution is certainly the most authoritarian thing there is; it is the act whereby one part of the population imposes its will upon the other by means of rifles, bayonets and cannon – authoritarian means, if such there be at all . . .', 'On Authority', *The Marx–Engels Reader*, pp. 730–3 at 733.

30 See Steve Wright's understanding of Autonomia as based on a refusal of the idea of the party vanguard as well as parliamentary politics, and an emphasis instead on creating a new non-party forms of organisation ('A Party of Autonomy', *Resistance in Practice: the Philosophy of Antonio Negri*, Timothy S. Murphy and Abdul-Karim Mustapha (eds) (London: Pluto Press, 2005), pp, 73–106.

31 Antonio Negri, *Insurgencies: Constituent Power and the Modern State*, trans. Maurizia Boscagli (Minneapolis, MN: University of Minnesota Press, 1999), p. 4.

32 See Negri, *Insurgencies*, p. 13.

33 See Voline in Guérin, *No Gods, No Masters*, p. 479.

34 Negri, *Insurgencies*, p. 13.

35 Ernesto Laclau and Chantal Mouffe, *Hegemony and Socialist Strategy: Towards a Radical Democratic Politics* (London: Verso, 2001), p. 159.
36 Laclau and Mouffe, *Hegemony and Socialist Strategy*, p. 162.
37 Laclau and Mouffe, *Hegemony and Socialist Strategy*, p. 162.
38 While making demands on the state does not necessarily confine politics to the state order – as I shall argue in Chapter 4 – there is little conception, in Laclau's and Mouffe's analysis, of the way that a certain radical framing of demands can presuppose the dissolution of state sovereignty and the invention of a political place beyond the state.
39 See Antonio Gramsci, *Selections from the Prison Notebooks*, ed. and trans. Quintin Hoare and Geoffrey Nowell-Smith (London: Lawrence & Wishart, 1971), pp. 238–9.
40 Gramsci, *Selections from the Prison Notebooks*, p. 253.
41 A similar point is made by Richard Day in *Gramsci is Dead: Anarchist Currents in the Newest Social Movements* (London: Pluto Press, 2005), p. 75.
42 See Chantal Mouffe, *On the Political* (London: Routledge, 2005), pp. 113–14.
43 See Schmitt, *The Nomos of the Earth in the International Law of the Jus Publicum Europeaum.*
44 Mouffe, *On the Political*, p. 118.
45 William Rasch, *Sovereignty and its Discontents: On the Primacy of Conflict and the Structure of the Political* (London: Birkbeck Law Press, 2004) p. 94.
46 See Rasch, *Sovereignty and its Discontents*, p. 16.
47 See Mouffe, *On the Political*, p. 21.
48 See Mouffe, *On the Political*, p. 23.
49 Miguel Abensour, *Democracy against the State: Marx and the Machiavellian Moment*, trans. Max Blechman and Martin Breaugh (Cambridge: Polity Press, 2011), p. xl.
50 Schmitt, *The Concept of the Political*, pp. 29–30.
51 Schmitt, *The Concept of the Political*, p. 33.
52 Abensour, *Democracy against the State*, p. xli.

Chapter 4

THE HORIZON OF ANARCHY: RADICAL POLITICS IN THE WAKE OF MARX

In Chapter 3, I explored the anarchist critique of Marxism – particularly on the question of state power – and elaborated, on the basis of this, the notion of a *politics of anti-politics*. In opposition to those who confine politics to the statist imaginary – and this includes Schmittian and neo-Schmittian conceptions of the 'autonomy of the political' – anarchism points to a politics beyond and against the state. *The autonomy of the political, if it is to mean anything, must mean a politics of autonomy.* At the same time, however, we can no longer conceive, as did the classical anarchists, of a pure social revolution against power. While we must reject the notion of a *political* revolution aimed simply at seizing the reins of the state and, in this way, perpetuating it, and while we must reject as entirely inadequate, parliamentary and reformist processes which work within the system of state power – we must at the same time question the idea of asserting an immanent, organic social principle against the impurities of politics. This does not mean that we cannot speak of movements at the level of civil society against the state – this is precisely where a postanarchist politics is situated. But the point is, as we shall see, that the politicisation of social forces involves at the same time a certain displacement of social identities – a certain dislodging or rupturing of normal social processes. Postanarchism can thus be seen as the attempt to free politics from the state – to conceive of a space for politics outside and against the state, and to see politics as an activity through which the principle of state sovereignty is radically questioned and disrupted. Postanarchism is, in this sense, a politics and an anti-politics: it is a politics that has no truck with politicians, parties, revolutionary vanguards and other self-proclaimed 'representatives of the people'; it is a way of using and democratising power without the desire to be *in* power; it proclaims an ethics of equality and liberty

103

beyond the limits of state authority, recognising that the state is the bloody altar on which such principles are sacrificed. From the classical anarchists we take the fundamental insight that the state is the eternal charnel house of revolutionary movements.

However, what does it mean to have a revolution – or as I suggested earlier, an insurrection – that has as its aim not the seizure of state power, but rather its dissolution and transcendence? Moreover, if we cannot rely on a natural social foundation to explain such a revolution, then how can it be conceived? Under what conditions does it emerge?

This chapter will address some of these questions, and it will do so through an engagement with a number of contemporary debates in radical political theory, particularly within the continental tradition. My contention here is that not only can a postanarchist approach shed light on some on the most pressing issues in radical politics today – such as questions of state power, the organisation of movements, the role of democracy, the place of the subject, the legitimacy of violence and the terrain of struggle – but also that contemporary thinkers such as Alain Badiou, Michael Hardt and Antonio Negri, Jacques Rancière and Giorgio Agamben, amongst others, draw upon a kind of anarchism without acknowledging it. This is not to say that they are anarchists *per se* – and, indeed, most of them would reject this characterisation – but that there are certain distinct anarchist elements in their approach to politics. It is a matter, then, of teasing out these anarchist threads to see where they might lead. Moreover, as I will attempt to show, an anarchist or postanarchist position would allow us to transcend the limitations of these approaches and provide a more consistent way of thinking about radical politics today.

THE FORGOTTEN LINK

As I suggested in Chapter 1, anarchism has always been a political heresy; its rejection of political authority and state sovereignty has confined it to the margins of politics. Nevertheless, we can speak of a libertarian current,[1] or undercurrent, that runs through radical politics, even influencing, as we have seen, elements of Marxism. However, the significance and innovation of anarchism has generally been overlooked. Indeed, there has often been a perplexing silence about anarchism in recent radical political thought. Elsewhere I have highlighted the anarchist themes that emerge in poststructuralist theory.[2] In thinkers like

Foucault, Derrida and Deleuze and Guattari, for instance, we find a kind of libertarian ethos: a critique of authoritarian political and social structures, and of the modes of thought and discourse through which their domination is organised. The movement of the nomadic 'war machines' against state capture in Deleuze and Guattari, Foucault's unmasking of the micro-practices of power, or Derrida's an-archic programme of deconstruction, all suggest a strongly anti-authoritarian tendency and the invocation of new, radical forms of politics beyond the confines of Marxism. Yet, the debt to anarchism here is never fully acknowledged. I believe that poststructuralist thought can be grounded consistently in anarchism: that is, that poststructuralism can be expressed politically as anarchism; although, as I have argued, this would be an anarchism of a different, non-essentialist kind.

We observe a similar silence about anarchism in more recent radical political thought, that which comes in the wake of poststructuralism. Indeed, in much contemporary continental theory we find a series of themes, preoccupations and debates which bear a strong resemblance to those of anarchism. Amid the ruins of Marxism – or at least of a certain institutionalised and statist form of it – there is a desire among many thinkers today to develop new categories and directions for radical politics. There is the attempt, first, to find new forms of radical political subjectivity no longer based on the Marxist notion of the proletariat. There is a recognition that such a category is too narrow to express the different forms of oppression, modes of politicisation and ways of relating to one's own work and existence that make up the contemporary world. However, there is also the recognition of the inadequacy of the ultimately liberal notion of 'identity politics' that characterised much new social movement theory. What is called for is new way of thinking about how, and by what processes, a subject becomes politicised – how does the subject become an egalitarian and collective subject? Secondly, there is, among many thinkers today, a rejection of authoritarian modes of political organisation – for instance, the centrally organised Marxist–Leninist vanguard party which would lead the proletariat to revolution, or the Communist and socialist parties in capitalist countries which sought to play the parliamentary game, thus abandoning any hope of emancipation from the state. There is a need, then, as Badiou would put it, for a politics without a party[3] – new forms of political organisation that are no longer structured around the model of the party, as the party always has as its aim the reproduction of state power. Related to this, therefore, is the question of the state itself: the immovability of state power, despite the revolutionary programmes which promised its 'withering away', and, moreover, the increasingly authoritarian character of the so-called liberal democratic state, show us that the state remains perhaps the central problem in radical politics. Radical thought, therefore, sees politics increasingly as being situated beyond the state – there is a desire to find a space for politics outside the framework of state power, a space from which the hegemony of the state would be challenged.

It seems to me that these themes and questions – political subjectivity beyond class, political organisation beyond the party and political action beyond the state – relate directly to anarchism. If these are the new directions that radical politics is moving in, then this would seem to suggest an increasingly anarchistic orientation. Indeed, this is a tendency that is being borne out in many radical movements and forms of resistance today. The emergence of the global anti-capitalist movement in recent times suggests a new form of politics, one that is much closer to anarchism in its aspirations and tactics, and in its decentralised, democratic modes of organisation. Also, the insurrections in Greece in December 2008 – which had an explicitly anarchist identification – are indicative of this libertarian moment in radical politics. It would seem that the prevailing form taken by radical politics today is anti-statist, anti-authoritarian and decentralised, and emphasises direct action rather than representative party politics and lobbying. Furthermore, is it not evident that there is a massive disengagement of ordinary people from normal political processes, an overwhelming scepticism – especially in the wake of the current economic crisis – about the political elites who supposedly govern in their interests? Is there not, at the same time, an obvious consternation on the part of these elites at this growing distance, signifying a crisis in their symbolic legitimacy? As a defensive or pre-emptive measure,[4] the state becomes more draconian and predatory, increasingly obsessed with surveillance and control, defining itself through war and security, seeking to authorise itself through a politics of fear and exception.

How should radical political thought respond to this situation, lagging behind – as it so often does – reality 'on the ground'? My contention is that anarchism – or more precisely postanarchism – can provide some answers here. Indeed, anarchism might be seen as the hidden referent for radical political thought today: while its importance is scarcely acknowledged amongst the thinkers referred to above, anarchism can nevertheless offer critical resources for radical political theory, allowing it to transcend many of its current limitations and, indeed, providing it with a more consistent ethical and political framework.

THE STATE AND THE PARTY

Central to anarchism, as we have seen, is the repudiation of state authority. The state is seen as a violent institution of domination – as a structure which sustains and intensifies other hierarchies and relations of power and exploitation, including economic relations. The state is always accompanied by a statist mind-set or political logic which affirms the idea of the necessity and inevitability of the state, particularly at revolutionary junctures, and prevents us thinking beyond it.

Yet thinking beyond the state is something we must do. Indeed, I see this as being the central task for radical politics today. As Badiou also recognises, the state, and the failure to transcend or escape its thrall, is one of the fundamental problems of radical politics:

> More precisely, we must ask the question that, without a doubt, constitutes the great enigma of the century: why does the subsumption of politics, either through the form of the immediate bond (the masses), or the mediate bond (the party) ultimately give rise to bureaucratic submission and the cult of the State?[5]

What must be explained, in other words, is the relation that ties us to the state and which leads to the perpetuation of state power. Like the anarchists, Badiou sees the state as more than simply an institution or series of institutions; it is also a certain relationship of domination to which people are bound through mechanisms like parliamentary democracy or organisations like the vanguard party. This is why, for Badiou, there is a certain link between the party and the state – the revolutionary party is a centralised and disciplined organisation structured around the aim of seizing state power; indeed, he refers to it as if it were the one entity – the party-state.[6] This critique of the state and the party has clear resonances with anarchism. As we saw in Chapter 3, anarchists regard the party as an authoritarian structure which is organised around the future goal of gaining state power; indeed, the party is a microcosm of the state itself, and an instance of the state even before it gets into power. If radical politics is to escape the pitfalls of state power and its inevitable authoritarianism, it must also eschew the form of the party.

We also find further parallels with anarchism in Badiou's understanding of the state and its relation to society. In Badiou's analysis, the state is seen as a certain way of representing a social situation, a way of including and counting as one – say through categories of citizenship, practices such as voting – the multiple elements or parts of that situation. Here, Badiou maintains, much like Stirner, that the state has no regard for the individual, for differences;[7] it simply incorporates the individual as an anonymous element in an overall structure, through the ordering and assigning of places and roles. We could say, for instance, that the state's surveillance of public places, its obsession with identification and information gathering, its management of crowds and movements of people, are measures designed to ensure that everyone stays put, that everyone is counted, that nothing escapes its incorporation. Furthermore, according to Badiou, while the state is a re-presentation of a situation structured by a particular set of social relations – say those of bourgeois society with its class hierarchies and capitalist economic exchanges – at the same time it is also distinct and separate from it, forming a kind of excrescence. For Badiou, however, the problem with the Marxist analysis of the state is that by focusing on this point of excess – on seeing the state as a coercive apparatus that can simply be seized in a revolutionary upheaval and later suppressed – is that the state is much more intransigent and inexorable than Marxists imagined, and that the revolution would simply lead to a changing of the guard:

> This is because even if the route of political change . . . is bordered by the State, it cannot in any way let itself be guided by the latter, for the State is precisely non-political, insofar as it cannot change, save hands, and it is well known that there is little strategic signification in such a change.[8]

Instead, radical politics must bear witness to the event, in which is revealed what Badiou calls the void of the situation: that which is not counted or formally included in the situation, its radical and destabilising excess.[9]

I shall return to this idea of the event and its political consequences later; but it would appear at this stage that there are certain parallels with anarchism in Badiou's approach to the question of the state in revolutionary politics. The idea that the Marxist seizure of state power will produce only a changing of the guard is, as we saw in Chapter 3, precisely the same warning given by anarchists in the nineteenth century. Rather than the state having a class or 'political' character – so that if the right class controlled it its oppressive character would be transformed – the state is, as Badiou puts it, 'non-political' in the sense that it cannot change in this way. In anarchist terms, this refers to the way that the state has its own specific structural logic of domination and self-perpetuation that is not reducible to class, and that cannot be displaced simply because representatives of a different class are at the helm. So, anarchists would share Badiou's point that what is needed is a different form of politics which is not 'guided' by the state: that is, which does not have as its aim the revolutionary seizure of state power through the vanguard party, but rather which seeks to overcome state power through the construction of a different set of relations. In other words, there is a need for a politics situated outside the state. Indeed, Badiou talks about the need for a politics that 'puts the State at a distance'.[10] This might take the form of non-party political organisations which shun involvement in parliamentary processes and which focus on specific issues, such as the status and rights of illegal migrants,[11] or an autonomous commune where new, egalitarian relations are made possible and whose existence constitutes a fundamental rupture with state-ordered society.[12]

Badiou's political thought, I suggest, invokes and draws upon a certain anarchism – indeed, it can be situated against an unacknowledged background of anarchism. It is curious, then, that Badiou is so dismissive of the anarchist tradition:

> We know today that all emancipatory politics must put an end to the model of the party, or of multiple parties, in order to affirm a politics 'without party', and yet at the same time without lapsing into the figure of anarchism, which has never been anything else than the vain critique, or double, or the shadow, of communist parties, just as the black flag is only the double or the shadow of the red flag.[13]

Perhaps we can detect here a certain sense of discomfort at the proximity of his own politics to anarchism; the sense in which there is an

inevitable association with anarchism in his idea of a politics of emancipation outside the state and 'without party'. Moreover, it is surely
unfair to characterise anarchism as merely a 'double' or 'shadow' of
communism. As I have shown, anarchism departed radically from the
Marxist tradition, developing its own political analyses and autonomous revolutionary practices, which, in many respects, tie in with
Badiou's own approach to politics. Indeed, while Badiou's politics is
grounded in a different tradition – Maoism – aspects of his political
thought could be more accurately situated, or rather, repositioned, as a
kind of anarchism.[14]

At the same time, however, we should be cautious here of too easy
an identification of Badiou's thought with anarchism; to do so would
be to elide the important ways in which it makes problematic certain
aspects of the revolutionary narrative of classical anarchism.[15] What
would be opposed in Badiou's account is the idea of the pure social
revolution that destroys state power in one giant upheaval. The spontaneous movement of social forces against the state is premised on
the Manichean division – central to classical anarchism – between the
natural social principle, and the artificial political principle, between,
in other words, society and the state. What this opposition neglects,
according to Badiou, is the deeper dialectical relationship between
these two forces. In a critique of what he saw as the libertarianism of
Deleuze's and Guattari's work, *Anti-Oedipus*, with its polar opposites
of Flux and the System, the Nomad and the Despot, the Schizo and
the Paranoiac – in other words, of the spontaneous, revolutionary
movement of desire against fixed, authoritarian structures and identities – Badiou argues that this simply leads to a sterile politics of resistance and opposition that leaves existing power structures intact.[16] The
critique referred to here was written in the 1970s, during Badiou's more
explicitly Maoist and also Marxist–Leninist phase; and, indeed, it is
interesting to note the major contrast between his earlier insistence on
the iron discipline of the vanguard party and its project of seizing state
power – in opposition to 'anarcho-desirers' like Deleuze and Guattari –
and his more recent attempts to conceive of a politics beyond the state
and the party. For all his criticism of the anarchist tradition, Badiou, it
would seem, has moved further in this direction in recent years, and I
can only add that, when compared with his earlier fetishisation of the
vanguard party, this is a good thing.

However, is there anything in this critique of left libertarianism

– what he denounced at the time, using the sectarian jargon of the day, as ultra-leftism[17] – that is worthy of more serious consideration? What I think can be taken from this is a certain problematisation of the absolute moral division between society and power that was central to classical anarchism. What Badiou's critique forces us to consider is the extent to which this sort of Manicheanism obscures a more complex relationship between the two forces; the way that – in a Foucauldian sense – there might be a more intimate interaction between the society and power, a realisation which would unsettle to some extent the revolutionary narrative of the great, spontaneous upheaval against state power. More specifically, anarchists would be forced to grapple with the realities of power: what does it mean to destroy state power?; how can this be concretely achieved?; can an overthrow of the state be realised without an engagement with other power relations?; to what extent is the idea of a totalising revolution against state power a comfortable illusion that condemns anarchism to a kind of purist position, that in reality is a position of impotence? In other words, such considerations would make it difficult for anarchism to sustain a position of pure anti-politics. However, we must not concede too much to Badiou here. To raise these questions is in no way to disqualify an anti-state, anti-authoritarian politics; it is not to suggest, as Badiou does in this particular critique (although as we have seen he later changes this position), that radical politics, if it is to be effective, must embrace the discipline of the vanguard party and gear itself towards the revolutionary seizure of state power. To say that anarchists must engage with the realities of power is not to say that they must work within the state and give up their opposition to it. Badiou says, in his critique of the libertarian position, that:

> the State is the only political question. The revolution is a radically new relation of the masses to the State. The State is a construction. A rupture without construction is the concrete definition of failure, and most often in the form of a massacre: the Paris Commune, the Canton Commune, the anarchists of Catalonia . . .[18]

In opposition to this, I would argue that the political question posed by the state does not pertain to how one should seize state power, but to how one should build a politics beyond its grasp: how one should build a politics which, in its very existence, presupposes the radical dissolution of the statist imaginary. Moreover, the need for construction does not entail the need for, or the inevitability of, the state, as if the state was the only way of achieving a political construction. Indeed, the examples Badiou gives of ruptures without a construction – the Paris Commune, the anarchist collectives in Spain, and so on – *were* precisely concrete non-state political constructions, regardless of their eventual defeat. To suggest that they failed because they sought an autonomous existence outside the party and the state entirely misses the point: that their political innovation, the way they gave us a glimpse of a new way of life, a new way of organising social relations and making political decisions, was possible only *because* they were autonomous from the party and the state. That is to say, their political value lay precisely in this autonomy – a point that Badiou himself later seems to accept, at least with regard to the Paris Commune.

What is really at issue here is the question of concrete political organ-isation, rather than a political construction that is imposed by, and con-fined to, the state. Rather than a spontaneous rebellion against the state that occurs everywhere, all at once, driven by forces that are immanent within the social body, an anarchist politics requires conscious and patient organisation: the building and defending of autonomous, collec-tive spaces outside the state; the experimentation with alternative forms of democratic decision making and egalitarian forms of exchange; and even a form of discipline, as long as it is a discipline imposed voluntarily and without coercion by the subject on him- or herself, rather than by a revolutionary leadership – a discipline that comes, for instance, with a commitment to a cause (here we might speak of a *discipline of indis-cipline*, an anarchist discipline). This is what I mean by an engagement with the realities of power. A postanarchist position calls into question the idea of an immanent revolution of society against politics; but on the other hand, it entirely rejects the idea that politics must take place within the framework of the state and the political party (whether it be of the parliamentary or revolutionary vanguard kind). Instead, it seeks, on the one hand hand, to detach the notion of politics from the state, and on the other, to detach society from a natural, moral foundation outside politics. In other words, postanarchism calls for an invention of a political space *between* society and the state, between the social order and the political order. This, I believe, is what Badiou, with his more recent motifs of the post-party organisation and politics at a distance from the state, is ultimately getting at.

THE DILEMMAS OF RADICAL POLITICS

The possibility of a politics that works outside the structures of the state and the party is central to contemporary radical politics and its future directions. As I have argued, a re-consideration of anarchism is vital for theorising this form of politics. Indeed, the question of anarchism has arisen in a recent debate between Simon Critchley and Slavoj Žižek. Critchley has made an argument for what he calls 'an-archic metapolitics', something that draws – albeit obliquely – on the anarchist tradition: this is a form of politics that takes a distance from the state, which makes demands upon it while working independently of it.[19] It avoids a head-on confrontation with the state, working instead in the interstices of state power, constructing spaces beyond its grasp. Žižek, ever the Leninist, writes in response:

> The ambiguity of Critchley's position resides in a strange non sequitur: if the state is here to stay, if it is impossible to abolish it (or capitalism), why retreat from it? Why not act with(in) the state? . . . Why limit oneself to a politics which, as Critchley puts it, 'calls the state into question and calls the established order to account, not in order to do away with the state, desirable though that might be in some utopian sense, but in order to better it or to attenuate its malicious effects'? These words simply demonstrate that today's liberal-democratic state and the dream of an 'infinitely demanding' anarchic politics exist in a relationship of mutual parasitism: anarchic agents do the ethical thinking, and the state does the work of running and regulating society.[20]

Instead of working outside the state, Žižek claims that a more effective strategy – such as that pursued by the likes of Hugo Chavez, or, indeed, Lenin – is to grasp state power and use its machinery ruthlessly to achieve one's political objectives. In other words, if the state cannot be done away with, then why not use it for revolutionary ends?

There is in this exchange an echo of the old debate between the anarchists and Marxists. This is not to suggest that Critchley is an anarchist in the classical sense. Nevertheless, this resurrection of the controversy over the state throws into sharp relief the dilemma confronting radical politics today: to take over the mechanisms of the state and use it to revolutionise society, or to work outside the state with the ultimate aim of transcending it through the development of alternative communities and practices. We have, with Žižek, the neo-Leninist vanguard approach, and with Critchley, an alternative approach that tends in the direction of anarchism.

Despite the obvious pitfalls of the Leninist vanguard strategy, we should nevertheless take Žižek's challenge to Critchley seriously: that, in other words, the problem with the strategy of working outside the state is that it may essentially leave the state intact, and entail an irresponsible and even self-indulgent politics of demand that hides a secret reliance on the state to take care of the everyday running of society. Is there some truth to this claim?

There are two aspects that I would like to address here. First, the notion of demand: making certain demands on the state – say for higher wages, equal rights for excluded groups, to not go to war or an end to draconian policing – is one of the basic strategies of social movements and radical groups. Making such demands does not necessarily mean working within the state or reaffirming its legitimacy. On the contrary, demands are made from a position outside the established political order, and they often exceed the question of the implementation of this or that specific measure. They implicitly call into question the legitimacy and even the sovereignty of the state by highlighting fundamental inconsistencies between, for instance, a formal constitutional order that guarantees certain rights and equalities, and state practices that in reality violate and deny them. Jacques Rancière gives a succinct example of this when he discusses Olympe de Gouges, who, at the time of the French Revolution, demanded that women be given the right to go to the Assembly. In doing so, she demonstrated the inconsistency between the promise of equality – invoked in a general sense and yet denied in the particular by the Declaration of the Rights of Man and the Citizen – and the political order which was formally based on this:

> Women could make a twofold demonstration. They could demonstrate that they were deprived of the rights that they had, thanks to the Declaration of Rights. And they could demonstrate, through their public action, that they had the rights that the constitution denied to them, that they could enact those rights. So they could act as subjects of the Rights of Man in the precise sense that I have mentioned. They acted as subjects that did not have the rights that they had and had the rights that they had not.[21]

While this was a demand for inclusion within the political order, it at the same time exposed a fissure or inconsistency in this order that was potentially destabilising, thus seeking to transcend the limits of that order.

Let's take another example: the demand to end draconian border control measures and to guarantee the rights of illegal migrants. While this is also a demand, to some extent, for the inclusion of those currently excluded from the national state order, it nevertheless comes from a place outside it – challenging the sovereign prerogative of the nation-state to determine its borders. It also highlights central contradictions and tensions within global capitalism and its relation to the nation-state: while global capitalism claims to promote the free movement of people (as well as capital and technology) across borders, it seems to be having precisely the opposite effect: that is, the intensification of existing borders and the erection of new ones, not to mention the more general control and restrictions placed on the movement of people within national territories. In demanding an end to increasingly brutal border control and surveillance measures, and in mobilising people around this issue, activist groups are engaging in a form of politics that ultimately calls into question the very principle of state sovereignty. The question of the excessiveness or 'irresponsibility' of such demands should be turned around: they are demands that are driven by an 'an-archic' *responsibility* for the liberty and equality of others.[22] While a radical politics of today would not be limited to the articulation of demands, and, indeed, would seek to go beyond this by building viable alternatives to the state, we should nevertheless acknowledge the radical potential of making demands and the position of autonomy already implicit within this practice.

The second aspect of Žižek's critique is the question of the extent to which an anarchist politics outside the state implicitly relies on the continuity of the state. To what extent does this sort of politics signify a retreat or withdrawal from the responsibilities of wielding state power, allowing things to continue as normal, or even to get worse if, for instance, far right forces manage to gain control of the state? In response to this, it could be argued that far right forces have, in the past, used both parliamentary and non-parliamentary means to gain power; and, indeed, the formal, parliamentary left has often been entirely ineffective in preventing this.[23] Resistance to far right forces can be effective only if a genuine political alternative is conceivable, and this would require the mobilisation of people not so much at the state level – that is, elections – but at the level of civil society. Moreover, one of the ways of demonstrating the capacity of non-state political alternatives is the development of autonomous communities, collectives and organisations that exist beyond the control of the state. The countless experiments in autonomous politics taking place everywhere – squatters' movements, social centres, indigenous collectives, land re-occupation movements, blockades, worker occupations, alternative media centres, communes, numerous activist networks and so on – are evidence of this possibility. It is here that I would want to push Critchley's argument beyond its own limits. Critchley is right to suggest that the state today is too powerful for full-scale assaults, and that a more effective strategy is working around it, at the interstices of state power. However, this does not mean that the state is a permanent, inevitable feature of political life – as Critchley seems to suggest.[24] If autonomous communities and organisations are increasingly able to perform the functions traditionally carried out by the state – for example, the way that in the wake of the economic crisis in Argentina in 2001, cooperatives and local assemblies provided basic social services in the absence of a functioning government – then the future of the state is by no means guaranteed. With the current economic crisis, the unwillingness or incapacity of governments to provide decent services for their populations will, I believe, increasingly expose the general inadequacy of the state in satisfying social needs. It is here that alternative forms of social organisation become conceivable.

While Žižek raises important questions about the efficacy of politics outside the state, the alternative he offers – revisiting ideas of the vanguard party, the proletarian dictatorship and revolutionary state terror, which I shall discuss later – is a completely defunct and outmoded model of politics, if indeed it ever had any emancipatory value to begin with. As I have suggested, radical politics seems to be heading today in precisely the opposite, more anarchic, direction.

SUBJECTIVITY BEYOND CLASS?

The question of new forms of politics which go beyond the Marxist and Leninist models, also throws up the question of new forms of political subjectivity beyond the Marxist notion of the proletariat. In Marxist theory, the category of the worker was understood in two senses: as a socio-economic category whose specific place in the industrial system embodied the general inhumanity of capitalism, as well as a revolutionary subjectivity politically constituted through a revolutionary vanguard party whose goal was the dictatorship of the proletariat. However, as we have seen, the classical anarchists questioned the consistency and even the revolutionary consciousness of this class subject, arguing that elements of the industrial proletariat had already taken on bourgeois and conservative values, and that other classes, such as the peasants and lumpenproletariat, should also be designated as revolutionary. The anarchists' emphasis on the heterogeneity and 'formlessness' of the collective revolutionary subject has become more relevant today. Many contemporary radical thinkers seek to describe the subject of emancipation in terms other than the proletariat, strictly defined in the Marxist sense.

However, this break with class as the determining element of radical political subjectivity is by no means to suggest that class is no longer important, or that class divisions no longer exist. Nor is it to suggest that economic inequalities, deprivations, exclusions and antagonisms are still not central to radical political struggles. Indeed, the emergence of the anti-capitalist movement in recent times shows that the dislocating effects of global capitalism are ever more central to the radical political agenda. Moreover, the idea of the heterogeneity of subjects should not lead us into some vague notion of 'identity politics'. While certain forms of identity politics – the struggles for recognition on the part of minorities – played, and continue to play, an important role in claiming equal treatment and rights, the point is that, in many Western societies at least, the simple assertion of a cultural, sexual or gender identity difference is no longer necessarily radical, and it is often all too smoothly accommodated within the state system.[25] Wendy Brown, for instance, shows how demands for recognition on the part of minority groups often bind them further to the state, making them more dependent on the state for the recognition of this identity and the protection of their rights, thus allowing the state to extend its power over life. For instance, the rights claims of certain feminist groups simply reaffirmed their status as 'victims' requiring the protection of the state. Brown asks: 'Might such protection codify within law the very powerlessness it seeks to redress?'[26]

What limits identity politics is not necessarily the way that demands are addressed to the state; as I have argued above, certain demands for the recognition of the rights of others – illegal migrants, for instance – can produce dislocating effects on the state system and call into question the principle of state sovereignty. What limits much identity politics is, rather, the way it is based around forms of identification that can be incorporated into the structure of power in 'multicultural' societies: gender differences, sexual differences, religious differences and the demand that such differences be 'respected' by institutions and other people. The state institutionalisation of this notion of respect not only de-politicises differences, but it also often leads to the restriction of the freedom of others – think, for instance, of the laws against 'hate speech' in the United Kingdom, or the myriad puritanical rules and coercions relating to sexual harassment in the workplace, or the discursive violence and fundamentalism of Political Correctness. Most importantly, identity politics is often unable to politicise capitalism, apart from a vague notion that capitalism is racist, sexist or homophobic. Here I think Žižek is right to suggest that many struggles for identity recognition, and the liberal multicultural politics that it leads to, take place against a background of an implicit de-politicisation of global capitalism.[27]

The terrain of radical politics has shifted in recent times in the direction of a more explicit problematisation of global capitalism and state power. This suggests new modes of political subjectification which challenge the various ways in which we are subordinated to capital, the ways in which capitalism subsumes and reconstitutes our everyday lives, relationships and experiences: from the constraints of the workplace, to the hierarchisation of social relations, the commodification and market rationalisation of daily activities, the privatisation of public spaces and the atomisation of our interactions with others. It also suggests forms of politics and subjectification which call into question authoritarian relationships, practices and institutions, particularly those that are concentrated within, and are sanctioned and organised by, the state. Indeed, this ethical and political critique of authority, and the desire to live without it, is what distinguishes the anarchist position from other left politics. Radical subjectification, therefore, involves not only a political critique of the state and its inherent violence and domination, but also a kind of ethical interrogation of one's psychological dependence on the state: as Stirner would put it, 'a working forth of me out of the established'.[28] Radical subjectification might be seen in terms of an insurrection of the self against the identities and roles imposed on us by the state; it is the process by which the subject 'takes a distance' from the state.

Furthermore, political subjectification increasingly invokes a universal dimension. This is not only in the sense that radical political struggles and movements emerge today on a terrain defined by globalisation, but also in the sense that they go beyond the mere assertion of a particular identity, and instead seek to form alliances, networks and solidarities with one another. A politics that is based around the assertion of an identity, or that seeks an institutional recognition of a specific difference, leaves largely un-contested economic relations and institutional power, as well as confines itself to a certain particularity, thus closing itself off from struggles and identities outside itself. What is foreclosed is an egalitarian, collective, democratic dimension which embodies a necessary openness to the other. Identity politics is often a form of sovereign politics – the assertion of a sovereign identity, self-contained in its difference. The act of subjectification becomes radical when the subject or group of subjects understand their suffering and struggles in relation to those of others. Indeed, the insistence on universality as a necessary dimension in political subjectification can also be found, in different ways, in Badiou, Žižek, Rancière and Laclau. For all these thinkers, there is the idea that for politics to take place, a part must come to express – if only temporarily or contingently – the iniquity of the whole and the struggle to rectify it; just as Marx saw the proletariat as the excluded part of capitalism that at the same represented the general catastrophe of capitalism and, therefore, the universal desire of humanity to be emancipated from it.

Yet, why is 'the proletariat' no longer an entirely sufficient category today to understand political subjectification? To say that class structures and divisions have been eroded or utterly fragmented would be too quick here. Obviously, even in our 'post-industrial' societies, there are still sectors of the population who do manual work and who are subject to terrible forms of exploitation – to say nothing about the countless millions of workers who live a desperate and deprived existence in poorer countries. Indeed, capitalist globalisation is producing, if anything, a *re*-proletarianisation of the entire world, where, increasingly, working conditions that one might have expected to find in the Third World – the worst kind of sweat shop labour, for instance – can be also found at the heart of developed economies.[29] Moreover, if we are to understand – as Marx himself did – proletarians as those who are excluded from the fruits of the wealth they produce and whose deprivation is the necessary structural feature of capitalism, then we can certainly retain this designation; although the lumpenproletariat (or sub-proletariat), or simply the global poor – the under-employed, casually employed or those completely excluded from employment and the market – might be a more accurate term to describe these 'disposable' millions. The issue here is not work itself or one's relation to work: work, its insecurities, or the sheer lack of it, is still obviously central to most people's lives. The problem with the notion of the proletariat relates to the way it was conceived in orthodox Marxist theory: both as a socio-economic category designating a specific class in society, as well as a political subjectivity which would be organised and led through the vanguard party. The proletariat was a specific sociological and political identity that was constructed in Marxist theory and imposed on workers, workers whose daily lives and experiences often did not conform to it: hence, for instance, Marx's emphasis on the role of the factory in producing a disciplined, united working class; Kautsky's economic reductionist view of class divisions; and Lenin's enthusiasm for Taylorism as a tool for the social rationalisation of labour. The proletariat had to be produced as a coherent, uniform identity which would be guided to revolution by the most enlightened, class-conscious sectors of the working-class movement.

Yet, we might question whether the proletariat was ever a uniform, coherent class in this way: it comprised multiple, heterogeneous and often conflicting struggles and identities – artisans who sought to defend traditional ways of life and work, workers who rebelled against the coercions and discipline of the factory system, engaging in machine breaking and other forms of industrial sabotage and so on. Indeed, it was more these spontaneous and immediate struggles against capitalism and the industrialisation process that anarchists celebrated, rather than subscribing to the Marxist narrative of workers embracing the technology and processes of industrial capitalism as the tools of their future liberation. Moreover, Rancière gives us a glimpse into the libertarian dreams and literary passions of French workers during the nineteenth century, the ways in which they resisted and problematised their identity as simply 'workers', seeking to escape rather than embrace the 'glories' of manual work.[30] Here Rancière displaces the very concept of class in the Marxist imaginary. Indeed, the subjectification that takes place here is a precisely a refusal of one's established identity as worker, and instead an active, even utopian experimentation in modes of artistic expression – particularly literature and poetry – that were deemed 'bourgeois' and unsuitable for workers. Subjectification is understood here in terms of a 'dis-identification', a displacement of one's socially defined role – something that produces a dissonance or disruption of the order of established identities and places. So, even in Marx's time class was perhaps never an entirely consistent, coherent or stable identity. We have no reason to imagine that the political designator of class would be anything but more fragmented, and less stable and consistent, today.

THE PEOPLE OR THE MULTITUDE?

If the proletariat no longer serves as an entirely sufficient category for radical politics today, what forms of subjectivity can take its place? It is here that I would like to examine two alternative ways of thinking about the subject: the *people*, as a heterogeneous ensemble contingently constructed around a chain of demands; and the *multitude*, as a political organism that, for Hardt and Negri, is immanent within the productive processes of post-Fordist capitalism.

For Laclau, the 'the people' should be seen as the central category of radical politics. In his work on populism, Laclau describes the discursive logics of articulation that go into the construction of 'the people':[31] he shows that this figure is not an empirical reality or an essence that emerges teleologically through the development of social and economic forces, as in Marxism. Rather, it is a political and discursive construct which emerges through the articulation of 'chains of equivalence' between different socio-political demands. Therefore, we cannot presuppose any sort of natural or essential unity between different identities, demands and antagonisms that emerge all around us on the political field; this unity has to be constructed in a contingent way around some sort of common political frontier. Moreover, in contradistinction to the Marxist position, the moment of political unity between identities and the demands upon which this unity is constructed, is *exterior* to capitalism. Laclau gives an example: 'The demand for higher wages does not derive from the logic of capitalist relations, but interrupts that logic in terms that are alien to it – those of a discourse concerning justice, for example.'[32]

In Chapter 3, I pointed out a number of parallels between the anarchist position and Laclau's and Mouffe's deconstruction of Marxist categories of class and economic reductionism. The value of Laclau's notion of populism for a post-anarchist analysis lies in its non-essentialist approach to the political subject – the way that a certain identity or position cannot be assumed to be immanent, and has to be constructed around political, ethical and discursive positions. However, where the notion of populist politics becomes more problematic from an anarchist point of view is that even though populist movements embody an anti-systemic dimension, they are generally organised around a leader: the desires, passions and aspirations of the movement are symbolically invested within the figure of the leader, or within a particular political party, which pitches itself in opposition to the existing political system. Indeed, the examples of left-wing populist movements that Laclau is especially fond of are Peronism in Argentina, and the movements in support of Chavez in Venezuela. Of course, such movements are not necessarily overtly authoritarian; although there is, I would say, an implicit authoritarian dimension in any populist movement. Yet, what makes this model of politics problematic is the notion of political leadership and representation, which is always a hierarchical and unequal power relationship, and the attempt to construct, sometimes coercively, a certain uniformity out of the desires of those who are 'represented'. Representation, for anarchists always ends up as a reaffirmation of the state, and consists of replacing one form of political authority for another. This is perhaps why populism has traditionally been a figure of the politics of the radical right;[33] and, moreover, is usually a politics confined – spatially and ideologically – to the nation state entity.[34]

As an alternative to the people, perhaps we can consider Hardt's and Negri's notion of the multitude, as formulated in their works *Empire* and *Multitude*. They argue that within the global Empire of capital, there is the growing hegemony of 'immaterial labour': labour that is increasingly aimed at the production of information and knowledge rather than material objects. Immaterial labour is not just a mode of economic production, but also a form of *biopolitical* production in which new social relationships and new forms of life are created through proliferating networks of communication and common knowledge. While these 'things' are produced under conditions of capitalism and private ownership, they are increasingly difficult to commodify and tend towards a 'being-in-common'. What is emerging with this form of production is, therefore, a new form of subjectivity defined by the possibility of a 'becoming-common' of labour. This commonality, which Hardt and Negri term the multitude, is a class concept, but one that, they argue, is different from the Marxist notion of the proletariat: it refers to all those who work under Empire, not simply or even primarily manual workers. Its existence, moreover, is based on a becoming or immanent potential, rather than being defined by a strictly empirical existence; and it represents an irreducible multiplicity – a combination of collectivity and plurality – rather than a unified identity like 'the people'. This immanent multiplicity has a tendency to converge into a common organism, a singularity, that will one day turn against Empire and emancipate itself.[35]

There are many aspects of Hardt's and Negri's argument concerning the multitude and emergent forms of politics that reflect anarchists themes. While they insist that they are 'not anarchists but communists',[36] their motif of a spontaneous insurgency of the multitude, which is not mediated through the vanguard party, and which emancipates itself from global capitalism and political sovereignty, seems to directly invoke a form of anarchism. Moreover, their emphasis on new forms of political commonality based on networked communication, affinity and direct democracy, seems to describe aspects of the global anti-capitalist movement and, indeed, many activists in this movement have recognised the relevance of their ideas. The form of politics they construct is informed to some extent by the libertarian Marxist or autonomist tradition, whose similarities with anarchism I have explored in Chapter 3.

Nevertheless, there are a number of problems with their approach. First, their idea of the multitude relies on an immanentism: the multitude is coming to the fore everywhere, due to the dynamics of Empire and the prevalence of 'immaterial labour'; new forms of commonality are emerging through biopolitical production and proliferating technologies. There is a kind of organic inevitability about the coming of the multitude and its transcendence of Empire through a general revolt. In many ways Hardt's and Negri's analysis parallels Marxist historical materialism: just as the proletariat merges into an identity and becomes class conscious through the dynamic of industrial capitalism, thus creating a revolutionary potential within capitalist societies through its tension with bourgeois relations of production, so the multitude forms into a commonality through the dynamic of 'immaterial' labour and production, creating a revolutionary potential within Empire. In each scenario, a particular agency harnesses the economic forces of capitalism in order to transform them and create a new series of social relationships. A postanarchist approach would question this narrative: the coming of the multitude cannot be simply assumed; its emergence is not entirely explainable by economic processes. Nor can its political commonality be guaranteed. To imagine this to be the case is to fall into a kind of essentialist or foundationalist argument, where there is a dependence on an ontological 'substance' or material foundation whose inner dynamic is the motor that generates certain forms of politics.

Secondly, we find in Hardt and Negri a rather suspect adoption of the idea of biopolitics. For Hardt and Negri, the postmodern Empire of global capitalism exercises a biopolitical control over life: for instance, the patenting of the human genome, corporate experimentations in biogenetics and cloning and so on, are just the most obvious examples of the way that capital subsumes and attempts to take control over the very biological basis of human life. In more general terms, capitalism's power over productive processes and our everyday activity at work is an aspect of biopower: a control asserted over the ways in which life reproduces the conditions of its existence. Paralleling Foucault's analysis of the transition from disciplinary power to biopower (the movement from disciplinary society to what Deleuze termed the 'society of control'), is the passage in Marx's theory from the formal subsumption to the real subsumption of labour under capital – in other words, the process by which capital invests not only the economic domain, but the entirety of social life.[37] So far so good. But where Hardt's and Negri's position becomes more problematic is in their view that biopolitics is at the same time the material field from which resistant subjectivities are constituted. Here they cite the analyses of autonomist thinkers such as Paolo Virno and Christian Marrazzi, which explore the ways in which biopolitics forms a new field of production, 'immaterial labour', and the way that this produces a social and communicative dimension of living labour, and with this, new, radical forms of subjectivity:

The immediately social dimension of the exploitation of living immaterial labour immerses labour in all the relational elements that define the social but also at the same time activate the critical elements that develop the potential of insubordination and revolt through the entire set of labouring practices.[38]

Put simply, biopower is oppressive and exploitative, but in the new forms of labour and production that it invests itself in and thus makes possible, it also creates the potential for our liberation from it. The multitude, in other words, is a biopolitical concept; it is an 'organism' whose conditions have been created by the excess of biopolitical life over the control exerted by biopower. However, the ambiguity here is the extent to which the multitude can actually achieve any real separation or distance from biopower in this way. Or will it always be defined by it; will it always be part of the substance of biopower without being able to constitute a break or discontinuity with it?[39] Foucault, who was the one who elaborated the concept of the biopower as a rationality of domination – a form of the regulation and government of life – would have been somewhat sceptical about seeing life itself, and particularly life defined by labour and production, as the material ground of resistance. Moreover, if we are to pay attention to Agamben's thesis that the biopolitical is always linked inextricably with the logic of sovereignty, to theorise radical politics from within the material field of biopolitics would be to confine it to what he calls 'bare life' and thus to leave it even more exposed to sovereign power.[40] It is perhaps because of the realisation that the multitude will always be caught within the field of biopower, that Hardt and Negri insist on the need for a radical mutation in the human subject – the formation of a new body incapable of submitting to dominant modes of normalisation; hence, their interest in the motifs of cyber-punk with its aesthetic mutilations of the body.[41] It is perhaps precisely because of the fear that the biopolitical multitude may amount to no more than bare life, that the body must be adorned (with piercings, technological prostheses, etc.); that it must mutate into something completely different. Hence, there is a fetishisation of the cyborg, a celebration of the way that technology leads to a mutation of the body and a supposedly creative melding between man and machine. While Hardt and Negri see a radical potential in such transformations, the technologically manipulated cyber-human may not signify so much an escape or exodus from biopolitical capitalism, as its ultimate fantasy.

Lastly, one could also raise questions about the terrain on which the insurgency of the multitude emerges. For Hardt and Negri, that terrain is the Empire of global capital, a smooth surface without an outside, a process of becoming in which national and economic divisions are in a process of erosion and decomposition. Aside from the question of whether Empire might be the most accurate way of describing the current situation – and here I think the notion of globalised capitalism would suffice, without having to go to the extremity of Hardt's and Negri's claim about a new global juridical sovereignty emerging – the notion of Empire as a smooth space defined increasingly by immaterial labour and production downplays the major divisions and antagonisms that continue to exist in the world and that, indeed, are intensifying rather than diminishing under capitalism. Such divisions are spatial and territorial: for instance, the aggressive reassertion of state sovereignty through intensified border policing measures; one should point here, as did Deleuze and Guattari, to the oscillation between deterritorialisation (through global capitalism) and reterritorialisation (the reassertion of fixed identities such as the State, Family, Nation).[42] These divisions are also economic, referring not only to differences between rich and poor, but to the existence of different economies and modes of production, differences that exist not just between the global North and South, but within these very sectors. Not only are there vastly different worlds of work and production – white-collar workers and computer programmers doing 'immaterial labour', alongside Fordist and even pre-Fordist modes of work, including slave labour[43] – but there are also the countless millions who are radically excluded from work and from Capital's circuits of productions and consumption: the disposable people who populate the slums, shanty towns and refugee camps of the global South. Given these divisions, how is it possible to speak of a common world of life and work, especially one that is defined by 'immaterial labour'? It should be noted that Hardt and Negri see the 'smooth space' of Empire as a process of becoming, an immanent reality that is unfolding rather than something that is already actual. However, there is little evidence to suggest that this is even a tendency: the processes of global capitalism seem to be creating as many divisions – walls, barriers, borders, economic antagonisms, exclusions – as they are breaking down. All this points to the difficulty in constituting a common political subjectivity: would the multitude not, on the contrary, be a highly fractured, divided subject based on a series of exclusions – for instance, those excluded from the world of work entirely, or those who were not engaged in 'immaterial labour'? Indeed, as George Caffentzis suggests, what lies behind the notion of the multitude is perhaps a kind of hidden Leninism, where the 'knowledge workers' as the most advanced strata within the multitude play the role of revolutionary vanguard.[44]

What we find with Hardt and Negri, then, is really a fetishisation of Empire. Just as, for Marx, capitalism was a progressive, modernising force whose preponderance was to be admired, so for Hardt and Negri, Empire is a stage through which we must pass on our way to emancipation and whose expansion must therefore not be impeded but, rather, encouraged; hence, for instance, Negri's support for the EU and for further European political integration. However, just as the classical anarchists were critical of Marx's enthusiasm for capitalism, industrialisation and technology – highlighting their devastating effects on people's lives – so we should adopt a critical distance with respect to Empire. This is not out of any nostalgia for cultural differences, or for the nation-state, whose demise cannot come quickly enough. Rather, it comes out of a critique of the Marxist stagism that finds its way into Hardt's and Negri's thesis, a stagism which suggests that the coming of the global multitudes will be an inevitable moment in history, and, therefore, that the spread of Empire, with its deployments of technology and new forms of work and life, should be promoted.[45] What one finds in Hardt and Negri is a fetishisation of Empire as a conceptual structure, a fetishisation which leads them to overlook the intensification of borders and economic divisions, or at least to dialecticise them back into this conceptual structure. As part of this, one also finds a fetishisation of technology and biopower, and a celebration of the melding of humanity with the machine in the production of a new revolutionary organism.

THE EVENT AND POLITICAL TEMPORALITIES OF STRUGGLE

If Empire is a system of control, surveillance and technological manipulation that is encompassing the entirety of life, then it should be resisted and opposed rather than welcomed. Indeed, if one rejects a Marxist determinist view of history – and I think we should – then it makes no sense, from a radical perspective, to support an increasing integration of political, social and economic structures and the increasing biopoliticisation of life. Rather, we should think in terms of moments of rupture and separation from Empire; moments of resistance, escape and 'lines of flight' from its regime of control. Rather than working through Empire, one must invent political spaces outside it. As I have said, this does not mean we should return to the ideas of national sovereignty and citizenship as bulwarks against Empire – one should resist the nostalgia, found in those like Schmitt, for the old 'pluriverse' of sovereign nation-states in the face of a new universal imperium, even if we acknowledge that they might at times take a more progressive form. A more radical project would be aimed, instead, at fostering the emergence of new autonomous political spaces, where communal and free relations can develop. This would involve an experimentation with new ways of living, different non-authoritarian political practices and structures, and even alternative economies. I will explore these proposals further in later chapters, but what must be emphasised is the idea of a break with the existing order here and now, rather than waiting for the coming multitudes.

This need to break with the existing order and to construct new spaces for politics is also recognised by Badiou, who argues that the autonomists inspired by Negri, 'are only the most spectacular face of recent adaptations to domination. Their undifferentiated "movement-ism" integrates smoothly with the necessary adjustments of capital, and in my view does not constitute any really independent political space.'[46] While it is somewhat unfair to lump together the whole of the anti-capitalist movement with Negri and the Italian autonomists, Badiou is correct in suggesting that the (Hardt and) Negri thesis to some extent mirrors and fetishises the fluxes and flows of global capital, and is thus unable to achieve any real separation from it. For Badiou, then, the moment of separation essential for radical politics must be theorised on a different ontological register, not that of History, but that of the Event: 'The idea of an overturning whose origin would be a state of a totality is imaginary. Every radical transformational action originates *in a point*, which, inside a situation, is an evental site.'[47] The event is a moment of unpredictability which, while conditioned by history and by the situation in which it arises, is not determined by them and exceeds them, leading to the emergence of something entirely new. If we take, for instance, the French Revolution as an event: it emerged in the context of a certain historical situation, yet could not be wholly accounted for or explained by the coordinates of that situation; it con-stituted a moment of rupture with the existing order in an ontological sense, creating a new and irreversible terrain for politics and thought. Specifically, the event – whose privileged sites for Badiou are art, politics, science and love – produces a new subject: the subject who participates in the event becomes riven through with it as if touched by Grace, to use Badiou's famous example of Saint Paul, and declares his or her commitment or fidelity to the event as a bearer of a process of truth. Indeed, it is through this fidelity to the truth of the event that one becomes a subject.[48]

What should we make of this quasi-religious ontology of the Event as deployed by Badiou? The notion of an event is an important one for radical politics, precisely because radical politics seeks a break with the existing order and thus implies a moment of unpredictability and disruption, and the invention of something new and unprecedented. Anarchism, in this sense, is a politics which, more so than Marxism, embodies this element of unpredictability: the emphasis in anarchism is, after all, on revolutionary spontaneity, although as we have seen in the case of classical anarchism, this spontaneous rebellion is at the same time conditioned by the development of rational social relations. Indeed, there is a certain tension here in anarchism that will be investigated in Chapter 5. However, we can say that the idea of the event as a moment of rupture resonates strongly with anarchism. Furthermore, Badiou points to the Paris Commune of 1871 as an instance of the event because it embodied the autonomous self-government of the workers, giving us a glimpse of a new way of life and thus constituting a rupture with the existing order. The commune is an event because it creates a political space that is autonomous from the state.

However, what is questionable and problematic in Badiou's notion of the event is its grandeur and rarity. For Badiou, the political event is a rare thing, so rare, in fact, that it almost never happens. Indeed, only a few historical moments attain the status of the Event: the French Revolution, which Badiou dates from 1792 and which includes as part of its 'sequence' the Paris Commune of 1871; the Bolshevik Revolution of 1917; the Chinese Cultural Revolution of 1966–76, and, as part of the latter's sequence, the student and worker uprising of May 1968 in France. It is as if all radical politics ended with the Cultural Revolution. Indeed, more recent events – events which in my view are equally important, such as the emergence of the global anti-capitalist movement – are treated with a strange and unwarranted contempt by Badiou.[49] Badiou's notion of the Event is highly idealised and abstract, bearing a kind of haughty disregard for concrete, more everyday forms of politics. One could say that genuine political events take place on an everyday basis: we can find genuine experiments in autonomous radical politics everywhere, in indigenous movements, land reoccupations, innovative forms of direct action, mass demonstrations and in courageous acts of civil disobedience, all of which Badiou seems either oblivious to or grandly dismissive of.

So while the idea of a political event is important, one should resist the temptation to romanticise and sanctify it in the way that Badiou does. One should instead affirm the 'everydayness' of the extraordinary: the idea that events are numerous and can take many forms. I agree that what is needed are forms of politics that break with the existing order and produce new emancipatory practices and identities – and here I believe anarchism is the appropriate figure today for this politics, precisely because it seeks a separation from the state order in a way that other modes of politics do not. The problem with Badiou is that he sets such an impossibly high and abstract standard for radical politics that in his eyes almost nothing lives up to the dignity of the Event, which, for him, is akin to the Pauline miracle.[50]

REVOLUTIONARY VIOLENCE AND TERROR

Indeed, such is the desire on the part of Badiou to assert the absolute separateness and singularity of the political Event that it would seem that it can be expressed only in the form of violence and revolutionary terror, as if Terror becomes the ultimate sign of the event's authenticity. One finds in Badiou's account a certain fetishisation particularly of the Jacobin Terror of 1793–4, along with a favourable treatment of the Cultural Revolution in China, an event characterised not only by excessive, irrational violence, but also by noxious leadership cults. Indeed, the names of authoritarian figures like Robespierre, Saint-Just, Lenin and Mao are invoked again and again by Badiou as symbols of genuine revolutionary fidelity and passion. Terror becomes, for Badiou, with Saint-Just in mind, the signifier of revolutionary virtue, its guarantee against weakness and corruption: 'what do they want, those who want neither virtue nor terror?'[51]

One finds a similar, indeed, even more explicit, admiration of terroristic politics in Žižek. For Žižek, the only way to institutionalise a democratic insurrection is through revolutionary terror.[52] Once again, terror becomes a sign of revolutionary authenticity for Žižek; violence is a signifier for a kind of ethics of the revolutionary act, of the commitment to 'go to the end' as he puts it, and to consolidate the revolution through a brutal suppression of its opponents. Thus, once again, Lenin, Mao and Robespierre become hallowed names for Žižek, invoked against his perennial targets the 'liberals', who want a 'revolution without a revolution', in other words a revolution without its violent consequences.[53]

The question of violence and revolutionary terror raises important questions for anarchism, which, historically, has been no stranger to terrorism, although this stereotypical association between the two has been grossly exaggerated. What should an anarchist response to violence be today? While acknowledging that certain forms of violence – particularly in the form of a defensive counterviolence against the violence of the state – might be part of an anarchist insurrection, the aim of an anarchist politics today should be the transcendence of violence. Non-violence, or a non-violent violence, similar perhaps to Walter Benjamin's notion of 'divine violence', should be its ethical horizon. The reason for this is that violence is an authoritarian, sovereign relationship, something that violates the autonomy of the other. For this reason, violence should not be considered as necessarily a sign of political authenticity.[54] The real problem, however, is not violence itself, but the use of violence by the state, or rather the statification of violence – this is when violence becomes Terror in the true sense of the word. The violence that is wielded by a revolutionary elite to consolidate power – as was the case in all the forms of Terror venerated by Žižek and Badiou, from the Jacobins to Lenin and Mao – has nothing redemptive about it; it cannot serve as a tool of liberation, and only ends up consolidating the most counterrevolutionary element of all, the state itself. Žižek is right to suggest that democratic insurrections be more than just a momentary transgression – that they must at some point construct a positive identity for themselves. Yet, he is wrong to claim that this institutionalisation can take place only at the level of the state and only through the Terror, and at the expense of individual liberty and autonomy. We should reject as outmoded the Jacobin paradigm for radical politics proposed by Žižek and Badiou. Instead, we should assert an anarchist politics and ethics against all forms of state violence; indeed, anarchism is, in my view, the only form of radical politics capable of avoiding the Terror.

Moreover, Žižek is even more mistaken in concluding that the Jacobin Terror is an example of what Benjamin termed divine violence.[55] The Jacobin Terror *was* precisely, in Benjamin's terms, a form of law-founding violence, a violence that established the power of the bourgeois state. By contrast, divine violence is a form of violence which breaks out of this dialectic of law and violence altogether; it is neither law making nor law preserving, but radically transcends this oscillation through which state power is reaffirmed:

> On the breaking of this cycle maintained by mythic forms of law, on the suspension of law with all the forces on which it depends as they depend on it, finally therefore on the abolition of state power, a new historical epoch is founded.[56]

Divine violence, therefore, invokes an anarchism: its violence consists not in the spilling of blood and the terrorism of revolutionary elites, but in the radical abolition and transcendence of state power. In opposition to the Jacobin Terror, we should also recall the words of Georges Sorel, for whom the violence of the proletarian general strike lay not in the sanctioning of killing and in the forceful imposition of a new order, but in a transformation of relations among workers seeking autonomy from the state. He draws a vital distinction between *force*, which is a form of bourgeois violence – and here he has in mind precisely the Jacobin violence of the early 1790s – and *violence*, which is the non-violent, transformative rupture of proletarians:

> the term violence should be employed only for acts of revolt; we should say, therefore that the object of force is to impose a certain social order in which the minority governs, while violence tends to the destruction of that order. The middle class have used force since the beginning of modern times, while the proletariat now reacts against the middle class and against the State by violence.[57]

In this chapter, I have tried to stake out a place for anarchism within contemporary debates in radical political theory. As I have shown, anarchism speaks to current attempts to formulate a radical politics in the wake of Marxism; a politics no longer confined to the parameters of the state, party and class. Yet, in resisting, on the one hand, the idea that emancipation is immanent within the dynamics of capitalism, and on the other, that emancipation must be ontologically grounded in the heroism of the Event and bloodiness of the Terror, anarchism establishes its own political and ethical terrain in the project of autonomy.

Yet, how do we think about this autonomy; how does it emerge, and where can it be established? From a postanarchist perspective, these spaces of autonomy are *political* – their emergence is not part of an inevitable unfolding of natural social forces or the articulation of universal rational and moral principles; rather, they depend upon a certain contingent disruption of the natural order of things. This is where postanarchism differs from classical anarchism. It will be the purpose of Chapter 5 to explore this divergence, and to delineate the postanarchist move – as elaborated in Chapter 2 – against other contemporary anarchist perspectives.

Notes

1 See Daniel Bensaid's review essay 'On a recent book by John Holloway', in which he refers to a libertarian current that runs through left wing and Marxist thought: *Historical Materialism*, 13(4), 2005, pp. 169–92.

2 See Newman, *From Bakunin to Lacan.*

3 See Alain Badiou, *Ethics: An Essay on the Understanding of Evil* (Appendix: 'Politics and Philosophy: An Interview with Alain Badiou'), trans. Peter Hallward (London: Verso, 2002), pp. 95–6

4 An example of this would be the arrest in early 2009 of members of an autonomous commune in rural France, known as the 'Tarnac Nine'. They were arrested on the bizarre charge of 'pre-terrorism'. The pre-emption by the state of experiments in autonomous politics is thus revealed as the true aim of the 'war on terror'. See Alberto Toscano's commentary 'The war against pre-terrorism: the Tarnac 9 and *The Coming Insurrection'*, *Radical Philosophy*, 154, March/April 2009.

5 Alain Badiou, *Metapolitics*, trans. Jason Barker (London: Verso, 2005), p. 70

6 See Alain Badiou, *Polemics*, trans. Steve Corcoran (London: Verso, 2006), p. 264.

7 See Stirner's critique of the liberal state: 'What is the meaning of the doctrine that we all enjoy "equality of political rights"? Only this, that the state has no regard for my person, that to it, I, like every other, am only a man, without having another significance that commands its deference' *The Ego and Its Own*, p. 93.

8 Alain Badiou, *Being and Event*, trans. Oliver Feltham (London: Continuum, 2005), p. 110.

9 This notion of the void, or un-counted of a situation relates to Badiou's use of mathematical set theory to theorise ontology: 'To put it more clearly, once the entirety of a situation is subject to the law of the one and consistency, it is necessary, from the standpoint of the immanence of the

situation, that the pure multiple, absolutely unrepresentable according to the count, be *nothing.'* (*Being and Event*, p. 53). So, in other words, the void is the element of pure multiplicity within a set which cannot be counted or represented, and yet whose existence is paradoxically necessary for the other elements to be counted and thus for the situation to achieve consistency.

10 See Badiou, *Metapolitics*, p. 145.

11 Badiou makes continual references to L'Organisation Politique (OP), a militant group he is involved in and which campaigns for the rights of undocumented migrant workers in France. See 'Appendix: Politics and Philosophy: An Interview with Alain Badiou', *Ethics*.

12 See Badiou's discussion of the Paris Commune in *Polemics*, pp. 257–90.

13 Badiou, *Polemics*, p. 321.

14 Indeed, Badiou is interested in the more libertarian tendencies in the Chinese Cultural Revolution, such as the Shanghai Commune of 1967. He sees the Cultural Revolution as unleashing new experiments in emancipative politics that challenged the authority of the party and the state. Yet this view is somewhat problematic given not only the violent excesses of the revolution, its re-education camps, its highly doctrinaire character, its pernicious cult of personality, but also that it was essentially authorised by Mao as a way of consolidating his personal power within the Communist Party. In other words, despite its libertarian and anti-authoritarian moments, it was a revolution instigated from above. There is, however, a distinct anarchist tradition in China that had an important influence on the 1949 Revolution and the legacy of democratic radicalism in that country. See Arif Dirlik's book *Anarchists in the Chinese Revolution* (Berkeley, CA: University of California Press, 1993).

15 See Ben Noys' discussion of the question of Badiou's relationship to anarchism in 'Through a Glass Darkly: Alain Badiou's Critique of Anarchism', *Anarchist Studies*, 16(2), 2008, pp. 107–20.

16 See Alain Badiou, 'The Flux and the Party: In the Margins of Anti-Oedipus', *Polygraph*, 15/16, 2004, pp. 75–92.

17 See Bruno Bosteels' article, 'Post-Maoism: Badiou and Politics', *Positions*, 13(3), 2005, pp. 575–634.

18 Badiou, 'The Flux and the Party: In the Margins of Anti-Oedipus', p. 80.

19 See Simon Critchley, *Infinitely Demanding: Ethics of Commitment, Politics of Resistance* (London: Verso, 2007), pp. 111–14.

20 Slavoj Žižek, 'Resistance is Surrender', *London Review of Books*, 15 November 2007.

21 See Jacques Rancière, 'Who is the Subject of the Rights of Man?', *The South Atlantic Quarterly*, 103(2/3), 2004, 297–310.

22 This notion of an-archic responsibility to the other clearly invokes

Levinasian ethics; it is an ethics also adopted by Critchley with his notion of the infinite demand.

23 Indeed, Badiou makes an important point when he talks about the way that the ineffectiveness of the parliamentary left in France to formulate any sort of genuine political alternative – precisely as a result of their incorporation into the capitalist-parliamentary order – was partly the reason behind their first round defeat by Le Pen in the 2002 presidential elections. Here Le Pen is seen as symptomatic of, and internal to, the capitalist-parliamentary order, rather than threatening it from the outside: 'But if Le Pen is homogeneous to our political system, then *it is the militants of emancipation who ought to be heterogeneous to it, so as to be really heterogeneous to Le Pen'. Polemics*, p. 81.

24 See Critchley, *Infinitely Demanding*, pp. 111–12.

25 This is not to dismiss the radical nature of a certain form of identity politics in many non-Western societies: asserting a Kurdish cultural identity in Turkey, for instance, or a homosexual identity in Iran, is obviously an infinitely more risky proposition than doing the same thing in the United Kingdom or the United States.

26 Wendy Brown, *States of Injury: Power and Freedom in late Modernity* (Princeton, NJ: Princeton University Press, 2005), p. 21.

27 See Slavoj Žižek's critique of liberal multiculturalism in *The Ticklish Subject: the Absent Centre of Political Ontology* (London: Verso, 1999).

28 Stirner, *The Ego and Its Own*, p. 280.

29 As Perry Anderson points out, the world's working class has effectively doubled to 3 billion since 2000. See 'Jottings on the Conjuncture', *New Left Review*, 48, November/December 2007, pp. 5–37.

30 See Jacques Rancière, *The Nights of Labour: the Workers' Dream in Nineteenth-century France*, trans. John Drury (Philadelphia, PA: Temple University Press, 1989).

31 See Ernesto Laclau, *On Populist Reason* (London: Verso, 2005).

32 See Laclau, *On Populist Reason*, p. 232.

33 Indeed, Žižek argues that there is a certain fetishistic dimension to the structure of populist discourse that lends itself to the politics of the radical right, and that distinguishes it from other forms of egalitarian mass mobilisations – such as the anti-globalisation movement, and the US civil rights movement. See the discussion on populism in *In Defense of Lost Causes*, pp. 264–333.

34 Laclau does, however, talk about the possibility of an internationalist politics, along the lines of the anti-globalisation movement (see *On Populist Reason*, p. 231). However, I would argue that it is the transnational and anti-sovereign nature of this movement which makes the designation 'populism' more problematic.

35 Michael Hardt and Antonio Negri, *Multitude: War and Democracy in the Age of Empire* (New York: Penguin, 2004), p. 101.

36 Michael Hardt and Antonio Negri, *Empire* (Cambridge, MA: Harvard University Press, 2000), p. 350.

37 See the chapter on 'Biopolitical Production', in Hardt and Negri, *Empire*, pp. 22–41.

38 Hardt and Negri, *Empire*, p. 29.

39 Alberto Toscano raises a similar query: 'it is not clear that the supposed fusion of distinct domains into a biopolitical continuum can really permit us to isolate, within the operations of the production and reproduction of life, a collective communist subject that wouldn't be shot through, incited and restricted by the innumerable dispositifs of biopolitical control'. See 'Always Already Only Now: Negri and the Biopolitical', *The Philosophy of Antonio Negri: Revolution in Theory*, Timothy S. Murphy and Abdul-Karim Mustapha (eds) (London: Pluto Press, 2007), vol. 2, pp. 109–28 at 113.

40 See Brett Neilson's discussion of the dispute between Agamben and Negri on this question, in 'Potenza Nuda? Sovereignty, Biopolitics, Capitalism', *Contretemps*, 5, December 2004, pp. 63–78.

41 See Hardt and Negri, *Empire*, p. 216.

42 See Gilles Deleuze and Felix Guattari, *Anti-Oedipus: Capitalism and Schizophrenia*, trans. Robert Hurley (London: Continuum, 2004), p. 37.

43 See George Caffentzis' critique of Negri's focus on 'techno-scientific labour' and 'knowledge work', which ignores the way in which these high-tech sectors depend upon the existence alongside them of low-tech forms of labour: 'Consequently, "new enclosures in the countryside" must accompany the rise of "automatic process" in industry, the computer requires the sweat shop, and the cyborg's existence is premised on the slave.' See 'The End of Work or the Renaissance of Slavery? A Critique of Rifkin and Negri' (spring 1998), available at: http://www.korotonomedya. net/otonomi/caffentzis.html.

44 See Caffentzis, 'The End of Work or the Renaissance of Slavery?'

45 See the critique of the Empire thesis in 'Barbarians: the Disordered Insurgence', by Crisso and Odoteo, available at: http://www.geocities. com/kk_abacus/ioaa/barbarians.html.

46 See Alain Badiou, 'Beyond Formalisation: an interview with Alain Badiou', trans. Bruno Bosteels and Alberto Toscano, *Angelaki*, 8(2), August 2003, pp. 111–36 at 121.

47 Badiou, *Being and Event*, p. 176.

48 See Badiou, *Ethics: An Essay on the Understanding of Evil*, p. 43.

49 Here, Alberto Toscano has suggested that global anti-capitalist politics may not be irreconcileable with Badiou's conception of politics. The politics of anti-capitalism does not have to be seen as emerging as an immanent

potentiality within the dynamics of global capitalism – an aspect of Hardt and Negri's thesis of which Badiou is particularly critical – but may operate as a political challenge to the transcendental regime of global capital in the name of an alternative vision (its slogan is after all 'Another World is Possible'). See 'From the State to the World? Badiou and Anti-Capitalism', *Communication & Cognition*, 37(3 & 4), 2004, pp. 199–224.

50 See Alain Badiou, *Saint Paul: the Foundation of Universalism*, trans. Ray Brassier (Stanford, CA: Stanford University Press, 2003). Daniel Bensaid also likens Badiou's event to a miracle.

51 Saint-Just cited in Badiou's *Metapolitics*, p. 128. See also Badiou's discussion on revolutionary terror as an expression of the egalitarian maxim in *Logics of Worlds: Being and Event, 2*, trans. Alberto Toscano (London: Continuum, 2009), pp. 25–7.

52 See Slavoj Žižek, *In Defence of Lost Causes* (London: Verso, 2008), pp. 418–19.

53 See Slavoj Žižek, 'Robespierre, or, the "Divine Violence" of Terror', Introduction to *Virtue and Terror*, by Maximilien Robespierre, trans. John Howe (London: Verso, 2007).

54 Moreover, many activists today consider violence to be counterproductive, and have for a long time been experimenting with various forms of non-violent direct confrontation. See David Graeber, 'The New Anarchists', *New Left Review*, 13, January–February 2002, pp. 62–73.

55 See Žižek, 'Robespierre, or, the "Divine Violence" of Terror', p. x.

56 Walter Benjamin, 'Critique of Violence', *Selected Writings, Vol. 1*, Marcus Bullock and Michael W. Jennings (eds) (Cambridge, MA: The Belknap Press of Harvard University Press, 1999), pp. 236–52 at 251–2.

57 Georges Sorel, *Reflections on Violence*, trans. T. E. Hulme and J. Roth (New York: Collier Books, 1999), pp. 171–2.

Chapter 5

DEBATING POSTANARCHISM: ONTOLOGY, ETHICS AND UTOPIA

In Chapter 4, I explored the relevance of anarchism to questions of radical politics today – particularly those arising within continental theory. Indeed, I suggested that many of themes and preoccupations of contemporary radical political thinkers – particularly the idea of a form of politics that is beyond state, party and class – reflect an unacknowledged anarchism. However, as I have shown, anarchism – in asserting an autonomous politics against the state – provides a more consistent theory of radical politics than that proposed by other thinkers. Central here is the rejection, in the name of greater revolutionary spontaneity, of the economic determinism, historical stagism and technological fetishism at the base of Hardt's and Negri's neoMarxist thesis. At the same time, anarchism refuses the desire to consecrate the political event in the form the Terror, a temptation that in the end only consecrates the state.

To propose an understanding of anarchism as that which asserts the autonomous dimension of politics might sound odd to some, particularly to anarchists themselves. Indeed, anarchism is usually seen as an *anti-politics*. Yet, as I have shown, anarchism has always found itself in the slightly paradoxical position of proposing the abolition of politics, while at the same time having to organise political movements and invent political strategies and programmes. Postanarchism works around this aporia between politics and anti-politics: indeed, it embodies the seemingly paradoxical position of a *politics of anti-politics*, or an anti-political politics, seeing this disjunction as generating new and productive articulations of politics and ethics. In this sense, the disjunction between politics and anti-politics is what might be called an 'inclusive' disjunction: a compound in which one proposition is true only if its opposing proposition is also true. Politics, at least in a radical, emancipatory sense, only has a consistent identity only if an anti-political, indeed utopian, dimension is also present – otherwise it remains caught within existing political frameworks and imaginaries. Conversely, anti-politics makes sense only if it takes seriously the tasks of politics: building, constructing, organising, fighting, making collective decisions and so on. Such practices are in no sense irreconcilable with libertarianism; on the contrary, they are its very condition. Put simply, a politics of anti-politics points to the possibility of a libertarian politics outside, and ultimately transcendent of, the state and all hierarchical structures of power and authority. To counteract such structures requires, however, the development of alternative libertarian and egalitarian structures and practices, coupled with a constant awareness of the authoritarian potential that lies in *any* structure.

Postanarchism also points to the productive disjuncture or tension between politics and ethics. On the one hand, it refuses attempts to eclipse politics in the name of ethics: a project that might be found, for example, in various global humanitarian and human rights ideologies; although here we should not discount the emancipatory potential of certain rights discourses, such as those supporting indigenous rights claims, or those of 'illegal' migrants, for instance. At the same time, a postanarchist perspective refuses to supplant ethics with politics entirely or to see politics as occupying a different domain to ethics. As we have seen, it opposes the Schmittian preoccupation with pure politics, in which politics is constructed as a power game played between antagonistic forces, friends and enemies. This paradigm reifies sovereignty and the state, and often plays itself out as a form of violent realpolitik. Rather, politics must be conditioned by ethics, not as a Heavenly tribunal that dispenses judgement, but as something which disrupts – in a Levinasian an-archic sense, as described in Chapter 2 – sovereign political identities, opening them to the possibilities of the Other.

POSTSTRUCTURALISM AND ANARCHISM

In this chapter, I will further clarify and elaborate a politics and ethics of postanarchism. I will do so by making clear the distinctions between postanarchism and other contemporary anarchist perspectives. I will suggest here that despite a number of important differences, much recent anarchist thought continues to work within the epistemological paradigm of classical anarchism, within its humanist and rationalist presuppositions. While I have argued that we cannot simply abandon these ideas, or the Enlightenment paradigm in which they were articulated, we should at least subject them to greater critical scrutiny. Moreover, as I shall show in this chapter, some of their limitations and inconsistencies become apparent when we look at how these categories continue to inform modern anarchist thought. Here we must stress that postanarchism is a moment of both continuity and discontinuity with classical anarchism: it retains from classical anarchism its equal-libertarian political ethos, its desire for revolt and its vision of a society of free association; while at the same time questioning classical anarchism's ontological and epistemological foundations. It is this movement beyond foundationalism, however, which places postanarchism on highly contested grounds within contemporary anarchist theory. Indeed, as we shall see, the influence of postmodernism, or, as I prefer to call it, poststructuralism, on anarchist thought,[1] has been strongly resisted by a number of important anarchist theorists.

In some ways, as I suggested previously, postanarchism can be seen as a response to the postmodern condition. While I have proposed that we take a certain cautious distance from postmodernism – a term that has been loosely and often unreflectively deployed in a wide variety of domains – we should nevertheless take account of a number of its key implications, particularly on the question of deep ontological foundations. To be more specific, anarchist thought should take into account several major insights from poststructuralist theory (and here I include deconstruction and Lacanian psychoanalysis), insights which I believe can be incorporated into an anarchist politics without losing or distorting its main tenets or principles:

(1) We should adopt, with Lyotard, a degree of scepticism towards metanarratives. In other words, we must subject to closer critical scrutiny the idea that there are universal moral and rational perspectives, or that there is a certain dialectical movement of historical forces that determines social relations. These notions are deemed to be totalising in the sense that they reduce, dismiss or repress differences and singularities. However, importantly, this does not mean that we must abandon a universal dimension for politics: simply that we can no longer regard this dimension as immanent, natural or historically determined; rather, it is something that must be deliberately constructed. Nor does this scepticism towards

metanarratives mean that we descend into nihilism, irrationalism or moral relativism, as poststructuralists are so often accused of. I shall explore this question later on in the chapter.

(2) We should also abandon the notion of essential identities: in other words, the idea that there is a constant, stable set of properties, characteristics and potentialities at the base of social identities and relations. Social identities are not necessarily fixed or stable; indeed, they are often indeterminate. The Man of Enlightenment humanism, the figure endowed with certain moral and rational characteristics or potentialities which would emerge as part of an historical process or a development of social forces, can no longer serve as an entirely convincing basis for politics. This does not mean that we reject 'humanity', or that we risk propagating inhumanity, but rather that we think about humanity in different and more diverse ways. Nor does it mean that we reject the idea of society itself or collective identities, but rather that social identities are contingent and discursively constructed.

(3) We therefore place a certain emphasis on the role of language and discourse in constituting social relations, practices and identities. However, rather than accepting the structuralist position that language is a fixed, totalising, all-determining system without an outside, we point to the way that discursive structures are themselves unstable, and often fragmented and incomplete. So, although the subject is conditioned by language as an external structure, he or she is not determined by it in an absolute sense and, therefore, has a large degree of autonomy and free agency. To point to the constitutive role of language does not mean that the subject is abandoned or reduced to a fixed 'position' within a structure. Discursive structures operate as both constraints on and conditions for freedom.

(4) Lastly, we accept the Foucauldian insight that power is constitutive (rather than simply repressive) and that it is more pervasive than we had perhaps imagined. To argue that power is coextensive with social relations and that it plays some role in constituting and defining social identities and practices, does not mean that politics is impossible or that domination is insurmountable, as many have alleged. Rather, it means that the revolutionary narrative is made somewhat more complicated and problematic, and that the 'game of freedom', to use Foucault's expression, is played within and against certain constraints.

These key points, which are incorporated into a postanarchist perspective, create certain difficulties for classical anarchism as I have already pointed out. In particular, they render problematic the notion of a rational social essence that unfolds and develops, either dialectically or in an evolutionary way, towards a harmonisation of social forces and the final liberation of humanity. However, at the same time, I do not consider these theoretical conditions to be either politically disabling or incompatible with anarchism. Rather, they mean simply that we must think about politics generally, and anarchist politics in particular, in new ways.

SOCIAL ANARCHISM OF LIFESTYLE ANARCHISM?

However, the poststructuralist ideas outlined above have inspired criticism in recent years from a number of anarchist thinkers, who have argued that they are antithetical to anarchism, robbing it of any effective normative basis for political action and consigning it to nihilism, irrationalism and moral relativism.[2] Indeed, despite their major differences, two major contemporary anarchist figures, Murray Bookchin and John Zerzan, are united in their condemnation of postmodernism/poststructuralism.

Bookchin, in his polemic, *Social Anarchism or Lifestyle Anarchism*, contends that anarchism is currently at a crossroads, confronted with two alternative articulations, between which there is an 'unbridgeable chasm'. These alternatives are a 'lifestyle' anarchism which centres around an irresponsible, selfish and nihilistic desire for personal autonomy and individual expression; and 'social' anarchism, which is a more politically committed, collectivist-oriented project of what Bookchin calls 'social freedom'. Whereas the latter retains the best traditions of socialist anarchism, exemplified by anarchists like Bakunin and Kropotkin, and embodied in the Spanish collectives and the libertarian workers movements of the nineteenth and early twentieth centuries, the former, into which category Bookchin places Stirner, Godwin, Nietzsche, Foucault, Emma Goldman and especially Hakim Bey, 'takes flight from all meaningful social activism and a steadfast commitment to lasting and creative projects by dissolving into kicks, postmodernist nihilism, and a dizzying Nietzschean sense of elitist superiority'.[3] The central thrust of his critique is that a certain individualistic, hedonistic and liberal-inspired strain has developed within anarchism, which has been influenced by different sources – such as existentialism (Stirner) and postmodernism (Foucault); which has taken different forms – such as Bey's anarcho-mysticism and Zerzan's primitivism; and which threatens to turn anarchism into a nihilistic, apolitical and narcissistic personal rebellion of disaffected bourgeois youth. What is in danger of being lost in this miasma of mysticism and hedonism, according to Bookchin, is the collectivist legacy of anarchism, in which questions of egalitarianism and social responsibility, rather than personal liberation, were at the forefront of revolutionary concerns, and in which politics was guided by sound Enlightenment-based rationalist principles. Particularly threatening to this rational legacy, then, is postmodernism, which, in Bookchin's view, celebrates irrationalism and relativism, and abandons revolutionary projects in favour of personal insurrections against localised sites of power.

There is much that could be said about Bookchin's polemic. It does betray a rather hopeless nostalgia for what Bookchin imagines to be a more authentic anarchism of the past. One also finds a kind of moral Puritanism here, in which the sense of social responsibility that supposedly characterised the early workers' and socialist movements,[4] is counterposed to the stereotypical image of rebellious youth, with their 'lifestyle zines' and destructive, nihilistic tendencies. This critique of what Bookchin imagines to be the egotistical irresponsibility and narcissistic self-indulgence of young people seems much at odds with his earlier critical writings on Marxism, in which he rejected as out of date the old model of the proletarian movement, proposing in its place new forms of libertarian politics based on the possibilities of a 'post-scarcity' and post-class society.[5] Furthermore, it is surely wrong to dismiss the recent forms of politics emerging with the anti-capitalist movement as simply 'lifestyle' politics, even though it is a politics no longer based strictly on class. Surely it would be contemptuous and unfair in the extreme to dismiss the many young people who participate in radical politics today as hedonistic egotists seeking destruction for its own sake, simply because they are not part of an identifiable working-class movement and may have read a bit too much Foucault and Debord for Bookchin's liking. Rather than their being driven by an irresponsible and selfish egoism or a nihilistic individualism, as Bookchin claims, the actions and practices of young activists today suggest precisely the opposite: an an-archic sense of solidarity and responsibility for those around the world exploited and excluded by global Capital.[6]

While Bookchin wrote this polemic several years before the 'Battle of Seattle' (1999) and the appearance of a global anti-capitalist movement, his spurious distinction between 'social' and 'lifestyle' anarchism is a gesture that is dismissive of new forms of anarchist politics and radical political practices that are no longer based solely on the labour movement and strictly defined working-class identities.

Furthermore, one should reject the distinction Bookchin makes between autonomy and freedom. Here he claims that while traditional 'social' anarchism sought *freedom*, which was understood collectively and socially, 'lifestyle' anarchism by contrast seeks a more 'liberal' notion of *autonomy*, based on the model of possessive individualism and embodying a selfish disregard for the needs of others. While freedom, for Bookchin, is socially-situated and an expression of collective egalitarian aspirations, autonomy is individualistic, solipsistic and often irresponsible, ranging from Stirnerian 'egoism', New Age spiritualism and self-development, to bourgeois yuppie 'me-ism'. We should point out, however, that this distinction between individual-based autonomy and socially- or collectively-based freedom was never part of classical anarchism. Even the anarchists whom Bookchin recruits on the side of collectivist social freedom – Kropotkin and Bakunin – never saw this as being in any sense irreconcilable with personal autonomy. Indeed, the two went hand-in-hand. As Bakunin said: 'I have in mind this liberty of everyone which, far from finding itself checked by the freedom of others, is, on the contrary, confirmed by it and extended to infinity.'[7] While this liberty was socially conditioned, emerging through an interaction of individuals with the social and natural forces of which they were a part, it was never meant to imply a collectivist subordination of the individual's liberty to social needs. Rather, the anarchist idea of freedom embodies and, indeed, maximises ('extended to infinity') the idea of individual liberty or autonomy, refusing to see it in opposition to the liberty of others or to the desire for social equality.

So, rather than finding an opposition between individual liberty (or autonomy) and social needs, I prefer to think in terms of 'equaliberty'. As I proposed in Chapter 1, equal-liberty implies the inextricability of liberty and equality, and refuses to see an opposition between individual freedom and collective, egalitarian freedom, between the one and the many; any constraint on one involves a constraint on the other. Indeed, I see this principle of equal-liberty as being central to anarchism, distinguishing it from liberalism, on the one hand, and socialism, on the other hand. Both these alternative ideologies imagine a tension between the individual and society, and between liberty and equality: liberalism tends to subordinate social needs to individual needs, and equality to liberty; while socialism tends to do the opposite. It is only anarchism that refuses this opposition. Bookchin, in resurrecting this distinction, and in attributing it, incorrectly, to the tradition of classical anarchism – or at least to some of its key proponents – betrays his socialist, rather than anarchist, leanings. Indeed, to equate the idea of individual autonomy with a bourgeois possessive individualism is something that even Marx rejected. Marx showed how this was an incredibly limited and ultimately self-contradictory way of thinking about freedom – boiling down to notions of private property, free trade and the freedom to exploit others – and that the abolition of bourgeois individualism under communism meant not the abolition of individual freedom and autonomy, or the subordination of the individual to the collective, but, on the contrary, an extension of the realm of individual autonomy, self-determination and freedom of expression beyond these narrow confines.[8] To see, as Bookchin does, notions of individual autonomy and liberty as being strictly part of the liberal tradition of Locke and John Stuart Mill, ignores the way in which individualism has a completely different resonance and importance in the radical tradition.

Here we should also reject Bookchin's equation of poststructuralist thinkers like Foucault, as well as Stirner, with liberalism and with liberal understandings of individualism. The importance of poststructuralist thought is in showing that the liberal, bourgeois individual is neither as consistent or autonomous as he or she imagines; that, as Foucault shows, the individual is often an 'effect' of relations of power, knowledge and regimes of truth that construct an identity for him or her. Indeed, this is precisely why Foucault questions the whole individualist discourse of personal rebellion and sexual liberation: because the 'essential self' that seeks to be liberated, or the Man of bourgeois rights and freedoms, 'is already in himself the effect of a subjection far more profound than himself'.[9] So, far from supporting the narcissistic rebellion of the self against power, as Bookchin claims, Foucault shows us that the project of personal liberation must be treated with much more caution. Similarly, with Stirner, we find not, as Bookchin suggests, a celebration of bourgeois individualism, but precisely a radical questioning of this subject. Indeed, for Stirner, the idea of the rational, utility maximising bourgeois individual is a constraint upon the much more radical possibilities of ego: here the ego should not be confused with the self-interested *homo economicus* of liberalism – this in itself is an abstraction of humanist and liberal discourses – but rather should be seen as a kernel of nothingness out of which different expressions of the 'self' can arise. Thus, Stirner's individualism is much too radical and idiosyncratic to be confined to the liberal conception.

While Bookchin makes some valid points about the apolitical emptiness and vapidity of certain New Age spiritual motifs of 'self-fulfilment'– to which we can only respond that these have nothing to do with a poststructuralist-inspired anarchism in any case – his thesis should in general be refuted. Anarchism, as I have suggested, sees no opposition between the collective interests of society and individual need for autonomy. To dismiss the latter as a bourgeois 'lifestyle' preoccupation has no legitimate basis in anarchist thought. The 'unbridgeable chasm' that he erects between 'social' and 'lifestyle' anarchism is an imaginary one, born of his own disdain for new, emergent forms of anarchism. Here, Bob Black refers to a certain 'paradigm shift' – in the Kuhnian sense – between the older, classical anarchism, represented in its last gasp by Bookchin, and what he terms New Anarchism, which he sees as consciously hedonistic, anti-political and post-leftist.[10] While I agree that there has been a certain shift to new understandings of anarchism – although here the notion of the paradigm shift is too strong to describe moments of both continuity and discontinuity with classical anarchism – and while I agree that Bookchin should be seen as part of the classical anarchist tradition, I do not see this 'shift' as occurring on the same terrain as Black does. That is to say, the difference between classical and 'new' – or as I prefer to call it 'post' – anarchism, is not between one that is political and 'leftist', and one that is hedonistic, anti-political and 'post-leftist'. This is in some senses to reflect Bookchin's own highly spurious distinction. If by 'anti-political' Black means 'post-political', in the sense of no longer being politically engaged, then he is certainly wrong. As I have suggested, the anti-political gesture does not mean an avoidance or withdrawal from political struggles, but rather the revolutionary abolition of formal politics and power (particularly in its statist form), and this is also obviously a *political* gesture; this is why it only makes sense to see anti-politics – even in its utopian dimension – as a certain type of politics. Furthermore, it makes no sense to me to see contemporary forms of anarchism as 'post-leftist', if by 'post-leftist' is meant an abandonment of the radical horizon of emancipation. While contemporary anarchism might be 'post-leftist' in the sense that it is no longer closely affiliated with the labour movement or the socialist tradition, it obviously still retains an anti-capitalist and egalitarian agenda.

Therefore, if there has been a 'shift' from classical to contemporary anarchism, it has taken place on a different terrain: on an *ontological* terrain. In other words, there has been an 'an-archic' dislodgement of the deep foundations of classical anarchist thought, a disturbance of its epistemological categories. As outlined above, we can no longer subscribe to ideas about human essence, the dialectic or the rational development of social forces. The 'paradigm shift' away from classical anarchism, therefore, involves an abandonment of the notion of the rational social object that formed the basis of its ethics and its revolutionary philosophy. Postanarchism refers to the orientation of anarchist theory and practice around precisely this rejection of a rational social totality.

THE ONTOLOGY OF 'SOCIAL ECOLOGY'

This notion of a rational social totality, and the reasons why it should be abandoned, become clearer if we turn once again to Bookchin, who, as I have argued, may be considered part of the classical anarchist tradition. Bookchin's central concept and programme of 'social ecology' embodies the idea that at the base of social relations there is a certain immanent and historically determined unfolding of rational and ethical capacities, which form part of what he calls an 'ecology of freedom'. This is an argument that closely parallels the developmental philosophies of classical nineteenth-century anarchists, in which one finds a certain narrative of freedom and progress driven by an unfolding of a social totality – an essence or capacity that is immanent within society, and whose emergence will bring about a rational harmonisation of social forces and the full humanisation of Man.

The same type of narrative can be found in Bookchin's *Ecology of Freedom*. Here he outlines a project of reconciling libertarian socialist – or anarchist – principles with the needs and prerogatives of an 'ecological society'. This involves harmonising humanity or the human-made universe (what he refers to as *second nature*) with non-human nature (*first nature*). The dialectical interaction between these two dimensions produces a rational synthesis which Bookchin calls a *third nature*: that is, a more complete, thinking nature in which are combined the principles of unity and diversity. This interaction takes place on the terrain of a rational wholeness or totality which was always immanent, although hitherto not fully realised:

> What makes unity in diversity in nature more than a suggestive ecological metaphor for unity in diversity in society is the underlying philosophical concept of wholeness. By wholeness, I mean varying levels of actualization, an unfolding of a wealth of particularities, that are latent in an as-yet-undeveloped potentiality. This potentiality may be a newly planted seed, a newly born infant, a newly born community, or a newly born society.[11]

Bookchin stresses that this notion of wholeness is not homogenising, but embodies a dynamic interaction of natural and social forces and particularities. However, the point is that this interaction of forces is determined dialectically as part of an unfolding rationality that is immanent in nature. Here Bookchin invokes Hegel's maxim, '"the True is the whole"', inverting it into the '"the whole is the True"':

> One can take this reversal of terms to mean that the true lies in the self-consummation of a process through which its development, in the flowering of its latent particularities into their fullness or wholeness, just as the potentialities of a child achieve expression in the wealth of experiences and physical growth that enter into childhood.[12]

Bookchin elsewhere refers to this logic of unfolding as *dialectical naturalism*: the process by which a certain latent potentially is realised, developing itself into its proper wholeness of fullness.[13] Bookchin's central thesis in his concept of social ecology is, therefore, the idea that the possibilities of a free society – a society without hierarchy and alienation – are contained within nature itself; moreover, they are unfolding in a rational way through a certain dynamic interaction between humanity and nature. This will culminate in a reconciliation between humanity and nature, and the realisation by human societies of libertarian and non-hierarchical principles of organisation which were already part of the natural order: 'Our continuity with non-hierarchical nature suggests that a non-hierarchical society is no less random than an ecosystem.'[14] Thus, the project of human freedom must be situated in relation to the natural world from which it emerges; its realisation is the fulfilment of a natural rational destiny, and a harmonisation of human with natural society.

This notion of the ripening of the conditions of human freedom through a rational process of enlightenment and social development is entirely consistent with classical anarchism. Here we might think of Bakunin's idea that freedom develops in accordance with natural laws, and that its realisation is possible only with the gradual discernment, through scientific observation and rational enquiry, of the way in which these laws constitute our very beings: 'In respect to Nature this is for man the only possible dignity and freedom. There will never be any other freedom; for natural laws are immutable and inevitable.'[15] Similarly, for Kropotkin, the principles of sociability and cooperation, which are the foundations upon which a free and ethical society are to be built, are found first in the natural world, where they function as principles of evolutionary survival among animal species. However, in these narratives, as in Bookchin's, there is a certain antagonism between these libertarian and mutualist principles rooted in nature and the forces of authoritarianism and hierarchy – forces which will nevertheless be overcome through a process of rational enlightenment and social revolution. Moreover, these narratives do not propose a simple return to nature, but, rather, seek to take advantage of technological developments and scientific progress to better harness and implement these natural principles.

However, can we assume that the possibilities of human freedom lie rooted in the natural order, as a secret waiting to be discovered, as a flower waiting to blossom, to use Bookchin's metaphor? Can we assume that there is a rational unfolding of possibilities, driven by a certain historical and social logic? This would seem to fall into the trap of essentialism, whereby there is a rational essence or being at the foundation of society whose truth we must perceive. There is an implicit positivism here, in which political and social phenomena are seen as conditioned by natural principles and scientifically observable conditions. Here I think one should reject this view of a social order founded on deep rational principles. In the words of Stirner, 'The essence of the world, so attractive and splendid, is for him who looks to the bottom of it – emptiness.'[16] In other words, rather than there being a rational objectivity at the foundation of society, an immanent wholeness embodying the potential for human freedom, there is a certain void or emptiness, one that produces radical contingency and indeterminacy rather than scientific objectivity. This idea has been elaborated by Laclau and Mouffe, who eschew the idea of society as a rationally intelligible totality, and instead see it as a field of antagonisms which function as its discursive limit. In other words, what gives society its definitional limit at the same time subverts it as a coherent, whole identity. Therefore, they argue, 'Society never manages fully to be society, because everything in it is penetrated by its limits, which prevent it from constituting itself as an objective reality.'[17] Antagonism should not be thought of here in the sense of the Hobbesian state of nature, as a war of everyman against everyman, but rather as a kind of rupturing or displacement of social identities that prevents the closure of society as a coherent identity.

To assert the indeterminacy and openness of social identities does not undermine the possibilities of radical politics. Anarchism does not require deep ontological foundations, such as those offered by Bookchin's concept of social ecology. On the contrary, this sort of foundationalism constrains politics by grounding it in a biological determinacy and an organic vision of society. My contention here is that we should no longer think of the politics of freedom and emancipation in these terms. To presuppose a harmonious, rational social order as the fundamental programme of politics, and to see this as being already immanent within social relations, entails the very closure of politics. It aims at a certain stabilisation, and, indeed, domestication of the political. Rather than seeing radical politics as part of a rational process, as moments in the unfolding of an objective totality, we should see it as unpredictable points of rupture with the existing social order. If we were to take Rancière's position here, we can see this idea of a determined social order as the order of 'the police', in opposition to which politics is always a moment of rupture, displacement and exteriority.[18] For Rancière, politics is democracy. However, democracy here has nothing to do with a stable regime of institutions, practices, identities and rights, but rather refers to the moment of dissonance or disjuncture created when the *demos* – the part that is excluded from the social and political order – demands to be included, and, importantly, does so on the basis of the presupposition of equality with the whole of the community. It is not, therefore, a matter of the smooth incorporation of a certain part into the whole, but rather the disjuncture between a part which has no place – the poor, illegal immigrants, for instance – and the order which cannot accommodate this part without disordering itself.

With certain qualifications, I regard Rancière's view of politics as being extremely useful for a rethinking of anarchism. This is because he sees politics itself as an *an-archic* displacement of the order of parts, semblances and identities. Can we speak, then, of an *an-archic* displacement of anarchism itself? This is what I have endeavoured to capture with the idea of postanarchism: a destabilisation of the ontological foundations and essential identities of anarchism. Furthermore, could we say, with Rancière, that any social order, even one based on anarchist principles, would be an order of the police? By 'police', Rancière is not referring to the coercive apparatuses of the state, but to a rational ordering of places, roles and identities within any community based on a certain 'distribution of the sensible': that is, a certain regime of signs that determines what is perceptible and what is not.[19] If we take this argument, we would have to concede that any form of social organisation will involve relations of power and exclusion – such relations are coextensive with society as such. No doubt the structures and contours of an anarchist community or society would be much more open, less exclusionary and restrictive, and more democratic than those of other societies. Yet, an anarchist politics must still be aware of the risk of new forms of power emerging in societies supposedly liberated from power. This does not mean, of course, that the project of building autonomous, libertarian communities is pointless and should be abandoned; rather, that anarchism should also be seen as an ethics in which power is continually problematised, and where borders are continually contested. Anarchism should remain sensitive to the possibilities of domination and to the inevitability of dissent and disagreement.

If we examine, for instance, Bookchin's idea of municipalism as the basis for a new politics of citizenship and democratic decision making, we find many interesting and appealing ideas for libertarian institutions and practices, including forms of council democracy and decentralisation. However, there is little acknowledgement of the possibility of new forms of power and exclusion emerging with such institutions. For instance, the category of citizenship, which often perpetuates such pervasive practices of exclusion and securitisation, is never really questioned or deconstructed in his account. Instead, we are presented with an image of the political structure of a rational ecological society of the future. As part of this confederalist vision, Bookchin invokes as examples of an 'authentic politics' models of political participation from Athenian democracy and New England town meetings, as well as the Arendtian and Aristotelian motifs of the properly political life.[20] While an anarchist politics can certainly draw upon the democratic forms and practices of the past, the problem lies more in the way that this confederalist vision of Bookchin's is imagined as part of a dialectical totality of social and political interdependencies that unfolds towards its own self-realisation.[21] This confederalist model is thus confirmed as the only political form a liberated society can take. However, if we are to understand anarchism not only as a way of thinking about future forms of a free society, but also as an an-archic disturbance of *all* political forms, then we would have to insist on a certain constitutive openness and a space of contestation and disagreement.

In considering Bookchin's politics, then, we should pay close attention to Rancière's critical analysis of classical anarchism:

> Historical anarchism oscillated between two fundamental attitudes: on the one hand it brought together the capacity for inventiveness of humans in association with schemas of historical evolution advanced by Marxist science. On the other, it presented itself, in the Proudhonian tradition, as the bearer of true social science, and of a social formula ready for future application . . . Murray Bookchin, for his part, seems to me to perpetuate the organicist vision to which anarchism has often been linked, a vision according to which the just society would be like a natural vegetable well embedded in its soil. This also means that he presents the anarchist solution as the application of a formula which is supposed to be a cure for the sickness of the state. I, for my part, do not believe in phrases ready-made for future application. I believe that there are current forms of opposition to the existing order which are developing future forms of being in common. The anarchist critique and forms of association linked to the anarchist tradition certainly take on a new importance since the failure of State Marxism and socialist parties. But this implies thinking the thing that historical anarchism judged contradictory: an anarchist political thought, an idea of anarchism as practical politics.[22]

If anarchism is to be seen as a *politics* in this sense, rather than as developmental narrative consecrated by scientific knowledge and natural law, then we would have to reject the ontological categories upon which Bookchin's political vision is founded. Because Bookchin's politics of social ecology is absolutised and made certain through the dialectic and through a rational, organic objectivity, it effects a closure of politics. To see anarchism as a 'practical politics' rather than as a social science, means that anarchism is practiced without these dialectical guarantees and naturalistic foundations; the emphasis is on contingency and practical innovation, rather than on understanding the organic basis and the rational *telos* of the story of human liberation. This move from a science of deep foundations to a politics of practices and contingencies is central to postanarchism.

ANARCHISM AS PRIMITIVISM

If we are to question the idea of anarchism as a discourse of rational progress and dialectical development, should we then see it as an anti-civilisational politics opposed to the very notion of progress? This is precisely the position adopted by the anarcho-primitivist, John Zerzan, who engages in a radical critique of civilisation in the name of a pre-civilisational Golden Age: that is, an image of man in Palaeolithic times as naturally free and unencumbered by the constraints of modern society. Zerzan's argument here is seemingly the direct opposite of Bookchin's: while the latter affirms the idea of technological innovation and progress, locating the possibilities of human liberation in a future ecological society, the former has an utterly dystopian vision of modernity, harkening back instead to a prelapsarian time of total freedom and oneness with nature, a state which it was our misfortune to ever abandon. For Zerzan, the hope of human liberation lies in a total destruction of technology and the trappings of civilisation, and a return to a primitive existence: an insurrection of the future primitive.[23] Moreover, it is because of his anti-civilisational stance, and his dystopian rejection of technology and the idea of progress, that Zerzan is condemned as a nihilistic 'lifestyle' anarchist in Bookchin's aforementioned polemic. Yet, these two thinkers have more in common than it may appear: they both hang on to the Enlightenment desire for *social fullness*. That is, the idea of a rational social harmony and the overcoming of alienation. Bookchin seeks this social fullness in the future, while Zerzan finds it in the past.

This similarity becomes more evident in their mutual opposition to postmodernism/poststructuralism. Like Bookchin, Zerzan equates postmodernism with nihilism, irrationalism and relativism. He refers to it as a 'catastrophe', arguing that it simply mirrors the abstraction, fragmentation and loss of reality generated by contemporary hyper-capitalism and consumerism. However, aside from the problematic conflation of a certain pop-culture notion of postmodernism – which I would agree largely consists in a fetishisation of capitalism and is incapable of providing any effective critique of it – with poststructuralism, which I see as more politically engaged, it is curious that Zerzan condemns postmodernism for its assault on Enlightenment humanism: 'Postmodernism subverts two of the over-arching tenets of Enlightenment humanism: the power of language to shape the world and the power of consciousness to shape a self.'[24] Yet surely the discourse of Enlightenment humanism, with its ideas of the rationally conscious individual and human emancipation, are products of the very civilisation that Zerzan so violently rejects. Indeed, in another essay, Zerzan claims that language itself is alienating and repressive because it abstracts us from the more immediate and authentic relationship with the world;[25] and yet he condemns postmodernism for undermining the power of language to shape the world. In what sense would rationality, and Enlightenment humanist notions of the autonomous subject, have any sort of meaning at all in the primitive, pre-linguistic societies Zerzan admires?

Such moments of self-contradiction aside, what becomes apparent in Zerzan's critique of postmodernism is the desire to preserve some notion of authenticity and presence; the idea that there is an essential reality – the thing in itself – beyond discourse and representation. What postmodernism undermines and disrupts, according to Zerzan, is the possibility of an authentic relationship with the world, a sensory appreciation of the real which is unmediated by language. The effect of strategies like deconstruction, according to Zerzan, is to make impossible 'unmediated contact or communication, only signs and representations; deconstruction is a search for presence and fulfilment interminably, necessarily, deferred'.[26] This is why Zerzan is also critical of Lacanian psychoanalysis, as it shows that pre-symbolic jouissance is impossible and unattainable because it is outside the order of language and representation.

Zerzan's desire to return to some authentic relationship with the world, some unmediated experience of the present, is like the desire to return to the pre-Oedipal state of bliss: the unmediated, harmonious enjoyment (jouissance) with the mother prior to the alienating intervention of the paternal signifier. Indeed, his descriptions of primitive hunter-gatherer societies in Palaeolithic times, for whom the constraints of civilisation, the burdens of gender and economic hierarchies and the violence and alienations of capitalism, technology and the division of labour were unknown, were societies of bliss, innocence and harmony, in which one experienced an authentic and immediate relationship with the natural environment. To live such an undomesticated existence, without technology, without involuntary work, without family structures, without even language and symbolic representation, is to experience a genuine freedom and a complete oneness with the world. According to Zerzan, such primitive hunter-gatherer societies were societies of leisure, abundance and egalitarianism.

This idea of a lost state of innocent enjoyment and authenticity has a powerful resonance today in the face of the pervasive intrusions and constraints of our technologically-saturated societies. Here we should not dismiss of the value of Zerzan's dystopian critique. We do, indeed, live a domesticated existence in our time of biopolitical capitalism, with its continual deployment of technologies of surveillance and control, its cynical commodification and manipulation of biological life itself and its devastation of the natural environment. Societies in the developed world increasingly resemble giant, hi-tech prisons, with their surveillance cameras, databases, biometric technologies and their enclosure of the commons. Are we not all haunted by the desire to destroy the chains that bind us, to escape these confines, to roam freely in wildness of a state of nature? Does not the desire to escape domestication recur as a powerful social fantasy? Indeed, this is how we should approach Zerzan's vision of authentic primitive societies. They should not be seen as actually existing societies; despite the abundance of anthropological studies that Zerzan cites as evidence for their existence, this is all pure speculation. Rather they should be seen as a kind of utopia, an antipolitical imaginary of freedom and autonomy that serves as a powerful basis for the critique of contemporary conditions. As Zerzan says, referring to the myth of the Golden Age, 'Eden, or whatever name it goes by, was the home of our primeval forager ancestors, and expresses the yearning of disillusioned tillers of the soil for a lost life of freedom and relative ease.'[27] We should, therefore, see Zerzan's utopia of primitive freedom and authenticity not as something that once existed, still less as something we can return to as part of an anti-civilisational programme, but as a kind of negative imaginary, a point of exteriority and excess that allows us to escape from the mental confines of this world and to reflect on its limits. As Zerzan himself says: 'To "define" a disalienated world would be impossible and even undesirable, but I think we can and should try to reveal the unworld of today and how it got this way.'[28] We cannot return to a primitive hunter-gatherer existence. As Rousseau said, we cannot return to the primeval bliss of the state of nature – once we had abandoned this Golden Age there was no going back. We can only go forward, working with what we have, resisting and destroying certain technologies, utilising and civilising others, but, more importantly, creating new spaces for autonomy and equality, new ways of life that resist and escape domestication.

However, where Zerzan's argument becomes problematic is in the essentialist notion that there is a rationally intelligible presence, a social objectivity that is beyond language and discourse. To speak in Lacanian terms, the pre-linguistic state of jouissance is precisely unattainable: it is always mediated by language that at the same time alienates and distorts it. It is an *imaginary* jouissance, an illusion created by the symbolic order itself, as the secret behind its veil. We live in a symbolic and linguistic universe, and to speculate about an original condition of authenticity and immediacy, or to imagine that an authentic presence is attainable behind the veils of the symbolic order or beyond the grasp of language, is futile. There is no getting outside language and the symbolic; nor can there be any return to the pre-Oedipal real. To speak in terms of alienation, as Zerzan does, is to image a pure presence or fullness beyond alienation, which is an impossibility. While Zerzan's attack on technology and domestication is no doubt important and valid, it is based on a highly problematic essentialism implicit in his notion of alienation.

To question this discourse of alienation is not a conservative gesture. It does not rob us of normative reasons for resisting domination, as Zerzan claims. It is to suggest that projects of resistance and emancipation do not need to be grounded in an immediate presence or positive fullness that exists beyond power and discourse. Rather, radical politics can be seen as being based on a moment of negativity: an emptiness or lack that is productive of new modes of political subjectivity and action.[29] Instead of hearkening back to a primordial authenticity that has been alienated and yet which can be recaptured – a state of harmony which would be the very eclipse of politics – I believe it is more fruitful to think in terms of a constitutive rift that is at the base of any identity, a rift that produces radical openings for political articulation and action.

THE ETHICS OF POSTANARCHISM

I have suggested that, despite their differences, both Bookchin and Zerzan work within an Enlightenment paradigm – similar to that of classical anarchism – which presupposes a rational social essence or fullness: one that is either lost and needs to be recovered, or one that will be realised in the future through a process of dialectical development. My argument has been that this ontological vision forecloses the dimension of the political, determining its direction and eliminating the openness and contingency proper to it. This idea of openness and contingency, moreover, also refers to the domain of ethics. As I have shown, ethics is what opens politics to that which is beyond its own limits, disturbing the sovereign*ising* tendency of political identities. In this sense, because postanarchism embodies a moment of an-anarchic disruption, it is a way of thinking about politics that is also deeply engaged with ethics. Postanarchism can be seen as a way of reflecting on the aporetic moment of tension between politics and ethics.

However, what do we mean by ethics here? Can we speak of a specifically postanarchist understanding of ethics, and how might this be different from other conceptions of ethics? The question of ethics and its relation to radical politics today becomes especially important in the face of what might superficially appear as two contradictory phenomena. On the one hand, there has been a delegitimising of universal moral categories, which can be found today in the plurality of moral positions, religious beliefs, ethical sensibilities and ways of life. On the other hand, we see the hysterical desire to reinvent moral absolutes: something that can be observed, for instance, in the construction of ethics – based on liberal notions of human rights – as a global ideology; or in the uncanny return of the worst kinds of religious dogmatism and conservatism. This is the paradoxical situation that confronts ethics under the conditions of postmodernity. While one can affirm, with Lyotard, the eclipse of metanarratives – including the Kantian universal moral imperative – the implications of this are often ambiguous. Rather than producing a liberation, it can at times lead to the imposition of a ferocious moral superego. Moral and religious fundamentalisms are in this sense symptomatic of the 'postmodern condition'. The decline of the traditional authority of moral law and universal injunctions is supplemented today with 'ethics committees' and New Age spiritualism in a desperate attempt to reinvent the place of authority, to cover over the lack in the symbolic order. The liberation promised with the decline of traditional moral and symbolic authority now ends up in a new series of constraints and prohibitions. In the words of Lacan, who reversed the maxim of Dostoyevsky, 'if God is dead, now *nothing* is permitted'.[30]

How might an ethically engaged form of radical politics like anarchism respond to this situation? An adequate response surely cannot be a naive libertarianism which celebrates the breakdown of traditional moral authority as a moment of existential freedom. Things are not so simple: as Lacan pointed out, the project of the libertine is often complicated by the emergence of new prohibitions and laws, a new desire for authority.[31] To transgress the law for its own sake only ends up reinventing it. As I will try to show, and contrary to what has been alleged, postanarchism does not amount to an amoral nihilism or relativism. Indeed, it builds upon the ethical possibilities of classical anarchism – particularly its ethics of solidarity and equality, the opposition to domination and a respect for the autonomy of others. Yet it does so without the ontological guarantees of universal moral and rational categories. While classical anarchism rejected the moral authority enshrined in religion, it proclaimed instead a moral authority based on nature, reason and science. For Kropotkin and Bakunin, nature contained moral and rational facts which could be discerned through scientific observation. When Kropotkin said that nature was the 'first ethical teacher of man', he was grounding an understanding of ethics in the certainties of biological evolution. While Godwin considered moral decision making to the be preserve of the autonomous individual who exercises the 'right to private judgement', he nevertheless saw this as being part of a process of universal moral and rational perfectibility.

However, if postanarchism questions this sort of moral foundationalism, can it still maintain a commitment to ethical action? Not according to Benjamin Franks, who argues that postanarchism leads to a radical subjectivism – a moral relativism where the individual, in a solipsistic fashion, determines his or her own moral coordinates – thus, making it unsuitable for developing ethical and political relations with others. This subjectivist position is attributed to Stirner, who, Franks argues, rejects the universal moral and rational discourses embodied in Enlightenment humanism and proposes in their place the supreme individualism and amoralism of the self-creating egoist:

However, the alternative [to consequentialist and deontological anarchisms] adopted by some egoist individualists and postanarchists, i.e. radical subjectivism, is inadequate on similar grounds. If subjectivism is right, then it restricts the possibility of meaningful ethical dialogue, recreates hierarchies between the liberated ego and the rest, and cannot adequately account for the creative ego, without recourse to the other social forms it rejects.[32]

However, aside from the question of the extent to which I base my understanding of postanarchist ethics *entirely* on a Stirnerite egoism, I nevertheless regard Stirner as useful for a rethinking of ethics in terms of singularities. Moreover, as I have suggested, Stirner's critique of morality should not be reduced to a simple selfish individualism: his understanding of the individual subject is more radical than that. I see Stirner as a kind of wrecking ball who demolishes the abstractions of humanism and rationalism erected in the place of God by Feuerbach. His point is to show that the moral and rational categories of modernity have an undiagnosed religiosity, a theological stain that continues to haunt their apparent secularity.[33] Morality is, therefore, an ideology, and it masks a certain relationship of domination. Thus, Stirner clears the ground for a reconsideration of ethics and politics beyond the categories of Enlightenment humanism and liberalism. Ethics and politics should be thought of at the level of singularities rather than universal abstractions; ethics must be open to a certain spontaneous and free self-determination by individuals, rather than imposed upon them from above through abstract moral codes and strictures. Moreover, the egoist who refuses to be subjected to these abstractions is not an immoralist, a position which simply reaffirms the binary established by morality. Rather, the egoist should be seen as an open dimension of subjectivity, a self-creating void that is always in the process of becoming, and in which all sovereign, fixed identities are destabilised. The subjectivity of the liberal bourgeois individual, with whom Stirner's ego is so often and so inaccurately associated, is itself undermined here.

However, does this egoism make ethical relations with others impossible, as Franks suggests? For Stirner, the egoistic removal of idealised abstractions like 'morality', 'humanity' and 'society' actually opens the possibility for new kinds of relations with other people, relations based on voluntary association rather than established bonds and obligations.

People will still come together, still fraternise, love one another and so on,

> but the difference is this, that then the individual really *unites* with the individual, while formerly they were *bound together* by a tie; son and father are bound together before majority, after it they can come together independently; before it they *belonged* together as members of a family, after it they unite together as egoists; sonship and fatherhood remain, but son and father no longer pin themselves down to these.[34]

While this social dimension of egoism is perhaps insufficiently elaborated and developed – Stirner makes certain references to the possibility of a 'union of egoists' – it is by no means ruled out in his account. Nor is there an implied hierarchy in Stirner's thinking, between the liberated ego and others, as Franks suggests. For Stirner, the possibilities of radical freedom offered by egoism and 'ownness' can be grasped by *anyone*; there is no Nietzschean sentimentality here for aristocracy.

As an alternative to both Stirnerite 'subjectivism' and moral universalism, Franks proposes a situated ethics: an understanding of ethics as situated within, and contingent upon, specific social practices, communities and organisations. Different situations demand different ethical relations and rules, rules which can nevertheless change over time, and are open to dialogue and critical negotiation.[35] I fully agree with this application of ethics, and I see it as a useful way of thinking about ethics in terms of autonomy and pluralism. However, what it lacks is an understanding of *ethical subjectivation* – in other words, the processes by which a subject becomes an ethical (and, indeed, political) subject. Therefore, I think the idea of a situated ethics needs to be supplemented with an account of the ethical subject. In an earlier chapter, I explored Levinas's anarchic account of ethics as a way of understanding ethical subjectivation: here the subject is held 'hostage' by the encounter with the Other, an encounter that unsettles and destabilises his or her sovereign identity. However, on the other side of this process are the micro-ethical and micro-political strategies that we engage in, and through which we constitute a relation to ethics. Here we must turn briefly to Foucault's 'ethics of the care of self'. While Foucault's focus on the ethical strategies that constitute the self might appear to be opposed to the Levinasian conception, in which the self is unsettled by the Other, my suggestion is that they are not as far apart as they seem: they both rely on a non-essentialist conception of the self and its relation to ethics. For Foucault, the ethical and ascetic strategies, such as *askesis*, that he explores in the later volumes of *The History of Sexuality*, are ways of thinking about the self, not in relation to an essential truth that the subject discovers within him or herself – a conception of the self which authorises regulatory and institutional practices into which the subject is inserted – but rather in relation to certain 'games of truth', rules of conduct and practices of care that the subject engages in. Put simply, these ethical strategies that Foucault discusses are ways that the subject *constructs*, rather than discovers, him- or herself. We find an important parallel here with Stirner's idea of the ego as a process of self-creation.

Moreover, although for Foucault, unlike Levinas, the care of the self is ontologically prior to the care of others, it nevertheless entails a certain ethical way of relating to others. In particular, it is a way of practising freedom in an ethical way: indeed, in this conception, freedom becomes an ethical problem. Freedom, for Foucault, cannot be a certain state beyond power that we finally reach through a moment of liberation. Rather, it must be an ongoing ethical practice, in which one's relationship with oneself and others is subject to a continual ethical interrogation:

> this practice of liberation is not in itself sufficient to define the practices of freedom that will still be needed if this people, this society, and these individuals are able to define admissible and acceptable forms of existence or political society . . . This ethical problem of the definition of practices of freedom, it seems to me, is much more important than the rather repetitive affirmation that sexuality or desire must be liberated.[36]

IS ANARCHISM A UTOPIA?

What remains insufficiently theorised within classical anarchism – with its narratives of the liberation and realisation of the human subject through a rational unfolding of social and natural forces – is precisely this idea of a micro-political ethics as suggested by Foucault. In other words, we cannot assume that a revolutionary project of liberation from oppressive political and economic conditions will be enough:

there will still be relations of power, requiring an ongoing ethical contestation, ongoing practices of freedom and the development of different modes of subjectivation. We must, therefore, consider again the question of utopia here. In previous chapters, I have suggested that postanarchism must retain a utopian dimension; indeed, this is vital to the anti-political horizon of radical politics. Yet this utopian dimension should be rethought. It should not be a concrete formulation of a liberated society; for instance, the idea of an ecological society with its municipal institutions, as proposed by Bookchin as the rational outcome of a process of dialectical unfolding. The utopian moment in anarchism should not seek to establish a scientific status for itself; it should not see itself in terms of a precise, scientific programme emerging inevitably from a rational process of social evolution. Rather, utopia gives itself over to the imaginary, providing a point of escape from the current order, a way of orienting and inciting (anti)political desire. Utopian thinking might be seen a way of puncturing the ontological status of the current order, introducing into it a moment of disruptive heterogeneity and singularity.

As I have argued, anarchism has always had a utopian dimension. However, one can also detect two different utopian moments in anarchism: one that might be termed 'scientific utopianism', in which a future anarchist society is founded on scientific and rational principles and will be the inevitable outcome of a revolution against the state; and another that might be termed 'utopianism of the here and now', in which the focus is less on what happens after the revolution, and more on a transformation of social relations within the present. Here the 'spiritual' anarchism of thinkers like Martin Buber and Gustav Landauer provides important ways of rethinking utopia. For instance, Landauer suggests that the state is more than simply an institution that can be overthrown in a revolution, and then replaced with an anarchist society. Rather, the state should be seen as a certain relation between people: a mode of behaviour and interaction. Therefore, it can be transcended only through a certain spiritual transformation of relationships: 'we destroy it by contracting other relationships, by behaving differently'.[37] If there is no such transformation, the state will be simply reinvented in a different form during the revolution. The focus must be, then, on creating alternative, non-statist, non-authoritarian relationships between people. We find an emphasis here, then, on a libertarian micro-politics and micro-ethics: as with thinkers like Étienne de la Boétie, Foucault and Stirner, Landauer shows us that the problem of 'voluntary servitude' – the state or political domination as a way of thinking and as a mode of relating to others – must be overcome in our heads and hearts before it can be overcome as an external institution; or rather, that the two processes would be concurrent. This suggests a utopianism of the immediate, of the here and now – one that builds on the possibilities of community that already exist, and yet whose ways of life presuppose what is non-existent or not yet existent.[38]

This 'micro-political' understanding provides us with an alternative, and I think more fruitful, way of thinking about utopia than that of scientific utopianism, in which the rational society of the future emerges as the inevitable product of the grand narrative of human liberation. However, this utopianism of the present should not be considered as an abandonment of politics, as if to imagine that the construction of autonomous communities and ways of life means that we can give up on the idea of politically confronting or contesting the existing order. The two must go together. Utopianism, while it is a means of escaping from the mental confines of the current order, should not be seen as a means of escaping from the responsibilities of political engagement. Indeed, we could say that a utopianism of the 'here and now' is also present in concrete forms of resistance to domination. For instance, to disrupt border control activities and to campaign for the rights of 'illegal' migrants is already a utopian act, because in such acts is presupposed the idea of a society of free circulation, without the tyranny of borders. So we must find ways of thinking about utopia that expresses both the desire for alternative forms of existence and the need to confront politically the dominations of the present.

CONCLUSION

In this chapter, I have further elaborated a politics and ethics of postanarchism through an engagement in debates with contemporary anarchist thinkers. I have shown that there is a continuity at an ontological and epistemological level, between classical anarchism and contemporary anarchist thinkers such as Bookchin and Zerzan, despite their many important differences. Furthermore, I have shown that if anarchism is to remain relevant to radical political struggles today, it must construct new understandings of politics, ethics, subjectivity and utopia which are not grounded in essentialist or rationalist ontologies, and which eschew the guarantees of the dialectic. In this sense, we should think about (post)anarchism in terms of utopian moments of disruption and contingency, rather than the unfolding of a rational project of social fulfilment. Chapter 6 will explore the ways in which a politics of postanarchism can be applied to contemporary radical struggles and issues today.

Notes

1 Here I refer not only to my own work, but also to that of other poststructuralist-inspired anarchist thinkers, such as Todd May and Lewis Call. See, respectively, *The Political Philosophy of Poststructuralist Anarchism* (Philadelphia, PA: Penn State Press, 1994); and *Postmodern Anarchism* (Lanham, MD: Lexington Books, 2003).

2 Other anarchist thinkers, however, have recognised the importance of poststructuralist theory for renewing anarchism. See for instance, Day's *Gramsci is Dead*. See also David Morland's essay, 'Anti-capitalism and poststructuralist anarchism', in *Changing Anarchism: Anarchist Theory and Practice in a Global Age*, Jonathan Purkis and James Bowen (ed.)) Manchester: Manchester University Press, 2004), pp. 23–54

3 Murray Bookchin, *Social Anarchism or Lifestyle Anarchism: an Unbridgeable Chasm* (San Francisco, CA: AK Press, 1995).

4 Here Bookchin asserts the slogan from the First International: 'No rights without duties, no duties without rights', sounding almost like a slogan for New Labour. (*Social Anarchism or Lifestyle Anarchism*, pp. 51–2).

5 See Bookchin, 'Listen Marxist!', *Post-Scarcity Anarchism*.

6 A similar point has been made by Simon Critchley, whose notion of 'anarchic metapolitics' embodies an ethics of responsibility: 'The conception of anarchism that I seek to defend, and which I think is what we find on the ground in activist practice, is not so much organized around freedom as around *responsibility*, an infinite responsibility that arises in relation to a situation of injustice.' *Infinitely Demanding*, p. 93

7 Bakunin, *Political Philosophy*, p. 270.

8 See Marx and Engels, 'The Communist Manifesto', pp. 485–6.

9 Michel Foucault, *Discipline and Punish: The Birth of the Prison*, trans. Alan Sheridan (London: Penguin, 1991).

10 See Bob Black, *Anarchy after Leftism* (Colombia, MO: CAL Press, 1997), pp. 144–50

11 Murray Bookchin, *The Ecology of Freedom: the Emergence and Dissolution of Hierarchy* Paolo Alto, CA: Cheshire Books, 1982), p. 31.

12 Bookchin, *The Ecology of Freedom*, p. 32.

13 See Murray Bookchin, *The Philosophy of Social Ecology: Essays on Dialectical Naturalism* (Montreal: Black Rose Books, 1990), p. 28.

14 Bookchin, *The Ecology of Freedom*, p. 37.

15 Bakunin, *Political Philosophy*, p. 94

16 Stirner, *The Ego and its Own*, p. 40.

17 Laclau and Mouffe, *Hegemony and Socialist Strategy*, p. 127.

18 See Jacques Rancière, *Disagreement: Politics and Philosophy*, trans. Julie Rose (Minneapolis, MN: University of Minnesota Press, 1999).

19 See Jacques Rancière, *The Politics of Aesthetics: the Distribution of the Sensible*, trans. Gabriel Rockhill (New York: Continuum, 2004).

20 Murray Bookchin, *From Urbanization to Cities: Towards a New Politics of Citizenship* (London: Cassell, 1995), p. 60.

21 See Bookchin, *From Urbanization to Cities*, pp. 254–5.

22 Jacques Rancière, 'Democracy, anarchism and radical politics today: An interview with Jacques Rancière', conducted by Todd May, Benjamin Noys and Saul Newman, trans. John Lechte, *Anarchist Studies*, 16(2), 2008, pp. 173–85 at 176–7.

23 See John Zerzan, *Future Primitive and Other Essays* (New York: Autonomedia, 1994).

24 See Zerzan, *Future Primitive*, p. 108.

25 See Zerzan, 'Language: Origin and Meaning', *Elements of Refusal* (Columbia, MO: CAL Press, 1999).

26 Zerzan, *Future Primitive*, p. 117.

27 Zerzan, *Future Primitive*, p. 29.

28 Zerzan, *Future Primitive*, p. 45.

29 A similar point is made by John Holloway, who sees negativity as the basis for a refusal of capitalism. While he retains the concept of alienation as characteristic of capitalism, he sees it as an operation which denies, not the original essence of the subject, but rather the subject's potentiality – a humanity to come, not a humanity to be recovered: 'Not a lost humanity, nor an existing humanity, but a humanity to be created.' See *Change the World Without Taking Power: the Meaning of Revolution Today* (London: Pluto, 2002), p. 152.

30 See Jacques Lacan, 'A theoretical introduction to the functions of psychoanalysis in criminology', *Journal for the Psychoanalysis of Culture and Society (JPCS)*, 1(2), 1996, pp. 13–25 at 15.

31 See Jacques Lacan, 'Kant with Sade', *October*, 51, 1989.

32 See Benjamin Franks, 'Postanarchism and Meta-ethics', *Anarchist Studies*, 16(2), 2008 pp. 135–53 at 148.

33 See Stirner, *The Ego and its Own*, pp. 45–6.

34 Stirner, *The Ego and Its Own*, p. 122.

35 See Franks, 'Postanarchism and Meta-ethics', p. 147.

36 Foucault, 'The Ethics of the Concern of the Self as a Practice of Freedom',
    pp. 282–3.
37 Gustav Landauer, quoted in Martin Buber, *Paths in Utopia* (New York:
    Syracuse University Press, 1996), p. 47.
38 We find a similar trope in Hakim Bey's notion of the 'Temporary Auto-
    nomous Zone': heterotopic spaces which exist in the present, or which can
    be created in the present, in which alternative, libertarian and non-statist
    forms of existence can be imagined. See *T.A.Z: the Temporary Autonomous
    Zone, Ontological Anarchy and Poetic Terrorism* (Autonomedia, 1991).

Chapter 6

CONCLUSION: POSTANARCHISM AND RADICAL POLITICS TODAY

In Chapter 5 I suggested that postanarchism occupies a certain utopian terrain. However, this was to be thought of as a *political* utopia, a utopia of the here and now; a utopianism that is deeply engaged in political struggles rather than retreating into passivity. In other words, it is important to think of the inevitable utopian dimension of radical politics in terms of action rather than stasis, engagement rather than escape; as a certain political space of insurgency and contestation through which the sovereignty of the existing order is confronted in the name of something other. The central challenge of this book has been to think politics outside the state – to explore the constituent principles and ethical contours of a political space which seeks autonomy from the order of the state. However, the desire for autonomy, which I see as the horizon of radical political struggles today, cannot be realised in any meaningful sense in the form of apolitical separatism, as a retreat from the world of struggle and contestation. The exodus from Empire that Hardt and Negri speak of will inevitably involve an active resistance to domination. The struggle for an outside, for another world, will always be the work of politics, and will involve a contestation with the limits of this world. We should think of autonomy, then, as an open-ended project – as something constructed through ongoing practices of opposition and democratisation.

The aim of this chapter is to chart the contours of the terrain of radical politics today: to briefly explore emerging forms of resistance to globalised capitalism and state domination, as well as to survey the threats and challenges that these movements of resistance face. My central contention is that an insurgent political space has already emerged, characterised by new and experimental forms of political practice and organisation that are anarchistic in orientation, although perhaps not consciously so. This observation is, of course, nothing new: for instance, much has been said already about the decentralised, democratic and non-authoritarian structures and practices involved in what is broadly termed the global anti-capitalist movement.[1] However, my aim here will be to show how these newly emergent radical struggles and movements can allow us to reflect on the limits of the political today. My suggestion is that we have reached a certain impasse in contemporary politics – a certain crisis of legitimacy in established political institutions and forms of democratic representation. The era of what has been termed by Rancière and others, 'post-politics', is upon us. This is a time in which the political domain, which used to be characterised by an identifiable ideological opposition between Left and Right, has been replaced by a technocratic rationality of government, constituted around the (now rather shaky) neoliberal economic consensus.

However, the time of 'post-politics' should not be greeted with pessimism but, rather, with a certain optimism: while the absolute nihilism at the heart of modern parliamentary politics is being ruthlessly exposed in, for instance, the embarrassing scandal over MPs' expenses in the United Kingdom, there are – and have been for some time – radical political movements and diverse struggles emerging on a global scale, in which new and more innovative forms of democratic life are being proposed and experimented with. We need only to shift our gaze to this alternative and dissenting world to see that this is not the era of post-politics at all, but rather one of intense politicisation.

At the same time, we should not be overly sanguine about the inevitability of radical social transformation, of global emancipation. Even though the current economic crisis is pointing to the very limits of capitalism – or at least of a particular hegemonic form of it – we cannot be certain about what forms of politics will come to dominate the contemporary horizon. We do not necessarily see signs of the immanent revolution of the multitude appearing everywhere. Indeed, one of the central aims of this book has been to question the idea of a pure social revolution that is determined by organically embedded principles, laws of science, the movement of historical forces or developments in the mode of production. The revolution – if we can still speak in those terms, as a singular event – is not immanent or inevitable; nor is it driven by a dialectical unfolding of natural or rational forces. Moreover, rather than thinking of a strict moral division between the social and political principle, as proposed by the classical anarchists, I have argued that it is more productive to highlight the antagonism that exists between politics and the state. The sovereign state is the order of de-politicisation: it is the principle of stabilisation and naturalisation, through which political conflicts are incorporated, sanitised, made safe or repressed; it is a certain forgetting of the antagonisms at the base of its sovereign foundations – a forgetting, as Foucault would say, of the blood congealed on the codes of law. Instead, I have argued that the political is the constitutive space *between* society and the state; and it is in this space that the current struggles against global capitalism and state authoritarianism must be situated.

This conceptualisation does not mean, though, that we cannot envisage a future transcendence of state authority; it does not mean that radical struggles are always caught in this in-between moment in the shadow of the state. Indeed, I would argue that the very existence and proliferation of such struggles, movements and autonomous communities already presupposes a certain dissolution or at least weakening, of the principle of state sovereignty. To situate the political in the space between society and the state has two functions. It points, first, to a rupturing of existing social relations, identities and roles, a certain moment of 'dis-identification' that I have spoken of before (in other words politics must signify a disruption or break with the idea of an established social order). Secondly, the positioning of the political in this interstitial space between two orders (society and the state) is a way of emphasising that the tasks of radical politics are not reducible to the overthrowing of state power; that even this revolutionary aim which was central to classical anarchist and, in a different sense, Leninist, politics is considerably more complicated and difficult to conceive now than it was a century or so ago. There is no more Winter Palace to storm, and radical politics is confronted with the problem of analysing, mapping and contesting forms of power that are more deterritorialised. The sovereign state continues to exist – indeed, its power has expanded rather than contracted – but its operation must be considered as part of a more dispersed and differentiated network of power. Moreover, as Foucault pointed out, the revolutionary seizure or even destruction of the state does not solve the problem of power.[2] The focus on the autonomy of the political highlights, then, the ongoing need to interrogate relations of power and to invent new practices of freedom. As I suggested in Chapter 5, the state should be thought of not simply as a series of institutions and structures of power, but as a certain authoritarian relationship, a particular way of thinking and structuring our lives – and so the idea of a politics of autonomy from the state involves the development of alternative non-authoritarian relationships, political practices, ways of thinking and modes of living.

So this is how we should think about the possibilities of radical politics today: no longer as laying the ground for a revolutionary event or a single, unified moment of global emancipation, but rather as a series of struggles, movements and communities whose existence is often fragile, whose practices are experimental, tentative and localised and whose continuity is by no means guaranteed. Nevertheless, they represent moments of potential rupture with the global order of power, and they embody – in their very singularity – the possibility of an alternative.

THE ORDER OF POWER: SECURITY, BORDERS, BIOPOLITICS

Radical politics is nevertheless confronted today by formidable forms of power. As if in anticipation of future insurgencies, the power of the state has exponentially increased in recent years. Securitisation becomes the dominant paradigm of the state; the matrix for an unprecedented deployment of strategies and technologies of control, surveillance and pre-emption, and for a permanent war-like mobilisation. The continual blurring of different forms of dissidence and protest into the idea of a threat to state security – climate change and anti-war protestors and activists being arrested under anti-terrorist powers, for example – suggests that the so-called war on terrorism has as its target all those who dissent from the state-capitalist order. At the same time, however, we should see this logic of securitisation and exception as a reaction to a certain crisis in the symbolic order of the nation-state under conditions of capitalist globalisation. The nation-state as the container of sovereignty is less certain; its boundaries and identity are less clearly delineated. Security, therefore, becomes a way for sovereignty to re-articulate itself in this more fluid global order. Through mechanisms of security, state power spills out beyond its own borders, constructing networks of surveillance, incarceration, control and war making that are no longer strictly determined by national boundaries. Prisons that are not prisons but camps, wars are no longer wars but 'policing' operations; global networks of surveillance and information-sharing – we are in the midst of, as Agamben would put it, a *zone of indistinction*,[3] in which national sovereignty blurs into global security while at the same time reifying and fetishising existing borders, and erecting new ones everywhere.

These developments open up two important sites for contestation. First, the logic of security itself, which has become so ubiquitous and omnipresent today, has to be seen as mechanism of de-politicisation: it is way of imposing a certain order on social reality which is self-legitimising and beyond question; it is an ideology that authorises the infinite accumulation of state power.[4] Moreover, as Foucault showed, the idea of security – as it functioned in liberal discourses of government in the eighteenth century – has become coextensive with the idea of freedom itself.[5] Today we have come to think of freedom only as strictly circumscribed by security; freedom and security become part of a binary, in which the former cannot be imagined without the latter, and in which the former always gives way to the exigencies and prerogatives imposed by the latter. The liberal idea of an appropriate balance between security and liberty is an illusion. The only vision the security paradigm offers us – with its pernicious technologies and its perverse logic which grips us in a double bind – is an empty, controlled, over-exposed landscape from which all hope of emancipation has faded, and where all we have left to do is obsessively measure the risks posed to our lives from the ever-present spectre of catastrophe. The security paradigm intensifies a micro-politics of fear, producing a kind of generalised neurosis.[6] It is against this state fantasy of security, and the affect of fear and despair that it produces, that radical politics must stake out its ground. It must reassert the hope of emancipation and affirm the risk of politics. This involves more than clawing back lost liberties, but rather inventing a new language of freedom that is no longer conditioned by security. Freedom must be discovered *beyond* security, and this can be achieved only through practices of political contestation, through forms of resistance, through modes of collective indiscipline and disobedience. For instance, the refusal and subversion of surveillance, and even the surveillance of surveillance,[7] become part of a new language of resistance that expresses the desire for a life that no longer seeks to be 'secured'.

Secondly, the question of borders emerges as one of the focal points for radical political struggles today. The symbolic crisis of the nation-state leads not to the erosion of borders but rather to their mobility, fluidity and ubiquity. Rather than the border disappearing, it appears everywhere, both internally and externally, intersecting with a vicious racist and anti-immigrant politics. Balibar refers to the polysemic and heterogeneous nature of borders: the fact that borders are experienced in different ways by different people, depending on race, nationality, social class and so on; and the fact that *some borders are no longer situated at the borders at all*, in the geographical-politico-administrative sense of the term'.[8] Here we might think of off-shore detention sites and processing centres for 'illegal' migrants: localities, 'heterotopias' of domination which find their strange counterpart in internalised borders – gated communities with elaborate security systems, or police blockades and security cordons at demonstrations; or the deterritorialised European border control and surveillance zones authorised by the Schengen Convention, borders which can be arbitrarily tightened or relaxed. Indeed, the border – symbolised by the infamous Israeli 'security fence' or the wall being constructed along the US–Mexico border – has become the most striking feature of a global order that claims to be about the free circulation of goods and people.

However, it is in contesting and disrupting these border control measures, in opposing practices of detention, or in fighting for the rights of 'illegal' migrants, that various activist groups and networks such as No Borders have highlighted this central contradiction and potential fault line in global state capitalism. Power today consists in the control and surveillance of movement – both internally and externally – and the mobilisation of borders. By asserting the right to move, to cross borders and territories freely, activist groups attempt to disrupt this deployment of power, thus calling into question the very sovereignty of the state. Moreover, the figure of the refugee (or illegal migrant) – the figure whom Arendt described as not even having the right to have rights because he does not belong to the political order of the state – embodies, I would argue, without wanting to diminish the extent of his or her suffering and vulnerability, alternative sites of politics; the possibility of a new postnational space from which radical demands can be made, and in which new collective political identities can be constructed.[9]

These various forms of power, and the struggles that have emerged against them, take place on the threshold of biopolitics. Without wanting to entirely buy into Hardt's and Negri's thesis about the total subsumption of life by capitalism, it is nevertheless apparent that the control, regulation and manipulation of life itself, down to its biological substratum, is – and has been for some time – the ultimate horizon of the state and capitalism. The conception of life as an organism whose desires are predictable and biologically determined, whose unseen dreams and dangerous pathologies can be gazed upon and whose behaviours can be controlled and manipulated through the application of biomedical and surveillance technologies – has become the overwhelming fantasy of our time.[10] Moreover, as Roberto Esposito argues, biopolitics can be understood only through a paradigm of 'immunisation', in which, just as the biological organism seeks to protect itself from contaminants, the political body seeks to secure itself against the outsiders that threaten its integrity[11] – accounting for the proliferation of figures of the enemy today, whether it be the terrorist, Muslim, illegal immigrant or criminal.

Radical politics today must come to terms with this logic of biopolitics and immunisation, and find ways of contesting its terms and coordinates. At the end of his lecture series *Society must be Defended*, in which he explores the genesis of biopower in the eighteenth century, showing how it intersected with eugenics, biologism and state racism in the nineteenth and twentieth centuries, Foucault charges (albeit somewhat unfairly) the socialist tradition – including anarchism – with a neglect of the problem of biopolitics and, thus, a hidden complicity with discourses of racism.[12] What might, then, an anarchist critique of biopolitics be? To formulate a conception of political community that does not seek to immunise itself against the other; and to invent modes of life and practices of freedom that are unpredictable and, thus, are resistant to discipline, remain the central problems for radical politics. Despite its early scientism – a scientism that was never, in any case, as absolute as that of Marxism – I would say that anarchism, with its focus on liberty and equality beyond the state, on its ethical, even spiritual dimension,[13] is best equipped to formulate notions of politics and subjectivity that exceed the grasp of biopolitics.

THINKING THE OUTSIDE

The politics of resistance to the biopolitical order of state capitalism suggests the possibility of an outside to this order; of points of rupture and anteriority in which we see a glimpse of alternative ways of life. While we must acknowledge the pervasiveness of this order and its formidable power, we should at the same time be able to discern its cracks, vulnerabilities and inconsistencies. Massimo de Angelis makes the important point – taking a certain distance from Hardt and Negri

– that the order confronted by radical political struggles today is not complete or all-encompassing: it is, on the contrary, subject to tensions, discontinuities and moments of rupture which leave openings for alternative social relationships to emerge. Indeed, he argues that there is more to our world than capitalism; that we *already* engage in social relationships that are not completely subsumed by capitalism, although their autonomy is always threatened by it.[14] It is a matter, then, of expanding the realm of these alternative practices, relationships and 'value struggles' – of expanding the dimension of what de Angelis calls the commons, in opposition to the colonising tendencies of capitalism. We should also recognise, with Foucault, the reversibility of power relationships, even those that seem so overwhelming; that while power might be ubiquitous, it is also characterised by instabilities and moments of resistance.

We can see instances of this outside in diverse struggle and movements of resistance appearing around the world. One might think here, for instance, of indigenous movements like the Zapatistas in the Chiapas region in Mexico,[15] or the Landless (Sem Terra) movement in Brazil, where there can be found innovative experiments in land sharing, communal grass-roots organisation, direct action and democratic decision making.[16] We find such moments of resistance in the numerous examples of people in poor countries fighting for local control over resources and to preserve their natural environment, in opposition to the privatising, neoliberal measures imposed by the state and multinational companies: for instance, the peasant insurgency mobilised against the proposed land seizure by a car company in West Bengal; or Amazonian tribes in Peru against the incursions of mining and logging companies; or poor farmers engaged in the sabotage of GM crops; or militant movements in the Niger Delta taking direct, sometimes violent action against Western oil corporations; or factory occupations by workers in countries in the global North.[17] One could also point to the emergence of transnational networks which try to develop links between activists around the world, as well as the numerous social centres, independent media centres, even squats and autonomous communes.[18] In all these various movements and struggles, despite their considerable differences, we see the attempt to construct autonomous political spaces – spaces defined by direct action, dissent and alternative social, political and economic relationships. Moreover, these various movements and identities articulate global issues and concerns – such as environmental devastation, the injustices of neoliberal economics, the excesses of corporate power and the intolerable nature of state violence and domination – through local struggles, while at the same time seeking to develop links of solidarity with other groups.[19]

MOVEMENT AND ORGANISATION

The construction of an outside to state capitalism, of an alternative series of political, social and economic spaces, requires some form of organisation. The idea of political organisation is not hostile to notions of autonomy and radical spontaneity, but on the contrary, is their very condition of realisation – a paradox that was recognised by Bakunin, who dreamt of creating an international organisation of workers' associations and peasants: 'But States do not crumble by themselves; they are overthrown by a universal international social organization.'[20] While, as I have said, we should question the idea of a grand overturning of state power, it is perhaps time to revisit Bakunin's dream of a transnational mass organisation. Today, such an organisation would be in the form of a movement rather than a party. It would be aimed at building alliances between people and activist groups around the world, rather than seizing state power. It would, moreover, take the form of a network or series of networks which allowed people to speak for themselves, rather than representing their interests to the formal channels of power. The central challenge of radical politics today, as I see it, is to propose forms of transnational organisation that are non-authoritarian, and which invent new modes of non-representative or direct democratic politics.

Indeed, the possibility of such an organisation has already been pre-figured, albeit in a nascent and imperfect form, in what has been broadly termed the Global Justice Movement, a movement that, although often fragmented, has managed at various moments to mobilise masses of people around the world in opposition to capitalist globalisation, and to articulate a certain common ground between different activist groups, interests and struggles.[21] Moreover, this movement – or 'movement of movements' – has displayed a new form of radical politics, one that is closer to anarchism than Marxism. What is remarkable about this movement has been not only its transnational scope, but also the way in which it manages to embody a certain vision of a global mass: a mass which, while being mobilised around an opposition to global capitalism, is no longer strictly identified with specific class interests, or even with any sort of identity politics as such. Indeed, this might be more accurately described as a form of 'post-identity' politics. Furthermore, the emphasis of this anti-capitalist politics has been on grass-roots mobilisations and participatory decision making rather than centralised leadership. The tactics adopted have usually been those of direct action – not only mass protests and creative forms of civil disobedience and non-violent confrontation, but also sabotage, the occupation of spaces (the Temporary Autonomous Zone) and other forms of subversion – rather than formal political representation. Importantly, then, while some activist groups and NGOs are engaged in political lobbying, the general focus of anti-capitalist movements has been on constructing forms of politics that are outside the state and which contest its hegemony from multiple points.

Let us take a slight risk here and call this an anarchist or, indeed, postanarchist form of politics. This is not because anarchist groups have been prominent in the movement – indeed, most activists would not necessarily identify themselves as anarchists, although many would acknowledge a certain affinity with anarchism[22] – but rather because its tactics, organisational principles and forms of mobilisation display a clear proximity to the anti-authoritarian and decentralist political ethos of anarchism. There is what might be termed an 'unconscious' anarchism that distinguishes anti-capitalist politics today: this is an anarchism that takes the form not so much of a coherent ideology or identity – the movement has also been influenced by ecologism, Marxism, indigenous and post-colonial perspectives, feminism and so on – but rather of a certain way of understanding and practising politics that seeks autonomy from the state, and that does not aim at the conquest of power but at its decentralisation and democratisation.

What is central here is the critique of the formal politics of representative democracy. Indeed, these movements of resistance might be seen in part as a response to the crisis of legitimacy in contemporary democracy. The chasm between ordinary people and political elites has never seemed wider or more stark. Therefore, the appearance of social movements on a global scale suggests the attempt to constitute an alternative political space, a new body politic: no longer the body of obedient citizens who respect the formal democratic mandate of power, but rather a rebellious, dissenting body – citizens who do not obey and who refuse to recognise the authority of those who represent them, thus breaking the bond between the subject and the state. Therefore, the anti-capitalist movement not only challenges the hegemony of neoliberal capitalism, but also the symbolic claim of the 'democratic' state to speak for its citizens. Radical movements today are not post- or anti-democratic, however: they simply find the current forms of democracy on offer inadequate, and seek to open the political space to alternative and more democratic modes of democracy. I shall return to this point later.

So we should regard contemporary anti-capitalist struggles and movements as constructing an alternative political space outside the established order of the 'democratic' state, as well as providing a basis for new non-authoritarian forms of political organisation? Indeed, if anarchism today takes the form of a movement, this would be a movement which radically opposes the idea of an external vanguard mobilising and leading the masses in a strategic way; rather, it would be self-organised and internal to the masses. Furthermore, as Agamben argues, the idea of the movement, following Aristotle's conceptualisation, embodies a certain lack and open-endedness: 'movement is an unfinished act, without telos, which means that movement keeps an essential relation with a privation, an absence of telos . . . The movement is the indefiniteness and imperfection of every politics. It always leaves a residue.'[23] This would be a way of understanding the notion of a radical movement in postanarchist terms, as embodying a certain lack and imperfection – a constitutive openness to the indeterminacy of the future – rather than the more prescriptive, disciplined and centralised forms of politics that characterise the vanguard party. The Jacobin temptation, fetishised by people like Badiou and Žižek, should be resisted.[24] It is here that Bakunin's warning against a revolution by decree becomes particularly pertinent. He argues that revolutions in the past have failed because they have sought to *impose* themselves on the masses in an authoritarian way, and this has led only to a narrowing and circumscription of revolutionary activity, and thus, to a stirring up of a rebellious hostility among the people against the revolutionary leadership. This might be symbolised, for instance, in the revolt of the Kronstadt sailors in 1921 against the authoritarian consolidation of the Revolution by the Bolsheviks. As Bakunin argues, it is impossible for the revolutionary party to fully understand the desires and interests of the people, 'just as it is impossible for the largest and most powerful sea-going vessel to measure the depths and expanse of the ocean'. This great, vast and sometimes enigmatic desire of the people cannot be adequately expressed in revolutionary decrees. That is why, as Bakunin says,

> *They* [revolutionary authorities] *must not do it themselves, by revolutionary decrees, by imposing this task on the masses; rather their aim should be that of provoking the masses to action. They must not try to impose upon the masses any organization whatever, but rather they should induce the people to set up autonomous organizations.*[25] (Italics are Bakunin's.)

This is exactly how we should approach the question of political organisation: it should be constituted around a refusal of revolutionary vanguardism and authoritarianism – instead fostering people's self-organisation. It should also retain a certain 'modesty', a certain prudence in attempting to articulate the desires of the people. Perhaps the Promethean politics of radical transformation ought to be tempered by a certain caution; while the idea of an event that transforms existing social structures and forms is an important one for radical politics, there must at the same time be a certain *attentiveness* to the details of a situation, and a certain respect for the desires, sensibilities, knowledge and traditions of ordinary people.[26] Radical transformation – and here we recall Bakunin's 'urge to destroy', which for him was also a creative urge – should be accompanied by a sensitivity to what exists, and a desire to conserve what needs to be conserved.

THE DEMOCRATIC ANARCHY-TO-COME

This way of thinking about political organisation as open-ended, as resistant to hierarchy and authoritarianism, and as embodying a certain care for the existent, even while it seeks to create what does not yet exist, points to a certain understanding of democracy. As I have argued, contemporary movements of resistance to global capitalism reject democracy in its current form; yet, they retain the horizon of democracy, while seeking to democratise it. We must acknowledge, then, that democratic experimentation today is largely taking place outside the 'democratic' state. Indeed, we could even go as far as to say that a certain autonomy from the state today is the very condition of democracy – that to be democratic today is to be, in some senses, in opposition to the state.[27]

Moreover, I would suggest that there is a certain link between anarchism and democracy – a link which, however, is aporetic in the sense that while anarchism seeks to democratise democracy in the name of egalitarianism, it is nevertheless sensitive to the danger that democracy can pose to individual liberty and autonomy. That is why, for anarchists, democracy must be conditioned by an ethics of equal-liberty, where neither liberty is subordinate to equality, nor equality to liberty. Better yet, an anarchist approach to democracy would insist that democratic mechanisms promote both equality and liberty in equal measure.

One way of thinking through this aporia is with the notion of autonomy. Throughout this book, I have understood anarchism as a politics of autonomy; indeed, I have seen the project of autonomy as being the horizon for all radical politics. But we need to think more precisely about what autonomy means today. It has to mean more than simply carving out a space – a territorial or political space – beyond the sovereignty of existing state institutions, although this would obviously be a precondition of autonomous politics. To insist simply on an autonomous and self-determined space avoids the question of the shape of social and political relations within that space; autonomous spaces can be subject to the worst kinds of authoritarian, repressive and fundamentalist politics.[28] It is clear, then, that autonomy must refer not only to the independence from the state of a particular political and territorial space, but also to the internal micro-political constitution of that space, to the organisation of social, political and economic relationships within it. The collective organisation of social life within an independent community cannot come at the expense of individual freedom, but, on the contrary, should be seen as coextensive with it. Is it possible, then, to talk about a politics of autonomy without invoking the ideas of voluntarism and non-coercion as the basic principles for organising collective life? Is it possible to think of autonomous politics without invoking the idea of the free commune, which I see as being at the heart of the radical political imaginary?

This is where democracy becomes important as a way of organising life collectively and freely in autonomous spaces. However, here democracy should be understood not primarily as a mechanism for expressing a unified popular will, but rather as a way of pluralising this will – opening up within it different and even dissenting spaces and perspectives. The point here is that we cannot imagine a democratic community as an entirely unified, transparent and coherent space, governed by established procedures, rules and mechanisms; nor should we see it as the realisation of some essential being-in-common. Rather, we should see it as a kind of non-space of possibility – a democracy of singularities which is open to different articulations of equal-liberty. Moreover, the realisation of forms of democracy beyond the state imposes a certain ethical responsibility upon people themselves to resolve, through ongoing practices of negotiation, tensions that may arise between majorities and minorities – a responsibility that until now has been taken out of their hands by the state.

There is a certain resonance here with Derrida's idea of the democracy to come (*l'avenir* or of *the future*), in which we find the attempt to detach democracy from state sovereignty and to think it beyond its current limits. For Derrida, democracy is always in tension with sovereignty because it embodies a multiplicity of wills, a more-than-one, whereas sovereignty always affirms a point of unity and oneness and thus an arbitrary determination of power. What is central to democracy, moreover, is its own *perfectibility*. As Derrida says: 'we do not yet know what democracy will have meant nor what it is'.[29] The democratic promise always exceeds its current articulations and representations; it cannot be satisfied with a number of minimum conditions or be completely embodied in a certain regime. Indeed, all actually existing democracies are found to be inadequate, to never be democratic enough. Therefore, democracy always points to a horizon beyond, to the future; it is always 'to come'. This does not mean that we should give up on democracy, or see it as continually deferrable. On the contrary, it means we should never be satisfied with existing forms taken by democracy and should always be working towards a greater democratisation in the here and now; towards an ongoing articulation of democracy's im/possible promise of perfect liberty with perfect equality.

We should also see at the heart of democracy the desire for autonomy – the desire of people to freely determine their own conditions of existence and to live without government. This idea of self-government has always been central to the very ideal of democracy, even as democracy has until now often been no more than a system for justifying power. Indeed, in democracy we catch a glimpse of the contingency and instability of all political power, the sense in which political power often hangs by a thread, needing the continual symbolic legitimation of the people. In this sense, the complete withdrawal from state democratic procedures – the mass refusal to vote for instance[30] – might be the ultimate democratic act. So, perhaps we should also see the democracy to come as a release from voluntary servitude – in other words, the realisation that the political power that dominates us is ultimately of our own making, and that we can free ourselves from it by refusing to recognise its authority, thus loosening the subjective bond which ties us to power and dispelling the thraldom and dependency that power induces in us.[31] In this sense, the democracy to come should be supplemented with a libertarian micro-politics and ethics that aims at dislodging our psychic investments in power and authority through the invention of new practices of freedom.

Democracy today consists in the invention or re-invention of spaces, movements, ways of life, economic exchanges and political practices that resist the imprint of the state and which foster relations of equal-liberty. The struggles that take place today against capitalism and the state are democratic struggles. At the same time, however, we might sound a certain note of dissatisfaction with the term 'democracy'. We can echo Bakunin, who finds the term *democracy* 'not sufficient'.[32] As Derrida himself said, '[A]s a term it's [democracy] not sacred. I can, some day or other, say "No, it's not the right term. The situation allows or demands that we use another term. . ."'[33] It is the contention of this book that the situation is changing, and that the new forms of autonomous politics that are currently emerging demand the use of another term – *anarchism*.

CONCLUSION

Postanarchism is not a specific form of politics; it offers no formulas or prescriptions for change. It does not have the sovereign ambition of supplanting anarchism with a newer name. On the contrary, postanarchism is a celebration and revisitation of this most heretical form of radical (anti)politics. Indeed, so far from anarchism having been surpassed, the radical struggles for autonomy appearing today on the global terrain indicate that, on the contrary, the anarchist moment has finally arrived.

One of the central claims of this book has been that anarchism, despite, or rather *because* of, its marginalised position at the outer limits of political theory, has something important to say about the nature of the political. In a sense, anarchism might be seen as the anti-political underside of other, more mainstream forms of politics – their critical conscience and their wild unconscious. Anarchism's basic contention that equality, liberty and democracy can never be adequately realised under the shadow of state authority, reveals the hidden and disavowed truth, for instance, of liberalism and socialism.

This truth, however, is no longer hidden (although it is still disavowed), and the crumbling and fragmentation of these ideologies, shipwrecked on the craggy shores of state power, now brings anarchism to the forefront of our political imagination. There has been a certain paradigm shift in politics away from the state and formal representative institutions – which still exist but increasingly as empty vessels, without life – and towards movements. Here a new set of political challenges and questions emerges (about freedom beyond security, democracy beyond the state, politics beyond the party, economic organisation beyond capitalism, globalisation beyond borders, life beyond biopolitics) – questions that anarchism is best equipped to respond to with the originality and innovation that this new situation demands.

It is because anarchism has come to light in this unprecedented way, as the horizon of politics today, that we must rethink some of its classical foundations in ways that are at the same time faithful to its basic ethos of liberty, equality, anti-authoritarianism and solidarity. My argument has been that anarchism has something new to teach itself. Anarchism is animated by a living, breathing 'spirit' of anarchy that disturbs its static foundations and fixed identities. Postanarchism reveals this joyous moment of anarchy within anarchism, using this, moreover, to think the political and the ethical in new ways between the twin poles of politics and anti-politics.

Notes

1 See for instance Graeber's, 'The New Anarchists'. See also the literature on the global justice movement and transnational activism from people like Donatella della Porta (ed.), *The Global Justice Movement: Cross-national and Trans-national Perspectives* (Boulder, CO: Paradigm Publishers, 2007) and Sidney Tarrow, *The New Transnational Activism* (Cambridge: Cambridge University Press, 2005).
2 See Michel Foucault, 'Truth and Power': Interview (June 1976), *Power: Essential Works of Michel Foucault, 1954–1984, Vol. 3*, pp. 111–33.
3 See Giorgio Agamben, *Homo Sacer: Sovereign Power and Bare Life*, trans. Daniel Heller-Roazen (Stanford CA: Stanford University Press, 1998).

4 See Mark Neocleous, *Critique of Security* (Edinburgh: Edinburgh University Press, 2008).

5 Michel Foucault in Michel Senellart (ed.), *Security, Territory, Population: Lectures at the College de France 1977–1978* (Basingstoke: Palgrave Macmillan, 2007), p. 48.

6 See Engin F. Isin, 'The Neurotic Citizen', *Citizenship Studies*, 8(4), September 2004, pp. 217–35.

7 One noticeable feature of the anti-G20 protests in London in 2009 was the ubiquitous presence of cameras – not only were police photographing protestors, but protestors were photographing police in an interesting reversal of the panoptic power relationship. In Germany in 2007, thousands of people demonstrated against growing state powers of surveillance and information gathering; their slogan was 'Liberty instead of Fear – Stop the Surveillance Mania!' (see http://www.edri.org/edrigram/number5.18/liberty-instead-of-fear, accessed 26 May 2009). Furthermore, the use of masks to cover the faces of protestors and activists is more than simply a defensive gesture against police identification, but points to a new politics of invisibility, where invisibility and anonymity themselves become symbols for resistance.

8 Balibar, *Politics and the Other Scene*, p. 84.

9 Todd May has explored the activities of an Algerian illegal migrants rights network (CASS) in Montreal, who, in the face of unbearable pressure exerted by state authorities, managed to effectively mobilise a politics of resistance and opposition to the government's deportation policies. See 'Equality Among the Refugees: a Rancièrean view of Montréal's Sans-Status Algerians', *Anarchist Studies*, 16(2), 2008, pp. 121–34.

10 As Foucault pointed out, the enigma of biopolitics is that as an operation of power whose function is to make life live, it produces death on a vast scale in order to achieve this: the other side to biopolitics is thanatopolitics. We can thus see ethnic cleansing operations and genocides as the other side of our obsessions in the West with the preservation and regulation of biological health and well-being. See Foucault, *Society must be Defended*.

11 See Roberto Esposito, *Bios: Biopolitics and Philosophy*, trans. Timothy Campbell (Minneapolis, MN: University of Minnesota Press, 2008), p. 46.

12 See Foucault, *Society must be Defended*, pp. 262–3.

13 It is in imagining alternative, utopian approaches to life – a life that exceeds scientific measurement – that the 'spiritual anarchism' of thinkers like Martin Buber and Gustave Landauer becomes important here in a critique of biopolitics.

14 See Massimo De Angelis, *The Beginning of History: Value Struggles and Global Capital* (London: Pluto, 2007), p. 34.

15 See Mihalis Mentinis's study of Zapatista politics in *Zapatistas: the Chiapas Revolt and What it Means for Radical Politics* (London: Pluto Press, 2006).

16 See Simon Tormey's discussion of the non-representative democratic polit-
    ical practices of the Zapatistas in '"Not in my Name": Deleuze, Zapatismo
    and the Critique of Representation', *Parliamentary Affairs*, 2006.
17 The recent practice of 'boss-napping' by workers in France is a new form
    of direct action in response to job lay-offs.
18 See Tom Mertes (ed.), *A Movement of Movements: Is Another World Really
    Possible?* (London: Verso, 2004).
19 The Zapatistas, for example, have successfully used the Internet to com-
    municate and develop links with activists and NGOs in the global North,
    calling for global solidarity with their struggle against neoliberalism.
20 Bakunin, *Political Philosophy*, p. 375.
21 See Nicola Montagna, 'The Making of a Global Movement: Cycles of Protest
    and Scales of Action' (draft paper submitted to *Global Geography*, 2009).
22 See Mark Rupert's discussion of the influence of anarchism on the Global
    Justice Movement in 'Anti-Capitalist Convergence? Anarchism, Socialism
    and the Global Justice Movement', in Manfred Steger (ed.), *Rethinking
    Globalism* (Lanham, MD: Rowman & Littlefield, 2003), pp. 121–35.
23 Giorgio Agamben, 'Movement' (8 March 2005) Multitudes web: http://
    multitudes.samizdat.net/Movement.html.
24 See, for instance, Peter Hallward's 'The Politics of Prescription', *The South
    Atlantic Quarterly*, 104(4), Fall 2005, pp. 769–89.
25 Bakunin, *Political Philosophy*, p. 398.
26 I borrow this metaphor of the Prometheus who steals fire from Heaven
    but with caution, from Bruno Latour. In discussing the concept of design,
    Latour distances himself from the Promethean heroic attitude of revo-
    lutionary rupture: 'A second and perhaps more important implication of
    design is an attentiveness to *details* that is completely lacking in the heroic,
    Promethean, hubristic dream of action. "Go forward, break radically with
    the past and the consequences will take care of themselves!" That was the
    old way – to build, to construct, to destroy, to radically overhaul: "*Après moi
    le deluge!*"' This desire must be tempered, even, and especially, in the case
    of revolutionary politics: 'President Mao was right after all: the revolution
    has to always be revolutionised. What he did not anticipate is that the new
    'revolutionary energy' would be taken from the set of attitudes that are
    hard to come by in revolutionary movements: modesty, care, precautions,
    skills, crafts, meanings, attention to details, careful conservations, redesign,
    artificiality, and ever shifting transitory fashions. We have to be radically
    careful, or carefully radical. . .'. 'A Cautious Prometheus? A Few Steps
    Toward a Philosophy of Design (with Special Attention to Peter Sloterdijk)',
    Keynote lecture for the Networks of Design meeting of the Design History
    Society, Falmouth, Cornwall, 3 September 2008, available at: http://www.
    bruno-latour.fr/articles/article/112-DESIGN-CORNWALL.pdf.

27 We should recall an idea from the early writings of Marx, that democracy is something which exceeds and in some ways opposes the principle of the political state, in the sense that the political state – even a democratic political state – can only be a *particularity*, a particular expression or form of the existence of the people, while the principle of democracy itself unities the general and the particular: 'The French have interpreted this as meaning that in true democracy the *political state is annihilated*. This is correct insofar as the political state qua political state, as constitution, no longer passes for the whole.' 'Contribution to the Critique of Hegel's Philosophy of Law', p. 30.

28 Here Žižek makes an important critical point against a fashionable tendency among certain Leftists to glorify the 'liberated territories' controlled by Hezbollah in Lebanon, or Hamas in Gaza, simply because they constitute points of resistance to Israeli aggression and because they provide social services to the people who live in these territories. The question that should be posed, according to Žižek, is not whether these organisations provide social services – much needed as they are – but whether they provide emancipatory possibilities for women and workers, for instance. See Interview with Žižek: 'Divine Violence and Liberated Territories: SOFT TARGET talks with Slavoj Žižek' (Los Angeles, 14 March 2007), available at: http://www.softtargetsjournal.com/web/zizek.php (accessed 1 June 2009).

29 Jacques Derrida, *Rogues: Two Essays on Reason*, trans. Pascale-Anne Brault and Michel Naas (Stanford CA: Stanford University Press, 2005), p. 9

30 See Žižek's discussion of Jose Saramago's novel, *Seeing* (2006), in which the mass submission of blank ballots in a parliamentary election throws the system of power into crisis. *Violence: Six Sideways Reflections* (New York: Picador, 2008).

31 This notion of voluntary servitude derives from Etienne de la Boëtie, for whom the problem of politics is to understand how we become slaves by choice: 'I should like merely to understand how it happens that so many men, so many villages, so many cities, so many nations, sometimes suffer under a single tyrant who has no other power than the power they give him; who is able to harm them only to the extent to which they have the willingness to bear with him; who could do them absolutely no injury unless they preferred to put up with him rather than contradict him.' *The Politics of Obedience: the Discourse of Voluntary Servitude*, trans. H. Kurz (New York, Free Life Editions, 1975), p. 46.

32 Bakunin, *Political Philosophy*, p. 223.

33 Jacques Derrida, *Negotiations: Interventions and Interviews, 1971–2001*, ed. and trans. E. Rottenburg (Stanford, CA: Stanford University Press, 2002), p. 181.

BIBLIOGRAPHY

Abensour, Miguel, 'An-archy between Metapolitics and Politics', *Parallax*, 8(3), 2002, pp. 5–18.

Abensour, Miguel, *Democracy against the State: Marx and the Machiavellian Moment*, trans. Max Blechman and Martin Breaugh (Cambridge: Polity Press, 2011).

Abensour, Miguel, 'Persistent Utopia', *Constellations*, 15(3), 2008, pp. 406–21.

Agamben, Giorgio, *Homo Sacer: Sovereign Power and Bare Life*, trans. Daniel Heller-Roazen (Stanford CA: Stanford University Press, 1998).

Agamben, Giorgio, 'Movement' (8 March 2005) Multitudes web: http://multitudes.samizdat.net/Movement.html.

Anderson, Perry, 'Jottings on the Conjuncture', *New Left Review*, 48, November/December 2007, pp. 5–37.

Arendt, Hannah, *The Human Condition* (Chicago, IL: University of Chicago Press, 1958).

Badiou, Alain, *Ethics: An Essay on the Understanding of Evil*, trans. Peter Hallward (London: Verso, 2002).

Badiou, Alain, 'Beyond Formalisation': an interview with Alain Badiou, trans. Bruno Bosteels and Alberto Toscano, *Angelaki*, 8(2), August 2003, pp. 111–36.

Badiou, Alain, *Saint Paul: the Foundation of Universalism*, trans. R. Brassier (Stanford, CA: Stanford University Press, 2003).

Badiou, Alain, 'The Flux and the Party: In the Margins of Anti-Oedipus', *Polygraph*, 15/16, 2004, pp. 75–92.

Badiou, Alain, *Being and Event*, trans. Oliver Feltham (London: Continuum, 2005).

Badiou, Alain, *Metapolitics*, trans. Jason Barker (London: Verso, 2005).

Badiou, Alain, *Polemics*, trans. Steve Corcoran (London: Verso, 2006).

Badiou, Alain, *Logics of Worlds: Being and Event, 2*, trans. Alberto Toscano, (London: Continuum, 2009).

Bakunin, Mikhail, *Marxism, Freedom and the State*, trans. K. J. Kenafick (London: Freedom Press, 1984).

Bakunin, Mikhail, *Political Philosophy of Mikhail Bakunin: Scientific Anarchism*, G. P. Maximoff (ed.) (London: Free Press of Glencoe, 1953).

Balibar, Étienne, *Politics and the Other Scene*, trans. Christine Jones, James Swenson and Chris Turner (London: Verso, 2002).

Benjamin, Walter, *Selected Writings, Vol. 1*, Marcus Bullock and Michael W. Jennings (eds) (Cambridge, MA: The Belknap Press of Harvard University Press, 1999).

Bensaid, Daniel, 'On a recent book by John Holloway', *Historical Materialism*, 13(4), 2005, pp. 169–92.

Bertolo, Amedeo, 'Democracy and Beyond', *Democracy & Nature*, 5(2), 1999, pp. 311–23.

Bey, Hakim, *Immediatism* (San Francisco, CA: AK Press, 1994).

Bey, Hakim, *T.A.Z: the Temporary Autonomous Zone, Ontological Anarchy and Poetic Terrorism*, Autonomedia, 1991.

Black, Bob, *Anarchy after Leftism* (Colombia, MO: CAL Press, 1997).

Bobbio, Norberto, *Democracy and Dictatorship: the Nature and Limits of State Power*, trans. P. Kennealy (Cambridge: Polity Press, 1989).

Bookchin, Murray, *From Urbanization to Cities: Towards a New Politics of Citizenship* (London: Cassell, 1995).

Bookchin, Murray, *Social Anarchism or Lifestyle Anarchism: an Unbridgeable Chasm* (San Francisco, CA: AK Press, 1995).

Bookchin, Murray, *The Ecology of Freedom: The Emergence and Dissolution of Hierarchy* (Paolo Alto, CA: Cheshire Books, 1982).

Bookchin, Murray, *Post-Scarcity Anarchism* (London: Wildwood House, 1974).

Bookchin, Murray, *The Philosophy of Social Ecology: Essays on Dialectical Naturalism* (Montreal: Black Rose Books, 1990).

Borch-Jacobsen, Mikkel, *The Freudian Subject*, trans. Catherine Porter (Stanford, CA: Stanford University Press, 1988).

Bosteels, Bruno, 'Post-Maoism: Badiou and Politics', *Positions*, 13(3), 2005, pp. 575–634.

Brockway, Fenner, *Britain's First Socialists: the Levellers, Agitators and Diggers of the English Revolution* (London: Quartet Books, 1983).

Brown, Wendy, *States of Injury: Power and Freedom in late Modernity* (Princeton, NJ: Princeton University Press, 2005).

Buber, Martin, *Paths in Utopia* (New York: Syracuse University Press, 1996).

Butler, Judith, *The Psychic Life of Power: Theories in Subjection* (Stanford, CA: Stanford University Press, 1997).

Caffentzis, George, 'The End of Work or the Renaissance of Slavery? A Critique of Rifkin and Negri' (Spring 1998), available at: http://www.korotonomedya.net/otonomi/caffentzis.html.

Call, Lewis, *Postmodern Anarchism* (Lanham, MD: Lexington Books, 2003).

Carter, Alan, 'Outline of an Anarchist Theory of History', in David Goodway (ed.) *For Anarchism: History, Theory and Practice* (London: Routledge, 1989), pp. 176–97.

Clark, Samuel, *Living without Domination: the Possibility of an Anarchist Utopia* (Farnham: Ashgate, 2007).

Crisso and Odoteo , 'Barbarians: the Disordered Insurgence', available at: http://www.geocities.com/kk_abacus/ioaa/barbarians.html.

Critchley, Simon, *Infinitely Demanding: Ethics of Commitment, Politics of Resistance* (London: Verso, 2007).

Crouch, Colin, *Post-Democracy* (Cambridge: Polity Press, 2004).

Day, Richard J. F., *Gramsci is Dead: Anarchist Currents in the Newest Social Movements* (London: Pluto Press, 2005).

De Angelis, Massimo, *The Beginning of History: Value Struggles and Global Capital* (London: Pluto, 2007).

Debord, Guy, *The Society of the Spectacle*, trans. Donald Nicholson-Smith (New York: Zone Books, 1995).

Deleuze, Gilles, *Difference and Repetition*, trans. Paul Patton (London: Continuum, 2001).

Deleuze, Gilles and Claire Parnet (eds), *Dialogues*, trans. Hugh Tomlinson (New York: Columbia University Press, 1987).

Deleuze, Gilles and Felix Guattari, *Anti-Oedipus: Capitalism and Schizophrenia*, trans. Robert Hurley (London: Continuum, 2004).

Deleuze, Gilles and Felix Guattari, *A Thousand Plateaus: Capitalism and Schizophrenia*, trans. Brian Massumi (London: Continuum, 2004).

della Porta, Donatella (ed.), *The Global Justice Movement: Cross-national and Trans-national Perspectives* (Boulder, CO: Paradigm Publishers, 2007).

Derrida, Jacques, *Positions*, trans. Alan Bass (Chicago, IL: University of Chicago Press, 1971).

Derrida, Jacques, *Negotiations: Interventions and Interviews, 1971–2001*, ed. and trans. E. Rottenburg (Stanford, CA: Stanford University Press, 2002).

Derrida, Jacques, *Rogues: Two Essays on Reason*, trans. Pascale-Anne Brault and Michel Naas (Stanford CA: Stanford University Press, 2005).

Dirlik, Arif, *Anarchists in the Chinese Revolution* (Berkeley, CA: University of California Press, 1993).

Engels, Friedrich, *The German Revolutions: the Peasant War in Germany* (Chicago, IL: University of Chicago Press, 1967).

Esposito, Roberto, *Bios: Biopolitics and Philosophy*, trans. Timothy Campbell (Minneapolis: University of Minnesota Press, 2008).

Feyerabend, Paul, *Against Method* (London: Verso, 1993).

Foucault, Michel, *The History of Sexuality VI: Introduction*, trans. R. Hunter (New York: Vintage Books, 1978).

Foucault, Michel, 'Governmentality', *The Foucault Effect: Studies in Governmentality*, Colin Gordon (ed.) (Chicago, IL: University of Chicago Press, 1991), pp. 87–104.

Foucault, Michel, *Discipline and Punish: The Birth of the Prison*, trans. Alan Sheridan (London: Penguin, 1991).

Foucault, Michel, *The Essential Works of Foucault 1954–1984, Volume 1: Ethics, Subjectivity and Truth*, Paul Rabinow (ed.), trans. Robert Hurley (London: Penguin, 2002).

Foucault, Michel, *The Essential Works of Foucault 1954–1984, Volume 3: Power*, James Faubion (ed.), trans. Robert Hurley (London: Penguin, 2002).

Foucault, Michel, *Society Must Be Defended: Lectures at the Collège De France 1975–1976*, trans. David Macey (London: Allen Lane, 2003).

Foucault, Michel, *Security, Territory, Population: Lectures at the Collège de France 1977–1978*, Michel Senellart (ed.) (Basingstoke: Palgrave Macmillan, 2007).

Franks, Benjamin, 'Postanarchism and Meta-ethics', *Anarchist Studies*, 16(2), 2008, pp. 135–53.

Freud, Sigmund, *The Standard Edition of the Complete Psychological Works of Sigmund Freud, Vol. 18* [1920–2], trans. and ed. James Strachey (London: Hogarth, 1955).

Godwin, William, *Anarchist Writings*, Peter Marshall (ed.) (London: Freedom Press, 1968).

Godwin, William, *Enquiry Concerning Political Justice* (Harmondsworth: Penguin, [1793] 1985).

Gordon, Uri, *Anarchy Alive!: Anti-authoritarian Politics from Practice to Theory* (London: Pluto Press, 2008).

Graeber, David, 'The New Anarchists', *New Left Review*, 13, January–February 2002, 62–73.

Gramsci, Antonio, *Selections from the Prison Notebooks*, eds and trans. Quintin Hoare and Geoffrey Nowell-Smith (London: Lawrence & Wishart, 1971).

Gray, Tim, 'Spencer, Steiner and Hart on the Equal Liberty Principle', *Journal of Applied Philosophy*, 10(1), 1993, pp. 91–104.

Guérin, Daniel, *No Gods, No Masters: an Anthology of Anarchism* (Oakland, CA: AK Press, 2005).

Hallward, Peter, 'The Politics of Prescription', *The South Atlantic Quarterly*, 104(4), Fall 2005, pp. 769–89.

Hardt, Michael, 'The Withering of Civil Society', *Deleuze and Guattari: New Mappings in Politics, Philosophy and Culture*, E. Kaufman and K. J. Heller (eds) (Minneapolis, MN: University of Minnesota Press, 1998), pp. 23–39.

Hardt, Michael and Antonio Negri, *Empire* (Cambridge, MA: Harvard University Press, 2000).

Hardt, Michael and Antonio Negri, *Multitude: War and Democracy in the Age of Empire* (New York: Penguin, 2004).

Hitchens, Christopher (ed.), *The Paris Commune 1871* (London: Sidgwick & Jackson, 1971).

Holloway, John, *Change the World Without Taking Power: the Meaning of Revolution Today* (London: Pluto, 2002).

Isin, Engin F., 'The Neurotic Citizen', *Citizenship Studies*, 8(4), (September 2004), pp. 217–35.

Kropotkin, Peter, *The State: Its Historic Role*, London: Freedom Press, 1943.

Kropotkin, Peter, *Ethics: Origin and Development*, trans. L. S. Friedland (New York: Tudor Publishing, 1947).

Kropotkin, Peter, *Revolutionary Pamphlets*, Roger N. Baldwin (ed.) (New York: Benjamin Blom, 1968).

Kropotkin, Peter, *Mutual Aid: A Factor of Evolution*, Paul Avrich (ed.) (New York: New York University, 1972).

Kropotkin, Peter, *The Conquest of Bread, and Other Writings*, Marshall S. Shatz (ed.) (Cambridge: Cambridge University Press, 1995).

Kropotkin, Peter, *Fields, Factories and Workshops Tomorrow*, Colin Ward (ed.) (London: Freedom Press, 1998).

La Boétie, Estienne de, *The Politics of Obedience: the Discourse of Voluntary Servitude*, trans. H. Kurz (New York, Free Life Editions, 1975).

Lacan, Jacques, 'Kant with Sade', *October*, 51, 1989.

Lacan, Jacques, 'A Theoretical Introduction to the Functions of Psychoanalysis in criminology', *Journal for the Psychoanalysis of Culture and Society (JPCS)*, 1(2), 1996, pp. 13–25.

Lacan, Jacques, 'Analyticon', *The Seminar of Jacques Lacan, Book XVII: The Other Side of Psychoanalysis*, Jacques-Alain Miller (ed.), trans. Russell Grigg (New York: W. W. Norton, 2007).

Laclau, Ernesto, *On Populist Reason* (London: Verso, 2005).

Laclau, Ernesto and Chantal Mouffe, *Hegemony and Socialist Strategy: Towards a Radical Democratic Politics* (London: Verso, 2001).

Latour, Bruno, 'A Cautious Prometheus? A Few Steps Toward a Philosophy of Design (with Special Attention to Peter Sloterdijk)', Keynote lecture for the Networks of Design meeting of the Design History Society, Falmouth, Cornwall, 3 September 2008, available at: http://www.bruno-latour.fr/articles/article/112-DESIGN-CORNWALL.pdf.

Lemke, Thomas, '"The Birth of Bio-politics": Michel Foucault's lecture at the Collège de France on neo-liberal governmentality', *Economy and Society*, 30(2), May 2001, pp. 190–207.

Lenin, V. I., *Collected Works, Vol. 5, May 1901–February 1902* (London: Lawrence & Wishart, 1961).

Lenin, V. I., *Collected Works, 1870–1924, Vol. 31* (London: Lawrence & Wishart, 1966).

Lenin, V. I., *State and Revolution* (New York: International Publishers, [1943] 1990.

Levinas, Emmanuel, *The Levinas Reader*, Sean Hand (ed.) (Oxford: Blackwell, 1989).

Locke, John, *The Second Treatise of Government*, J. W Gough (ed.) (Oxford: Blackwell, 1956).

Lyotard, Jean-François, *The Postmodern Condition: a Report on Knowledge*, trans. Geoffrey Bennington and Brian Massumi (Manchester: Manchester University Press, 1991).

Marchart, Oliver, *Post-Foundational Political Thought: Political Difference in Nancy, Lefort, Badiou and Laclau* (Edinburgh: Edinburgh University Press, 2007).

Marshall, Peter, *Demanding the Impossible: A History of Anarchism* (London: Harper Perennial, 2008).

Marx, Karl and Friedrich Engels, *Collected Works, Vol. 3* (London: Lawrence & Wishart, 1975).

Marx, Karl and Friedrich Engels, *The Marx–Engels Reader*, Robert Tucker (ed.) (New York: Princeton University Press, 1978).

Marx, Karl and Friedrich Engels, *Collected Works, Vol. 11* (London: Lawrence & Wishart, 1979).

May, Todd, *The Political Philosophy of Poststructuralist Anarchism* (Philadelphia, PA: Penn State Press, 1994).

May, Todd, 'Equality Among the Refugees: a Rancièrean view of Montréal's Sans-Status Algerians', *Anarchist Studies*, 16(2), 2008, pp. 121–34.

May, Todd, *The Political Thought of Jacques Rancière, Creating Equality* (Edinburgh: Edinburgh University Press, 2008).

Mentinis, Mihalis, *Zapatistas: the Chiapas Revolt and What it Means for Radical Politics* (London: Pluto Press, 2006).

Mertes, Tom (ed.), *A Movement of Movements: Is Another World Really Possible?* (London: Verso, 2004).

Montagna, Nicola, 'The Making of a Global Movement: Cycles of Protest and Scales of Action' (draft paper submitted to *Global Geography*, 2009).

Morland, David, 'Anti-capitalism and Poststructuralist Anarchism', *Changing Anarchism: Anarchist theory and practice in a Global Age*, Jonathan Purkis and James Bowen (eds) (Manchester: Manchester University Press), pp. 23–54.

Morland, David, *Demanding the Impossible? Human Nature and Politics in Nineteenth-Century Social Anarchism* (London: Cassell, 1997).

Mouffe, Chantal, *On the Political* (London: Routledge, 2005).

Mouffe, Chantal, *The Democratic Paradox* (London: Verso, 2000).

Negri, Antonio, *Insurgencies: Constituent Power and the Modern State*, trans. Maurizia Boscagli (Minneapolis, MN: University of Minnesota Press, 1999).

Neilson, Brett, 'Potenza Nuda? Sovereignty, Biopolitics, Capitalism', *Contretemps*, 5, December 2004, pp. 63–78.

Neocleous, Mark, *Critique of Security* (Edinburgh: Edinburgh University Press, 2008).

Newman, Saul, *From Bakunin to Lacan: Anti-authoritarianism and the Dislocation of Power* (Lanham, MD: Lexington Books, 2001).

Noys, Ben, 'Through a Glass Darkly: Alain Badiou's Critique of Anarchism', *Anarchist Studies*, 16(2), 2008, pp. 107–20.

Noys, Benjamin, 'Anarchy-without-Anarchism' (October 2006). Available at: http://leniency.blogspot.com/2009/06/anarchywithoutanarchism.html.

Pogge, Thomas, 'Equal Liberty for All?', *Midwest Studies in Philosophy*, XXVIII, 2004, pp. 266–81.

Poulantzas, Nicos, 'The Problem of the Capitalist State', *New Left Review*, 58, 1969.

Poulantzas, Nicos, *Political Power & Social Classes*, trans. Timothy O'Hagan (London: NLB and Sheed & Ward, 1973).

Proudhon, Pierre-Joseph, *What is Property?*, Donald R. Kelley and Bonnie G. Smith (eds) (Cambridge: Cambridge University Press, 1994).

Rancière, Jacques, *The Nights of Labour: the Workers' Dream in Nineteenth-century France*, trans. John Drury (Philadelphia, PA: Temple University Press, 1989).

Rancière, Jacques, *Disagreement: Politics and Philosophy*, trans. Julie Rose (Minneapolis, MN: University of Minnesota Press, 1999).

Rancière, Jacques, 'Who is the Subject of the Rights of Man?', *The South Atlantic Quarterly*, 103(2/3), 2004, pp. 297–310.

Rancière, Jacques, *The Politics of Aesthetics: the Distribution of the Sensible*, trans. Gabriel Rockhill (New York: Continuum, 2004).

Rancière, Jacques, 'Democracy, anarchism and radical politics today: An interview with Jacques Ranciere', with Todd May, Benjamin Noys and Saul Newman, trans. John Lechte, *Anarchist Studies*, 16(2), 2008, pp. 173–85.

Rasch, William, *Sovereignty and its Discontents: On the Primacy of Conflict and the Structure of the Political* (London: Birkbeck Law Press, 2004).

Reich, Wilhelm *The Mass Psychology of Fascism* (New York: Farrar, Straus & Giroux, 1980).

Richards, Vernon (ed.), *Errico Malatesta: His Life & Ideas* (London: Freedom Press, 1993).

Rothbard, Murray, 'Robert Nozick and the Immaculate Conception of the State', *Journal of Libertarian Studies*, 1(1), 1977, pp. 45–57.

Rupert, Mark, 'Anti-Capitalist Convergence? Anarchism, Socialism and the Global Justice Movement', in Manfred Steger (ed.), *Rethinking Globalism* (Lanham, MD: Rowman & Littlefield, 2003), pp. 121–35.

Schmitt, Carl, *The Concept of the Political*, trans. George Schwab Chicago, IL: University of Chicago Press, 1996).

Schmitt, Carl, *The* Nomos *of the Earth in the International Law of the* Jus Publicum Europeaum, trans. G. L. Ulmen (New York: Telos Press, 2003).

Schmitt, Carl, *Political Theology: Four Chapters on the Concept of Sovereignty*, trans. G. Schwab (Chicago, IL: University of Chicago Press, 2005).

Schürmann, Reiner *Heidegger on Being and Acting: From Principles to Anarchy*, trans. Christine Marie Gros (Bloomington, IN: Indiana University Press, 1987).

Sorel, Georges, *Reflections on Violence*, trans. T. E. Hulme and J. Roth (New York: Collier Books, 1999).

Spencer, Herbert, *Social Statics* (London: Chapman, 1851).

Spencer, Herbert, *The Man versus the State* (Harmondsworth: Penguin, [1884] 1969).

Stirner, Max, *The Ego and Its Own*, David Leopold (ed.) (Cambridge: Cambridge University Press, 1995).

Tarrow, Sidney, *The New Transnational Activism* (Cambridge: Cambridge University Press, 2005).

Tocqueville, Alexis de, *Democracy in America*, trans. J. P. Mayer (ed.), G. Lawrence (London: Fontana Press, 1994).

Tormey, Simon, '"Not in my Name": Deleuze, Zapatismo and the Critique of Representation', *Parliamentary Affairs*, 2006.

Toscano, Alberto, 'From the State to the World? Badiou and Anti-Capitalism', *Communication & Cognition*, 37(3&4), 2004, pp. 199–224.

Toscano, Alberto, 'Always Already Only Now: Negri and the Biopolitical', *The Philosophy of Antonio Negri: Revolution in Theory*, Timothy S. Murphy and Abdul-Karim Mustapha (eds) (London: Pluto Press, 2007), vol. 2, pp. 109–28.

Toscano, Alberto, 'The war against pre-terrorism: the Tarnac 9 and *The Coming Insurrection'*, *Radical Philosophy*, 154, March/April 2009.

Vaneigem, Raoul, *The Revolution of Everyday Life*, trans. Donald Nicholson-Smith (London: Rebel Press, 2006).

Vattimo, Gianni, *The End of Modernity: Nihilism and the Hermeneutics in Post-Modern Culture*, trans. Jon R. Snyder (Cambridge: Polity Press, 1988).

Wolff, Robert Paul, *In Defense of Anarchism* (Berkeley, CA: University of California Press, 1998).

Woodcock, George, *Anarchism: A History of Libertarian Ideas and Movements* (Harmondsworth: Penguin, 1986).

Wright, Steve, 'A Party of Autonomy', *Resistance in Practice: the Philosophy of Antonio Negri*, Timothy S. Murphy and Abdul-Karim Mustapha (eds) (London: Pluto Press, 2005), pp. 73–106.

Zerzan, John, *Future Primitive and Other Essays* (New York: Autonomedia, 1994).

Zerzan, John, *Elements of Refusal* (Columbia, CO: CAL Press, 1999).

Žižek, Slavoj, *The Ticklish Subject: the Absent Centre of Political Ontology* (London: Verso, 1999).

Žižek, Slavoj, 'Divine Violence and Liberated Territories' Interview with SOFT TARGET (Los Angeles, 14 March 2007), available at: http://www.softtargetsjournal.com/web/zizek.php.

Žižek, Slavoj, 'Resistance is Surrender', *London Review of Books*, 15 November 2007.

Žižek, Slavoj, 'Robespierre, or, the "Divine Violence" of Terror', Introduction to *Virtue and Terror*, by Maximilien Robespierre, trans. John Howe (London: Verso, 2007).

Žižek, Slavoj, *In Defence of Lost Causes* (London: Verso, 2008).

Žižek, Slavoj, *Violence: Six Sideways Reflections* (New York: Picador, 2008).

INDEX